Living in Truth, Beauty, and Goodness

Living in Truth,
Beauty, and Goodness

Values and Virtues

Jeffrey Wattles

Foreword by
Stephen G. Post

CASCADE *Books* • Eugene, Oregon

Cascade Books
An Imprint of Wipf and Stock Publishers
199 W. 8th Ave., Suite 3
Eugene, OR 97401

www.wipfandstock.com

PAPERBACK ISBN: 978-1-4982-3971-4
HARDCOVER ISBN: 978-1-4982-3973-8
EBOOK ISBN: 978-1-4982-3972-1

Cataloguing-in-Publication data:

Wattles, Jeffrey.

   Living in truth, beauty, and goodness : values and virtues / Jeffrey Wattles;
foreword by Stephen G. Post.

   xiv + 220 pp. ; 23 cm. Includes bibliographical references and index.

   ISBN 978-1-4982-3971-4 (paperback) | ISBN 978-1-4982-3973-8 (hardback) |
ISBN 978-1-4982-3972-1 (ebook)

   1. Life. 2. Philosophy. 3. Virtues. I. Title.

BD431 .W245 2016

Manufactured in the U.S.A.   07/20/16

Contents

Part II. Walking in Beauty

Part III. Participating in Divine Goodness

Foreword

I FIRST MET PROFESSOR Jeffrey Wattles at least fifteen years ago in one of his philosophy classes at Kent State University, where I was witness to his remarkable ability to engage students in a way that helped them gain perspective on the direction and meaning of their lives. They took him seriously not simply as an intellectual, but as someone who could coax them to live better by reflecting deeply on important matters of virtue and purpose in life. Professor Wattles is successful because while his motives and thought have their grounding in his basic Christianity, he is a Christian "inclusivist" in Paul Tillich's sense of the term—someone who is going to appreciate the work of God in other traditions consistent with core Christian values. How else can anyone seriously engage our cosmopolitan and interspiritual age? Wattles is equally comfortable connecting with students who represent Hinduism, Buddhism, Taoism, and other traditions, including secular philosophy. He is not a simple-minded "pluralist" who endorses anything and everything, but a discerning thinker who looks for God's work in a range of cultures and spiritualities.

I had already learned much from Wattles's exceptional book *The Golden Rule* (Oxford University Press, 1996), in which he surveys the diverse historical contexts of the rule and delves into a number of the world's religions as well as secular philosophical thought over the recent centuries. *The Golden Rule* is quite simply the authoritative study on the subject, weaving together science, history, ethics, and religious thought at a time when this approach was much rarer than it is now. On the back cover of *The Golden Rule* there is a brief biosketch that concludes with this line: "His next book will present a philosophy of living based on concepts of truth, beauty, and goodness." Two decades after this promise, his second book has finally taken shape in *Living in Truth, Beauty, and Goodness: Values and Virtues.* Now

retired from his teaching career, Wattles has found the time to write this
equally impressive and unique book. It is well worth reading and discussing.

Living in Truth, Beauty, and Goodness arises from his years of teaching
students from diverse backgrounds who really want to be challenged to find
new philosophies of living that will enhance their lives. Wattles has developed an excellent website to accompany this book at http://UniversalFamily.
org. Living in Truth, Beauty, and Goodness is designed to be a guide for those
perplexed by the spiritual and philosophical emptiness of modern culture
and materialism, and their journey can continue forward after they finish the
book with the many postings on the accompanying website.

True to his previous writing, Wattles presents a philosophy of living
grounded in the trinity of truth, beauty, and goodness. In Part I. Living the
Truth, he asks us to examine the character strengths and virtues of three
very different individuals each deeply committed to following their quest
for truth with integrity—Darwin, Socrates, and Jesus. The chapter on
Darwin underscores how the pursuit of fact and accuracy shaped the life
and character of Darwin as it does for any true scientist, even when critics
abound. His chapter on Socrates highlights the philosopher's lifelong drive
for rational truth, even to the point of accepting death in integrity rather
than fleeing Athens. This theme of integrity reaches a clear crescendo in
a chapter on the life and teachings of Jesus on spiritual truth. While each
chapter includes careful interpretation of the thought worlds of their subjects, the greater emphasis is on their lives, their values and virtues, which
help us live out everyday life to the fullest. We see three profiles in truth and
courage in widely different contexts but all conjoined, for Wattles wants us
all to seek truth in scientific fact, in philosophy and wisdom, and in spirituality. He sees no conflict between these three pursuits, and asks us each
to be diligent in all these domains, for ultimately, truth is truth, approached
empirically, rationally, or spiritually.

In Part II. Walking in Beauty, Wattles invites us to examine the character strengths and virtues of two individuals deeply committed to following
their quest for beauty—John Muir and Johann Sebastian Bach. Muir pursued beauty as the nation's first great modern naturalist, and of course, Bach
is Bach. As one who has read much about Bach and played at least some of
his lute suites, I can attest that I have not found anything as thoughtful as
Wattles's treatment of Bach. In this chapter all of Bach's biographical wanderings and his immense creativity come together in his character strengths
and his profound theological insights. This chapter brings to mind Jaroslav
Pelikan's great work Bach Among the Theologians. The reader comes to know
what it means to pursue beauty despite hardships and challenges in a spiritual quest.

In *Part III. Participating in Divine Goodness*, Wattles draws on the great New Testament exegete, physician, and medical missionary Albert Schweitzer, whose love for life was unsurpassed. Here Wattles returns us to some of the themes from *The Golden Rule*, but with a level of depth and insight at the affective, rational, and spiritual levels that could only emerge from deep reflection over many years since the first book was written. Wattles also focuses a chapter on Pitirim Sorokin, the greatest twentieth-century sociological and integrative thinker on the centrality of love, and especially of our experience of God's love. As a scholar of Harvard's Sorokin myself over many years, and having met the man as a boy when he was speaking in New Hampshire, I can safely state that Sorokin's vision about a human future that must break through at the level of spiritual experience and practical application to the ways and power of divine love is very clearly and persuasively presented in Wattles's chapter. Over the years, Professor Wattles and I have had many discussions of the nature of Divine *agape* love and the various expressions of it, and I have emphasized Sorokin's work in conversations going back to 2000. Only now, in reading *Living in Truth, Beauty, and Goodness*, do I feel that I grasp the spiritual essence of this great man.

But I must end this foreword by stressing how easily readable this book will be to everyday people who just want to live better and more meaningful lives. The chapters are connected by the narrative of Wattles's own quite remarkable spiritual journey around the globe from youth, and with anecdotes from his many delighted students who were able to find their way to deep living with his mentorship and guidance. In summary, Wattles is a seeker, and he wants us to understand all that being a seeker implies. He has found himself in a very profound Christianity. Wattles joins the ranks of those humble believers who want to not just tolerate, but engage, various spiritual traditions and philosophical modalities. He is a humble man who has written a book that should be read by every college student and every thoughtful person concerned about the destructive drift of our materialistic, sensate, and increasingly dangerous world where growing up seems harder to do, and the future less certain than ever before.

Stephen G. Post, PhD

President, The Institute for Research on Unlimited Love
(www.unlimitedloveinstitute.org)
and Professor, Stony Brook University School of Medicine

Preface

AFTER A HEALTHY AND devout early childhood, I consecrated myself at the age of seven to becoming perfect. For the most part, I continued to enjoy education, religion, and life generally. I was happily immersed in my high school studies in Charlottesville, Virginia, when one spring morning my English teacher gave our class some silent time to think. Truth, beauty, and goodness suddenly manifested for me not as intellectual ideas but as a trio of luminous realities. The experience was intuitive, utterly clear, and perfectly calm.

When I went to college and met Plato in the course on Western civilization and discovered the power of logical analysis in ethics, philosophy swept over me like a wave, and I was determined to be a professor. My next few years of study were a headlong plunge into a new quality of thinking. The patient analysis, clarity, impressive arguments, and depth of concept made a tremendous appeal to my intellect. But I abandoned my religious rudder. I fell in love with Nietzsche, whose brilliant boldness struck me as insightful. Taking his ideas as my philosophy of living proved a disaster: without faith, I lost my moral compass and then my sanity. I did not realize that my philosophical passion was a quest for God.

Gradually, the pieces came together. I deepened my study of Plato and began to practice Transcendental Meditation, and my spiritual perspective brightened. In graduate school, I found God and started all over again, building my philosophy of living around concepts of truth, beauty, and goodness. I soon found my inquiry leading me into a meadow of joyous discovery; and I vowed to write a book to share the bountiful treasure.

After graduate school, with the mind of a philosopher and the heart of an evangelist, I spent some time in seminary and joined a group engaged in evangelism, going door to door and doing some street preaching. When I needed to get serious about my career, I went back to philosophy and began working to subordinate my religious fervor to the will of God. My passion for high-quality thinking was unswerving, but I had a new message for people: "You are a divinely created, infinitely loved, spiritually indwelt, evolutionary, free-will son or daughter of God."

After my forays into Western philosophy, I immersed myself for several years in the profound and beautiful simplicities of Eastern philosophy with Lao Tzu, Confucius, Mencius, Chu Hsi, and Wang Yang-ming. Later, I had the chance to teach units on Latin American philosophy and African philosophy.

Each layer of my education enabled me to better understand and identify with new groups of people. My travels in Europe, Asia, Africa, and Latin America; living for extended periods in France, Belgium, and Switzerland; working for seven years at a small international school in Berkeley, California, where I taught world history, world literature, humanities, English, business, and psychology; marrying a Japanese person and savoring the treasures of Japanese culture—these experiences strengthened my bonds with people, all kinds of people. Looking for what was true and beautiful and good yielded an abundant harvest.

My last fifteen years as a teacher were especially rewarding for bonding with diverse individuals and promoting discovery. I had gradually been learning to integrate concepts of truth, beauty, and goodness into my courses, and I started to center them on experiential projects based on these concepts. I would select the most universally appealing concept from the philosophy or religious tradition that we were studying and invite the students to modify that concept until they felt good about applying it in their own lives. For example, in the world religions course we would begin with the Bhagavad Gita of Hinduism and the Dhammapada of Buddhism, and the first project was on centered and compassionate living. For a centering practice, a person could select from alternatives ranging from conscious breathing to seeking the kingdom of God within. Conscious breathing simply means taking time to allow the attention to rest on the breath; described in this way, the practice is free of spiritual or religious connotations. My students were mostly Christians and atheists; classes might also include agnostics, Buddhists, Jews, Muslims, and people exploring spirituality independently. I made sure that they all felt supported no matter what they believed or did not believe about religion.

During the first week or so when students were thinking creatively about how to apply the assigned and personally modified concept in their lives, I would tell them that the greatest growth comes from tackling our front-burner issue, our biggest growth challenge—within the limits of psychological wisdom about not taking on too much. Most students did tackle their number one issue, and this was one of the main reasons why so many of them had transformative experiences. I repeatedly emphasized that growth has its own rhythm and cannot be forced. They were warned about feeling pressure to achieve a dramatic breakthrough. The essential thing was to give evidence of sincere and persistent effort to *cultivate the soil* for growth.

Week by week, students would journal about what happened as they put the concept they had chosen into practice (journals were always private). After a month and a half, they would turn in papers that related the readings to their experience. I would read these immediately, usually moved to tears by the challenges that some of them had chosen to confront and the triumphs they achieved. I would make selections representing the range of experiences that seemed most educational, ask permission from each student to read their selection anonymously in class, and then dedicate the next class meeting to letting the students hear their classmates' amazing achievements. Those days of sharing were the highlight of my life.

How do I know that the students were not faking? A very few did and were caught. But the class was based on such a quality of interpersonal relating that most students—as far as I could tell—were drawn into the atmosphere of openness and trust. During office hours, many shared their lives with me. In their writing I would normally see a special kind of eloquence combining blunt factual description with the freshness of discovery. The writing had a spontaneous quality; it was not the rhetoric of skilled writers, but the mark of having sincerely followed through on a project. Usually about two-thirds of the students reported major breakthroughs. It was a privilege, a struggle at times, a tremendous learning experience, and a profound satisfaction to lead these experiential courses for over three thousand students.[1]

Now, in retirement, I continue with my mission. My goal is to interact in ways that give tastes, promote discoveries, and whet appetites for projects of any duration, from minutes to years. My voice in these pages is more overtly religious than was my conduct in class, but it offers the same invitation to you, the reader: to create your own philosophy of living. Using the tools that this book provides, you can most effectively leverage your personal growth and planetary contribution by wrestling with these ideas, adapting them to what you honestly feel good about putting into practice,

1. About 10 percent of the students seemed to engage only superficially; in addition to the roughly two-thirds whose experiences were transformational, the rest reported positive but modest experiences. All the students were exposed for sixteen weeks to an uplifting environment of high meanings and values.

addressing your front-burner issue, and going forward with your own creative experiments in truth, beauty, and goodness.

Upon completing the reading of a chapter, it is wise to create for yourself some kind of summary so that you are not left with a pile of challenging ideas and an ever more daunting list of virtues to cultivate. To symbolize the whole of a chapter, a part, or book, you can create your own image, diagram, mind-map, gesture, phrase, or work of art that stands for the whole.

The chapters are designed with easy access on the ground floor and with high ceilings above so that the windows offer an expanded vista. The secret to success is to remember that even modest progress is rich in meaning and value; whenever a microproject or something more ambitious leads to a satisfactory result, it is appropriate to give thanks and take a victory lap.

The philosophy of living in truth, beauty, and goodness presented here is more than any one book can put into words and more than any one author can produce. Some of the needed work has already been done by men and women who have gone before; other students, scholars, authors, specialists, generalists, and interested persons are needed to bring this philosophy to fullness. Some will do projects in one or more of the seven areas featured here and share their experience. Some will use experiential education to help students discover and actualize these values. Some will contribute as I have tried to do, helping to build the new philosophy of living. Potentials for teamwork beckon on the horizon. I plan to make available more opportunities: a podcast series, YouTube videos, free online courses based on these chapters, with ongoing conversation on my weblog, http://UniversalFamily.org.

This book is full of resources for your voyage into truth, beauty, and goodness. Life introduces everyone to these values. Now let's go with them to the next level!

Introduction

Setting Out on a Path to
Higher-Quality Thinking

I KNOW WHAT IT is to be moved by high-quality thinking. A relaxed satisfaction comes over me when I find writing that clarifies a muddled topic and awakens the urge to explore further. The flow, the quiet logic, the confident handling of information, the flavor of insight skillfully shared—such excellence has led me to some good decisions with far-reaching implications. I have seen good thinking spark enthusiasm in others too, and I see evidence of more and more people caring about improving the way their minds function.

The desire for quality thinking is not merely an esoteric passion shared by an elite group of intellectuals; it also affects popular culture, where we speak of smartphones, information technology, and the knowledge economy. The nationwide restaurant chain Chipotle prints brief essays on burrito bags in a series titled "Cultivating Thought"—a branding move that would be unthinkable unless their market research showed that it resonates with the interests of their clientele.

But cultivating one's mind does not succeed as an isolated venture. Intimate connections exist between thinking, feeling, and doing. Neuroscience has found that our brains are wired to connect the parts of the brain involved in thinking with the parts of the brain associated with feeling. We can't think clearly if our emotions are in turmoil. Nor does thinking go well if we are caught up in an episode of selfishness and materialism. Think better, and you'll feel better; feel better, and you'll act better. These three aspects of our lives flourish together.

Our thinking, feeling, and doing are not random; they are oriented to values. Although the values we seek are diverse, we can classify them under three suitable headings. When we wrestle with a problem and break through to the answer, we may speak of "intuition" or "insight," words implying *truth*, which is sought in thinking. When we keenly enjoy listening to music or quietly contemplate the night sky, we may use words such as "cool" or "awesome," expressing shades of *beauty*, which attracts feeling. When we get involved in doing something for others and speak of "making a difference," "giving back," or doing something "to make the world a better place," the phrases imply *goodness*, expressed in doing.

Truth, beauty, and goodness are lofty and down-to-earth, universal and local, timeless and timely, celebrated and longed-for. They are values that we feel and ideas that we debate. We usually do not have them in mind when we are engaged in activity, but they are always present. They are living realities bearing dynamic potentials for a future that we can help create. Our sense of them affects the way we see things, how we feel and act, and the kind of person we become. To seek a higher quality of thinking about these values is therefore to seek a philosophy of living.

Our naturally developing philosophy

In a casual sense, we develop our own philosophy simply by growing up. An example is Sydney Jordan's response to an assignment I gave my students during the first week in a philosophy class: Write about an experience that has given you an intuitive understanding of truth.

> For me, truth is a feeling of satisfaction. Not in the way of feeling full and satisfied after a meal, but rather a sense of wholeness. For example, my family has a rather large garden that we work every summer. This past summer was the first time I was allowed to have a crop of my own. The feeling I got from the start when the ground is first turned to the harvest is a sense of completeness. At the end of each session in the garden I am dirty, sweaty, and tired, but it is my hard work and dedication that produces something good. People that do what I do need determination, hard work, patience. Being in the garden every summer is a truth for me. We plant it, care for it, wait, and it grows then feeds us and others. Truth is what is there when all of the fancy is taken away. Truth is understanding the value of things, that all things have value and are in some way connected.[1]

1. Sydney Jordan's experience report is quoted with her permission.

Here we see blended cognitive, emotional, and practical experience, nurturing character growth and leading to an expanded understanding of truth.

When our understanding is functioning well, we feel no need for wisdom to help us put the pieces together. But we run into difficulties that make us think, and think hard. We develop our philosophy of living further in our late teens and twenties as we face the challenges of adult life; we "make choices that lead to the creation of a pattern of life that lasts for almost 20 years."[2]

Later on, when we wrestle with ethical dilemmas, struggle in relationships, question religion, or cope with loss, big questions loom. What is the meaning of life? Where is our world heading? Which values are worth committing to? Caught up in such questions, we want more than knowledge and quick solutions; we want wisdom. We become hungry for the power of high-quality thinking and spiritual realization that can lift us to a new level of emotional harmony and practical effectiveness. We become ready to develop our philosophy more deliberately.

A special opportunity for philosophy today

Once we become interested in a philosophy of truth, beauty, and goodness, our inquiry starts to overlap with what philosophers have been discussing for thousands of years. The project of developing such a philosophy goes back at least as far as Plato. In his dialogue, the *Symposium*, we find some ideas akin to what is proposed here—for example, intellectual insight into truth as a stepping stone to the realization of beauty, and reflection on beauty as leading to the realization of goodness.[3] These values continued to be discussed by Thomas Aquinas and other medieval philosophers and theologians in the Catholic intellectual tradition down to the present day. The concepts are called transcendentals, because they transcend every category and apply to everything in every category: everything has a measure of truth (including being and unity), goodness, and beauty.[4] Then, beginning in the eighteenth and nineteenth centuries, German idealists, along with kindred minds elsewhere, rethought these concepts in terms of our human capaci-

2. The study of late teens and twenties developing a philosophy of living is mentioned in Buford, *Personal Philosophy*, v.

3. These insights are found in Plato, *Symposium*, 210d–212b and 204c–206a.

4. For a brief introduction to the transcendentals, see Kreeft, "Lewis's Philosophy." Ramos, *Dynamic Transcendentals*, takes theoretical and applied perspectives in the direction of the philosophy set forth here. Jaroszyński, *Beauty and Being*, gives fine discussions of truth and goodness as well as beauty. Nichols, *Key to Balthasar*, summarizes the contributions on these themes by a major twentieth-century theologian.

ties to make judgments. They probed aesthetics, ethics, and philosophy's disciplines regarding truth, including philosophy of science, epistemology (knowledge-ology), and philosophy of religion—all essential ingredients in a philosophy of living.

Today the conversation is global, as philosophers around the world also draw on non-Western traditions. Philosophic sagacity is recognized as one of the four traditions of African philosophy, alongside ethnophilosophy, postcolonial philosophy, and professional philosophy. And for thousands of years, Asian philosophy has kept in touch with philosophy of living concerns.

The present age gives philosophy a new opportunity. Limited philosophies clash in their specific emphases on science, or on humanistic values, or on religion, but a more inclusive philosophy can play the role of a peacemaker. Although there is no peace between truth and error, most conflicts are between positions that have a mix of truth and error in them. Philosophy can lift up the truths in opposing positions, and it can speak to persons of different religions and no religion.

What is needed is a philosophy that takes high concepts of truth, beauty, and goodness, and makes them accessible for practical living. But contemporary Western academic philosophy—with all its marvelous resources and its disciplines of clarity, careful reasoning, conceptual coherence, and comprehensiveness—does not address the need. In the ancient world, philosophies of living flourished, but philosophers today find their discipline organized into specialties, none of which synthesizes philosophy into something livable. The philosophy of living is not yet recognized as a specialty alongside aesthetics and ethics in the way that medicine recognizes the specialty that is variously called primary care, general practice, or family medicine. And most of the philosophy of living found in the popular marketplace is being written by persons with little background in philosophy.

Since professional philosophy is not organized to address the need for a full philosophy of living, most people on a wisdom quest turn elsewhere. Many people who know God get their philosophy of living from books on spirituality as it is taught and practiced in any number of traditions. Seekers commonly look to the philosophies associated with Hinduism and the practice of yoga, Buddhism, and the practice of mindfulness, or Taoism and the practice of naturalness. Many turn to New Age explorations of integrated living or self-help. The philosophy of living being developed here has a strong core that can preserve its integrity even as it remains open to welcome genuine insights from these and other sources. Ancient Greek philosophy served for centuries as a resource for Jews, Christians, and Muslims;

and the new philosophy emerging here could conceivably provide a shared language for a global conversation.

Before we continue, let's distinguish three things that are closely related: (1) The general term *the philosophy of living* refers to a field of inquiry that may be done from any philosophical perspective whatsoever.(2) When I talk about *this new or emerging philosophy of living*, I refer to an approach centered on concepts of truth, beauty, and goodness, found in science, philosophy, spiritual experience, nature, the arts, morality, and character;[5] and (3) *my interpretation* of this emerging philosophy as set forth in this book.[6]

Philosophy as a friend of spirituality

One of philosophy's traditional strengths is its broad accessibility, its capacity to reach out to all thoughtful persons no matter what they believe or do not believe; but we must make a watershed decision about spirituality and religion. Philosophy traditionally aspires toward an integrated understanding of the full spectrum of human experience, but many experiences of truth, beauty, and goodness are spiritual experiences—so what are we to make of spiritual experience?[7]

---

5. The blueprint for *Living in Truth, Beauty, and Goodness* comes from the Urantia Foundation, *Urantia Book*, 43. This book has deeply informed my work on this project. In it we see the concepts of truth, beauty, and goodness expanded to embrace science, philosophy, spiritual experience, nature, the arts, morality, and character. I have also learned much from other books on truth, beauty, and goodness (in addition to those mentioned previously on the transcendentals). First is the book that merits its position as the market leader: Gardner, *Truth, Beauty, Goodness Reframed*. Wilson, *Preaching as Poetry*, develops these themes in postmodernist and applied ways. McIntosh, *Presence of the Infinite*, synthesizes traditional, modern, and postmodernist approaches in an evolutionary spirituality. Brown, *Restoration of Reason,* provides a sturdy history of philosophy perspective; Pelikan, *Fools for Christ*, takes a cultural history approach; and Ross, *Gift of Beauty* and *Gift of Truth,* presents an elegant, postmodernist philosophical perspective.

6. Existentialism addresses the philosophy of living, if not in the fullness proposed here; and it has the merit of avoiding the formulation of a static, intellectual system. This book staves off that fate in many ways—by its concept of the mystery of each unique personality; its openness to contributions from every tradition; its embrace of the spiritual dimension; its concept of evolution and recourse to ever-developing science; its future-oriented and sometimes pragmatic approach; and its emphasis on personal experience in religion, education, and concept formation. Nevertheless, this book is systematic in setting forth its sequence of chapters. This outline is of course not intended to function as a pattern for other expressions of the emerging philosophy.

7. For recent books on the philosophy of living, see Seachris, *Exploring Meaning of Life*; Eagleton, *Meaning of Life*; Cottingham, *Meaning of Life*; Klemke and Cahn, *Meaning of Life Reader*; Kekes, *Art of Life*; Nozick, *Examined Life*; Thomson, *On the Meaning*

Prior to considering this question, it helps to clarify two terms. Many truth lovers have become disillusioned with religion, and identify themselves as "spiritual but not religious." They see bad religion loose in the world, with its fanaticism, moralism, intolerance, and ignorance, all of which make it hard to imagine that good religion, real religion, could be essential to the cure. When I use the term "spiritual," I refer primarily to supreme values and to their source—the Source whose spirit is present within us. In spiritual experience, divine reality holds sway, no matter what the person believes or does not believe. When I call a person "religious," I do not have organized religion in mind; I mean that the person holds a faith-based concept of God or some equivalent ideal, an ideal that I find in much of Hinduism and Buddhism. By extension, the new philosophy I set forth is religious philosophy. The term *religion* connotes more explicit associations with tradition; but true spirituality is the living heart of real religion, and the religious affirmation of a supreme Deity is essential to an adequate understanding of spirituality.

Religion tends to regard spiritual experience as a gift of God, while secularism generally dismisses religious experience, reducing it to biology and psychology. Reality is many-sided, and no one perspective tells the whole story. Diverse sciences, philosophies, and religions *all* contribute to understanding spiritual experience. The new philosophy of living in truth, beauty, and goodness does not take the secular option; it is a religious philosophy, and one that keeps inquiry alive on all levels.

We all have experiences of tasting the flavor of truth, being touched by beauty, or acting for the greater good. These experiences are often so blended that we might not even identify our tastes and touches and doings in these terms. In our most deeply satisfying experiences, when we are living at our best, we are consciously or unconsciously in touch with a wonderfulness within. Known by persons of every religion and of no religion, this wonderfulness within is a center of meaning and value, a source of energy, power, wisdom, peace, insight, love, joy, creativity, purpose, and guidance. Responding to these blessings, many people begin to sense the presence of something or *someone*, most commonly referred to as God, who often seems elusive but sometimes enters human experience as decisively real.

The goal of spiritual development is often understood to be a way of living; and core values of that spiritual way are set forth in this book. The simple thesis of this emerging philosophy is that truth, beauty, and goodness are qualities of God and values that we can live. Working with a concept of

of Life; Lurie, *Tracking the Meaning*; White, *Heart of Wisdom*; and Runzo and Martin, eds., *Meaning in World Religions*.

God, we can think of truth, beauty, and goodness as the language God uses to communicate with our thinking, feeling, and doing. The more we live these values, the better we can listen to what God is saying, and the better we can hold up our end of the conversation.

In every major cultural arena where you might expect to find it, this philosophy of living is lacking. The field of philosophy needs it conceptually; religions and other spiritual paths need it experientially. It displaces none of them, and contributes to all.

This book's special features

As we pursue truth, beauty, and goodness, we grow toward a strong character that unifies intellectual, spiritual, aesthetic, and moral virtues. This book leads the reader along a path of cultivating growth in these traits as we pursue the correlated primary values. Our guides (through biographical sketches) are Darwin, Socrates, Jesus, Bach, and other world-class pioneers, whose strengths inspire us to develop to a level that fits our gifts and opportunities. Each chapter explains and illustrates a set of basic principles to help the reader do what conduces to success. Each chapter also has a section titled "From my journey," which tells stories of my growth struggles toward some of the qualities under discussion. Having learned so many things the hard way, I hope that this openness, along with the careful unfolding of a path of growing in virtue, will enable readers to save time by learning some lessons an easier way.

Living in Truth, Beauty, and Goodness has a theoretical framework, but it focuses more on practical application. Philosophy gives rational support for its conclusions by describing examples, reasoning logically, and refuting objections; and these methods are used here. But the real proof that truth, beauty, and goodness are livable qualities of God comes from personal experience. My main goal in these pages is to give an accessible and inviting path to that experience. My way of expressing that path challenges the reader to transplant concepts presented with my interpretation and language into the context of his or her own garden of concepts, interpretation, and language—and then creatively put the resulting meanings and values into practice.

The reader can learn here to integrate science and religion, make wiser decisions, experience a deeper relationship with God, develop an outstanding aesthetic appreciation of nature, live more artistically, find new meaning and dynamism in the golden rule of treating others as we want to be treated, and love with divine motivation and enhanced maturity.

The vista ahead

When we contemplate the seemingly solid tangle of planetary problems that crowd in upon us, we may sense the magnitude of the wisdom, power, creativity, courage, and love it will take to untangle them. In another thousand years, things should be much better. By our mistaken choices, humankind has usually learned things the hard way; but that can change. There is an easier way. That easier way is rugged, but it is vastly superior to the hard way of barricaded folly. Inspired leadership and teamwork could save our world from mountains of needless suffering. We could change this world's direction in one generation.

To achieve that new direction, the first requirement is for individuals to get into closer touch with the divine source of our essential needs. Only by developing our spiritual awareness can we learn that each one of us is infinitely loved, and each has a role to play in the universal family. Every one of us can exercise our awesome privilege of being part of the plan that the Creator is guiding to fulfillment. We can experience spiritual insight, joy, and activation, and know that we walk in the corridors of cosmic power.

If we face a confusing mix of truths, half-truths, and lies, *truth* befriends us and empowers us (if we cooperate) to put the confusing mix in order. If we suffer from unstable attitudes, superficial attractions, and conflicting emotions, *beauty* attracts us toward emotional maturity that includes relaxed good humor and awe in the presence of the sublime. If we are overcommitted to our projects and undercommitted to the will of God, divine *goodness* leads us into paths that fit our gifts with others' needs.

Our thinking, feeling, and doing are being quietly uplifted. Whatever the state of our current philosophy of living, abundant help in developing it further is available from human and divine sources. Welcome to the collaborative quest!

Part I. Living the Truth

1

Facts, Causes, and Evolution

Charles Darwin and Scientific Living

THE BEAUTY OF THIS vast, starry universe encourages us as we take up the challenge of living here. On our world, organisms have evolved with increasing powers of mind; now humankind is walking the earth, going through the life cycle, and beginning to take responsibility for the planet's future. Our challenge is that the universe is a place where material forces tend to dominate. We may be potentially more spiritual than we realize, but we are also more material than we know, as science increasingly teaches us. We work with a mind that is intertwined with brain process; and our behavior is affected by genetic, biochemical, environmental, and social factors. We wonder how our best thinking is to gain the upper hand; but we may suspect that our problems conceal within them the call of destiny.

In response to our collective challenges, what one person can contribute is a life well lived. Such a life comprises several components, and facing the facts of our problems launches the first component, scientific living—acting in the light of the relevant truths of science. But when we look at our personal problems and the problems of our world, they can seem overwhelming. The hectic pace of modern life makes it hard to focus effectively. We are not taught while growing up how to live scientifically. And the books on harmonizing science and religion are mostly theoretical, not practical.

In response to these difficulties, we can observe virtues of scientific living that Charles Darwin developed in his life of pursuing truth and develop these qualities to the degree that is realistic for us by applying them in our daily lives. In this chapter, after an experience report on my own scientific living project, we will consider this challenge and then examine a four-step approach to scientific living. The last step pioneers ways to integrate science and religion in practice, with examples from cosmology, biology, psychology, and history.

From my journey

My recent venture in scientific living has sometimes been a wild ride, with magnificent discoveries and sobering disappointments. Once I retired, I realized that I had overplayed my religion card and my philosophy card—used these responses in situations that called for something else. Having often blundered by failing to give adequate attention to the material facts of the here and now, I came to the realization that I needed to give scientific living a new level of priority in my life. Focusing fully on the task in hand is the basis for excellence in scientific living, and I had a tendency to get lost in thought while driving, which I picked as my primary activity to work on. The effort to balance philosophical and spiritual interests with scientific living opened up a new phase of growth.

I was familiar with some scientific findings about attention.[1] For example, we don't pay attention to things we find boring (so I found ways to make driving more interesting); our attention span is limited (so I didn't need to feel bad if my attention wandered a bit); multitasking interferes with concentration (it was easy to turn off the radio but hard to turn off the stream of philosophical reflection). I learned that effective focus does not mean fixing my gaze on the car immediately ahead of me; a policeman told me that it was better—and more relaxing—to look at the horizon on the road ahead, trusting that peripheral vision would alert me to anything important that was closer. He also recommended that I occasionally I sweep my attention from side to side. His suggestions gave me a sense of freedom of movement as I interacted with the scene unfolding around me, but I needed more than technique.

One breakthrough I'll never forget: On long trips, my wife and I usually take turns driving two-hour shifts so that no dangerous fatigue sets in. But one morning, I had to drive to Chicago, six and a half hours from our home in Ohio, and Hagiko was in Japan; and I enjoyed what was for me an unprecedented sustained focus on the road. Fatigue never threatened; distraction was almost nonexistent. I was immersed in spiritual love. And I needed only one break to eat and enjoy an hour of profound rest. One thing

---

1. These findings come from Medina, *Brain Rules*, chapter 4. People's attention spans are becoming shorter, according to mounting research; multitasking harms our ability to pay attention to things. The culture conspires to give us all some degree of attention deficit disorder.

that helped was to take advantage of the little opportunities to communicate with other drivers along the highway—for example, flashing my high beams at truckers to let them know that they had passed me completely and it was safe to pull back into the right lane. I sent love to each driver who came near, and when I arrived in Chicago, I was exhilarated.

Peak experiences underscore broader truths, in this case about the interweaving of practical and spiritual dimensions in the everyday reliable driving that I have finally attained, thank God. This ongoing project has led to improvement in other areas. In general, I am gradually getting better at being faithful in big and little things. Cosmically, I find increasing power in the idea of a friendly universe. Biologically, I am finding it more mean-ingful to maintain healthy habits. Psychologically, I'm growing in listening and adjusting my communication to people's receptivity. I recognize more quickly when my unbeautiful emotions are rumbling and my brain is get-ting its energies out of balance; and responding to these situations as they arise allows me to let go of ugly thoughts, mobilize truth, invite a new divine invasion, and cleanse the inner life. And I have a sharper sense of what I can contribute in the current phase of history.

Darwin's hunger for the truth of fact

This biographical sketch of Darwin, like others in this book, makes limited claims. No one person exemplifies every virtue connected with scientific living, and I don't know to what extent Darwin practiced his virtues as a scientist in the rest of his life. Nor do I aim to give a balanced estimate of Darwin's character or to suggest that he was a solitary genius without sub-stantial debts to others. I do not take sides in the controversies about Dar-winism beyond the limited use made of his ideas here. Our brief glimpse into Darwin's life is designed simply to help us grow. Above all, we should not let his achievements, or those of anyone else profiled in this book, lead us to form unreasonably high expectations of ourselves.

Charles Darwin (1809–1882) became a great scientist thanks to his extraordinary gifts, a fine scientific education, decades of experience in re-search—and because he developed the virtues of scientific living to a world-class level. Fortunately, we do not need his gifts, education, and experience to approach those same qualities.

Darwin understood that science is an activity to which nonscientists can contribute. He encouraged Navy officers to assist in his research, and found that with only a little preparation and equipment, they could make systematic observations of the causes of geological change. They could observe "sedimentary deposition, erosion of cliffs, icebergs, coral reefs. . . . They should collect dust that settled on the deck, and, ashore, concentrate on fossils, volcanoes, and coal samples."[2]

Darwin had been well trained and educated in the skills and knowledge of geology and biology, but went beyond academic norms in his voracious and innovative pursuit of facts. In search of evidence of biological mutation, he "followed up hearsay stories of exceptional hounds, silkworms, hybrid geese, feral and farm animals in the colonies—anything in fact on selection, inheritance, and breeding. . . . He looked anew at the gamekeepers' familiar fare: agricultural shows, animal husbandry, farmhouse lore, and the *Poultry Chronicle*. And he began quizzing those who knew most about breeding and inheritance: fanciers and nurserymen."[3] Darwin found that through a profession or hobby or just keen observing, persons without any specialized academic background might acquire knowledge of scientific value.

In science, one quality rises above the others: hunger for truth. Truth is the value whose wholehearted pursuit is the main scientific virtue. Human motivation is rarely single, but it is hard to avoid the impression that a most diligent passion for truth spurred Darwin on, from his early studies in Edinburgh and Cambridge through his voyage on the *Beagle* to his later prodigious researches. In his autobiography, after modestly acknowledging his limitations, Darwin set forth his strengths: "noticing things which easily escape attention, and . . . observing them carefully"; observing and collecting facts; and being consistent and passionate in his "love of natural science."[4]

Strengths are interconnected. Hunger for truth motivates concentration, hard work, and patience. For example, beginning in 1846, Darwin spent nearly eight years of physically demanding labor studying barnacles; describing one species after another with minute care, he found tiny variations in their sexual characteristics that provided another piece to the puzzle of how evolution works. Darwin wrote of his habit of concentrating and working energetically on whatever he was engaged in.[5]

A truth seeker needs courage, and the love of truth inspires courage. Darwin's courage enabled him to rise above severe, chronic stomach troubles and to confront opposition from elements in his society whose respect mattered to him. He pursued unpopular lines of thinking, which shows particular courage in his case, since he was a kind and tactful man,

2. Desmond and Moore, *Darwin*, 352.

3. Ibid., 426; cf. 565.

4. Darwin, *Autobiography*, 68.

5. Ibid., 39.

not the aggressive or polarizing sort. His theory of evolution was not only controversial, but it was also linked to Lyell's unsettling geology of gradual change over enormous stretches of time. This idea competed with the traditional biblical view, which assumed a young earth some six thousand years old and posited an early era of catastrophic upheavals with volcanoes and earthquakes, in order to make sense of the relative geologic stability that has historically been observed.

To seek truth efficiently, Darwin needed to organize his inquiries. Every foray was strategic, part of his quest to puzzle out the causes of things. He described his own habits as methodical, and the trait was evident in his scholarship. In dozens of large scrapbooks, he collected and sorted by topic the facts he had gathered. He made an index of key facts in any book he bought; when he borrowed a book, he would make his own summary of it. Thus, before writing on a particular topic, he could review all his prior research.[6]

Willingness to test hypotheses thoroughly and follow truth wherever it leads fostered Darwin's humility. He was always ready to revise his cherished ideas; in response to a well-argued criticism of his writing, he deleted passages that he had hoped were true, noting that a scientist should have no regret about letting go of false beliefs.[7] "I have steadily endeavoured to keep my mind free so as to give up any hypothesis, however much beloved (and I cannot resist forming one on every subject), as soon as facts are shown to be opposed to it. Indeed, I have had no choice but to act in this manner, for with the exception of the Coral Reefs, I cannot remember a single first-formed hypothesis which had not after a time to be given up or greatly modified."[8]

When it was called for, Darwin had no trouble acknowledging the weakness of his case, and he sometimes added a dash of gentle humor. To a friend who found a flaw in his reasoning, Darwin replied, "You speak of finding a flaw in my hypothesis. This shows you do not understand its nature. It is a mere rag of a hypothesis with as many flaws and holes as sound parts. But I can carry in it my fruit to market for a short distance over a gentle road; . . . and a poor rag is better than nothing to carry one's fruit to market in."[9] In *The Origin of Species*, Darwin admitted the fact that the geological record does not adequately support natural selection as the primary mechanism of evolution. "He who rejects these views on the nature of the

6. Ibid., 65–66.
7. Desmond and Moore, *Darwin*, 457.
8. Darwin, *Autobiography*, 68.
9. Ibid., 475, modifying the spelling.

geological record, will rightly reject my whole theory. For he may ask in vain where are the numberless transitional links which must formerly have connected the closely allied or representative species, found in the several stages of the same great formation." A mark of Darwin's greatness was his unpretentious lucidity, which enabled him to write, "I am well aware that scarcely a single point is discussed in this volume on which facts cannot be adduced, often apparently leading to conclusions directly opposite to those at which I have arrived."[10]

Darwin's humility was combined with tenacious loyalty to the idea of evolution that he was developing. When research on one explanatory hypothesis went badly, he would be crestfallen; but he would push on to invent and pursue another hypothesis with characteristic vigor. The balance of these virtues in his character is evident in *The Origin of Species*: "Long before having arrived at this part of my work [chapter 6, "Difficulties on Theory"], a crowd of difficulties will have occurred to the reader. Some of them are so grave that to this day I can never reflect on them without being staggered; but, to the best of my judgment, the greater number are only apparent, and those that are real are not, I think, fatal to my theory."[11] This combination of confidence and humility liberates inquiry.

Hunger for truth leads to a thoroughgoing identification with reality, as we see in an account of Darwin late in life, when he was immersed in experiments on the movement of plants.

> Spring turned the study into a pungent jungle, with seeds sprouting in biscuit tins on the chimneypiece, cabbages and runner beans in floor pots, and nasturtium, cyclamens, cacti, and telegraph plants scattered on tables. Charles was in his element, infatuated with every rootlet and blossom. All these were his companions; he had a feeling for their "aliveness." He talked to them unselfconsciously, praising their ingenuity or twitting the "little beggars" for "doing just what I don't want them to." Sometimes a flower caught his eye, and he would stroke it gently, childlike in his "love for its delicate form & colour." The plants moved him, like the romances [his wife] Emma read aloud in the afternoons, and when the plants moved themselves they stirred him most of all.[12]

Here the mind of the researcher fills with the life he investigates. A pervasive feature of scientific living is the passion of the very life of inquiry itself, in

10. Darwin, *Origin of Species*, 308 and 96.

11. Ibid., 202.

12. Ibid., 631.

which there are repeated attempts, ups and downs, perseverance, and progress. Darwin's identification with life hints at a kinship between the striving scientist and the evolving world he studies.

Nothing is more basic to science than what Darwin called "hard, unbending facts";[13] nevertheless, a collection of facts by itself is not science. Darwin knew that skins and bones and "isolated facts soon become uninteresting."[14] To move from extensive collections of facts to science, he would work to explain the facts, "grouping them so that general laws or conclusions may be drawn from them." Indeed, he could legitimately claim, as he did in *The Origin of Species*, to have created with massive supporting evidence and argument a remarkably broad unifying vision: "All living and extinct beings are united by complex, radiating, and circuitous lines of affinities into one grand system."[15]

Darwin's drive to piece together a grand narrative of evolution was combined with a scientist's resolve to keep his broad theory based on facts. He did not dabble in untestable speculation and had a keen sense for the crucial difference between well-supported fact and speculative theory. "Unlike the atheists, seeking an alternative to Anglican Creationism in a chemical soup, Darwin kept ultimate origins out of the picture. Life's initial appearance was inscrutable, he implied to [Robert] Hooker. All that should concern the naturalist was its subsequent change."[16] He avoided speculation about chemical evolution, the idea that living organisms arose spontaneously from inorganic, chemical elements.

Darwin's sensitivity to beauty and commitment to goodness

The virtues of scientific inquiry appear to stand as a cluster on their own. But a perusal of the journal that Darwin wrote in his twenties during the years on the *Beagle* shows his scientific virtues enmeshed with his classical education: his love of Milton, Shakespeare, and other poets as part of his general aesthetic sensitivity; his broad reading and general anthropological interests; his religious faith; and his ethical humanity.[17] The strengths of scientific living flourish best when integrated with other virtues.

13. Ibid., 284.
14. Desmond and Moore, *Darwin*, 190.
15. Darwin, *Origin of Species*, 377.
16. Desmond and Moore, *Darwin*, 412.
17. Darwin, *Journal*.

During his voyage on the *Beagle*, Darwin had many profound experiences of natural beauty. "He had climbed the Andes, stood on volcanic rims, seen glaciers crashing into the sea, waded along coral reefs, but with all said and done, none of these exceeded 'in sublimity the primeval forests.' He had sat enraptured in lush creeper-strewn jungles, 'temples filled with the varied productions of the God of Nature.' He had been filled with religious awe: 'No one can stand unmoved in these solitudes, without feeling that there is more in man than the mere breath of his body.'"[18]

The breadth of Darwin's bond with all of life was accompanied by strong ethical feelings for his fellow man. Darwin's profound respect for human beings enabled him to observe anthropological differences while retaining his core convictions. He had a revulsion against the mistreatment of any person, no matter how "savage." Although he surveyed what he regarded as a continuous spectrum of humanity, and even though he traced humankind to the apes, he retained a lifelong abhorrence of slavery, a strong, intuitive, visceral indignation. Darwin did not force science to proclaim his ethical message, but neither did he let science subvert his moral intuition.

Darwin developed and exercised virtues useful in any kind of inquiry:

- Hunger for truth and whole-souled identification with the real
- An approach to problem-solving that is alive, exploratory, and resourceful
- The habit of testing one's ideas by patient, methodical inquiry, accurate reasoning, and careful attention to fact
- Keen perception and concentrated observation
- The ability to distinguish fact from theoretical speculation
- Humility, freedom from prejudice, and openness to diverse views
- Teamwork
- Courage

Further study expands this list. For example, Louis Caruna takes a different and fruitful approach that yields five virtues:

> First, the virtue of living with due respect both toward common sense . . . and to the more sophisticated scientific world-views; second, the virtue of living in a way that gives [balanced] importance both to what is universal [as set forth in grand theories

18. Desmond and Moore, *Darwin*, 191. It is well known that the religious faith of Darwin's early years waned later on; apparently his growth in spiritual experience did not keep pace with his intellectual advancement.

such as the physics of Newton and Einstein] and to what is particular [to guard against overgeneralization]; third, the virtue of
prudential risk-taking that is aware of both the strong points
and weak points of our intellectual faculties [willingness to exercise both a healthy skepticism about empirical claims and also a
healthy trust about what reason can achieve]; fourth, the virtue
of living in a way that acknowledges the [many factors that affect
our views of things]; fifth the virtue of heuristic courage [we
need to trust tradition and the continuity of scientific progress
and also to recognize that we must be ready for discoveries that
carry us beyond conventional thinking].[19]

Barbara McClintock's virtues as a scientist

Feminist philosophy of science celebrates the way that keen perception develops intuitive power through long and loving practice. These virtues of
scientific living, glimpsed in Darwin, are notably exemplified by Barbara
McClintock, as portrayed by Evelyn Fox Keller in *A Feeling for the Organism*. McClintock was a specialist in the genetics of maize. She knew the
corn plants in her field with a naturalist's intimacy and made discoveries
in genetics that anticipated the work of later generations of biochemical
researchers. A fellow Cornell cytogeneticist, Marcus Rhoades, once said to
her: "I've often marveled that you can look at a cell under the microscope
and can see so much!" What was her secret? After coming to a key insight
regarding a cellular reproductive process in a particular plant, her experience of looking at the cells changed:

> Where before she had seen only disorder, now she could pick
> out the chromosomes easily. "I found that the more I worked
> with them the bigger and bigger [they] got, and when I was
> really working with them I wasn't outside, I was down there. I
> was part of the system. I was right down there with them, and
> everything got big. I even was able to see the internal parts of
> the chromosomes—actually everything was there. It surprised
> me because I actually felt as if I were right down there and these
> were my friends." . . . She spoke of the "real affection" one gets
> for the pieces that "go together": "As you look at these things,
> they become part of you. And you forget yourself. The main
> thing about it is you forget yourself."[20]

19. Caruna, *Science and Virtue*, 110–11.
20. Keller, *Feeling for the Organism*, 69 and 117.

Keller recalls that during her interviews, McClintock said over and over again that one must have the time to look, the patience to "hear what the material has to say to you," the openness to "let it come to you." Above all, one must have "a feeling for the organism." To be sure, one doesn't acquire such perception only by perceiving. McClintock explained, "I have learned so much about the corn plant that when I see things, I can interpret [them] right away." Her seeing went back and forth between the microscope and the field:

> [One must understand] how it grows, understand its parts, un-derstand when something is going wrong with it. [An organism] isn't just a piece of plastic, it's something that is constantly being affected by the environment, constantly showing attributes or disabilities in its growth. You have to be aware of all of that. . . . You need to know those plants well enough so that if anything changes, . . . you [can] look at the plant and right away you know what this damage you see is from—something that scraped across it or something that bit it or something that the wind did.
>
> No two plants are exactly alike. They're all different, and as a consequence, you have to know that difference. . . . I start with the seedling, and I don't want to leave it. I don't feel I really know the story if I don't watch the plant all the way along. So I know every plant in the field. I know them intimately, and I find it a great pleasure to know them.[21]

Scientists differ, as do branches of science, in the proportion of attention given to empirical particulars and to rational structure. McClintock's grasp of particulars also nourished, and was nourished by, her grasp of the logic that explained her amazingly reliable intuitive solutions.

Many of the virtues that we observe in scientists can readily be trans-lated into principles: Concentrate on the task at hand. Pay attention to the facts that define and surround your situation. Explore causes. Seek for a big-picture integration of all relevant data.[22] Balance common sense with sci-ence and universal theories with attention to particulars. Have confidence

---

21. Ibid., 198.

22. Another principle I have found helpful comes from a scientist friend of mine, James Edward Blessing: solve problems as they arise. For example, if you are working on a problem that seems to take only a few steps for its solution, and along the way an additional, unforeseen problem crops up, then turn to focus on that. If the path to solv-ing the new problem turns up yet another one, turn to that with the same dedication, and so on. Finally, the intermediate problems will all be solved, resulting in the original problem being solved with an uncommon thoroughness. However, it is necessary to keep things in perspective; if too many problems show up, at some point it becomes unreasonable to continue to pursue a particular course of action.

in the power of reason alongside healthy skepticism about human intellectual weaknesses. Trust the wisdom of tradition but be ready to innovate.
These habits are useful for any type of inquiry and for scientific living.

To learn the fine art of taking insights about scientific virtues into the
laboratory of life, it helps to distinguish four stages of scientific living and
see examples that guide us to approach our own goal of scientific living
more concretely and confidently.

Scientific living basics

Scientists' practices challenge us as we recall that scientific living means acting in the light of the relevant truths of science. The truths of science are
truths of fact. Scientific living begins with stage one: being aware of fact,
understanding fact at a level that is normally satisfactory for practical purposes, and focusing effectively on the task at hand. When we focus well, we
notice facts that would be easy to overlook, face facts that are hard to deal
with, and establish important facts with care instead of jumping to conclusions. Exploring facts leads us to causes. We do what we reasonably can
to figure out causes and their effects; and thinking about these leads us to
consider factors that operate in our situation, the resources we can bring to
bear, and the consequences of alternative courses of action.

Our intuitive, stage-one understanding of fact is continually revised
by our forays into the later stages of scientific living: bringing to mind the
scientific information we already have, acquiring new knowledge, and putting things in a broad perspective. As we have need and time, we enter the
second stage of scientific living: getting explicit about which science or sciences are relevant to our task, and bringing to mind and applying what we
already know of the relevant scientific knowledge. For example, a student
of mine whose project in scientific living was to quit smoking classified the
temptations that arose as biological, psychological, or sociological. Simply
identifying and classifying temptations empowered him to overcome them
more readily. He did not study more science; he simply brought to mind
what he already knew and made use of that knowledge.

The difference between using what we know and neglecting what
we know is great. Consider a more detailed example. A student notices a
problem: it is harder to concentrate in class when he is hungry. He immediately sees the cause, notes its practical implications, and then recognizes
the solution: he needs to eat adequately before coming to class. He identifies the relevant science as biology. He states the relevant truth of science
in a general and positive way: proper nutrition is required for the brain to

efficiently support learning. He already knows that coffee and a doughnut do not make a good breakfast. He realizes that if he disciplines himself to take time for proper nutrition, he will feel better, learn better, and contribute better. In order to form the habit of eating a healthy breakfast, he recognizes his need to develop virtues of time management and self-mastery (note that this need makes another science, psychology, relevant to his project).[23]

The third stage of scientific living involves learning more of science and applying it in practice. Continuing the previous example: the student goes online, does a search for "nutrition brain learning," and from the results selects resources that bring him new knowledge, enhance his perspective, enable him to make a better selection of foods, and boosts his motivation.[24]

In the fourth stage of scientific living, we develop a perspective that integrates science with philosophy and religion, a perspective centered on a concept of evolution. Once biology set in motion the idea of evolution, the idea was taken up by other sciences. The picture of a long, gradual, and challenging process leading to the appearance of higher forms of life struck a responsive chord. The concept of evolution was expanded by Henri Bergson, Pierre Teilhard de Chardin, and others, to become a cosmic concept embracing all levels of life.[25] Today we can build on their achievements to affirm the outworking of divine purpose in the interconnected realms of energy and matter, biological development, personal growth, and planetary history. In its fullness, scientific living participates in that multidimensional evolutionary process.

Those of us who aspire to live the truth in its fullness do well to spend some time cultivating scientific habits of mind. Consider this testimony from Albert Schweitzer, who described what it was like to enter medical school, having already distinguished himself as a musician, philosopher, and theologian.

> I was at last in a position to acquire the knowledge I needed in order to feel the firm ground of reality under my feet in philosophy!
>
> But study of the natural sciences brought me even more than the increase of knowledge I had longed for. It was to me a spiritual experience. I had all along felt it to be psychically a danger that in the so-called humanities with which I had been concerned hitherto, there is no truth which affirms itself as

23. This example comes from the project of David Paulik.

24. See the article by Philippa Norman, "Feeding the Brain."

25. For a contemporary version, see McIntosh, *Evolution's Purpose*, 168, and Wattles, "Teleology Past and Present."

self-evident, but that a mere opinion can, by the way in which it deals with the subject matter, obtain recognition as true. The search for truth in the domains of history and philosophy is carried on in constantly repeated endless duels between the sense of reality of the one and the inventive imaginative power of the other. The argument from facts is never able to obtain a definite victory over the skillfully produced opinion. How often does what is reckoned as progress consist in a skillfully argued opinion putting real insight out of action for a long time!

To have to watch this drama going on and on, and deal in such different ways with men who had lost all feeling for reality I had found not a little depressing. Now I was suddenly in another country. I was concerned with truths which embodied realities, and found myself among men who took it as a matter of course that they had to justify with facts every statement they made. It was an experience which I felt to be needed for my own intellectual development.[26]

Schweitzer discovered that he needed a scientific foundation, along with his philosophy and religion, in order fully to experience living the truth. We will learn more about Schweitzer in chapter 6.

If we are developing a religious philosophy, we can, when scientific discovery is mixed with an antireligious philosophy, transplant the scientific discovery into our own garden. We can regard science and religion as complementary. Science observes the outer world of things and leads the mind toward the invisible realm of microprocesses and mathematical law; religion takes the mind to the inner world of values. Science makes statements about the body and about observable behavior; religion makes affirmations about soul, spirit, and the whole person. The matter of science responds to physical gravity; religious experience responds to another kind of attraction. Mind spans the gap between brain and spirit, and philosophy spans the gap between science and religion. For philosophy to harmonize scientific realism with spiritual idealism, it helps to see that philosophy can interpret any fact of science as being consistent with any truth of religion. Material fact and spiritual truth do not contradict each other.

In practice, working with a multidimensional concept of evolution leads us to calm down, seek the long-range view in any situation, temper spiritual idealism with scientific realism, study to know the proper sequence of events, discern what projects are timely, and be patient with the long-term gradual unfolding. When we find ourselves in a decline, we work to slow it down. When we can lead an advance, we do not get too far ahead of

26. Schweitzer, *My Life and Thought*, 104.

those we hope to lead. The reward for scientific living is that when we act in accord with universe law and the wisdom of evolution, we gain stability and power.[27]

Cosmology and a friendly universe

As we participate in evolution concretely, we get involved in cosmology, biology, psychology, and history. Each item of scientific knowledge within these disciplines contributes to a big picture; and the widest framework for scientific thinking is cosmology, an account of the cosmos as a whole.

Each generation tends to project its cosmology in the light of the science or discipline that is most impressive at the time. The ancient Greeks, from Pythagoras through Ptolemy, beheld a universe of geometry, regularity, and proportion. Theologians in the Middle Ages saw creation as expressing the purposes of God, the First Cause. During the period from Galileo through Newton, an image arose of the creation as a mechanism like a clock, described in terms of the causal laws of classical mathematical physics. Then Darwin's theory of evolution stimulated concepts of the cosmos as a whole, sometimes in combination with postclassical physics of relativity and merely statistical laws at the micro level. Ecology also stimulates the cosmological imagination to see the earth as a living whole, and mother nature as an embracing and nurturing source with which we must learn anew to live in harmony. We can synthesize all these historical contributions in a concept of the cosmos. In that case, our wisdom synthesis would envision a universe of statistical laws at the micro level, which yield causal regularities at the perceptual level, supporting evolving life in an interconnected web, expressing the purpose of God.

We participate in cosmic evolution by our choice of attitude: we can regard the universe as friendly. From our human perspective, we experience much that strikes us as indifferent or hostile to human interests; but such experience does not require us to draw an atheistic or pessimistic conclusion about human destiny in the cosmos. Science by itself does not answer the question regarding a friendly universe, but there is evidence to support a belief in a wise, strong, and loving Creator of a universe that is being managed with our long-range best interests in mind.

Consider what cosmologists call fine-tuning: life as we know it requires a universe in which basic physical constants must be very precisely what they are; slight deviations would make life impossible. It is as though

27. A philosophically and spiritually expanded concept of evolution can symbolize this entire philosophy of living.

creative intelligence fine-tuned four basic forces. *Gravitation* is just strong enough to hold galaxies together and weak enough to allow the universe to expand. The *weak nuclear force* slows down the rate at which stars burn their hydrogen, so that stars last long enough for life to evolve. The *strong nuclear force* is strong enough to bind together the protons and neutrons in an atom, but its range is limited; it does not draw electrons close to the nucleus, so electrons are available to form bonds with other atoms. The *electromagnetic force* holds electrons in their precise orbits so that these bonds form stable molecules.[28]

Fine-tuning also seems evident in the way that the properties of water fit the requirements of life. Water covers three-quarters of our planet and makes up 90 percent of our body mass. It stores heat and helps maintain the temperature equilibrium required for planetary life, both in the individual organism and in the environment. When an animal perspires and the water evaporates, the heat carried off with the vapor brings efficient cooling to the skin. Unlike other liquids, water expands when it freezes; thus, because ice is less dense than its liquid form, it floats. In the winter, ice on lakes and rivers insulates the deeper water from heat loss and thereby protects marine life, without which no organism could exist. Water vapor is one of the atmospheric devices for filtering out harmful radiation from the spectrum of radiation that the sun pours forth, and for transmitting precisely the wavelengths that life requires.

Despite evidence of the universe being fine-tuned for life, scientific cosmology has no room for the hope of everlasting life. Consider the Second Law of Thermodynamics, which has been interpreted to predict the "heat death" of the universe as a result of increasing entropy, disorder. The idea is that in all energy reactions, some energy is always reduced to heat. Heat is the simplest, most rudimentary, most "degraded" or disorganized form of energy—molecules randomly bumping against other molecules. Heat thus represents a loss of organization; due to this loss, no engine can be 100 percent efficient or run by itself forever. Another example of entropy is the reduction of an eggshell to pieces when it is broken; the previous order is replaced by fragmentation. Even organisms take more energy from the environment than they embody in their own highly ordered ("negentropic") structures and activities. If the Second Law were extended to the cosmos as a whole, it would predict that the universe will eventually run down and the final state of energy organization in the universe will be molecules or more primitive particles randomly bumping into one another. The scenario

28. For explanations and additional examples, see Rolnick, *Origins*, on which I rely for this description. Particularly helpful on the topic of fine tuning are writings by philosophers Robin Collins and John Leslie.

in which entropy has the final word assumes that the universe is a closed system in the sense that it receives no sustaining infusion of energy and mind-guided order.

Science itself evolves. The truths of science are as dependable as anything in this world; but scientific knowledge is growing and scientific theories are changing. Although an exclusively scientific discourse about cosmology must abstain from any talk of a Creator's purpose, we may consider modifying a key assumption in scientific cosmology: the idea of the physical universe as a closed system, unaffected by anything beyond itself and capable of being explained entirely in its own terms. To assume a closed universe shuts down the hope of everlasting life.[29]

But what if the universe is open? What if an infinite and eternal Creator continuously nourishes the created universe with ordered energy? If such energy does in fact pour forth, and if, in addition, these energies are being intelligently managed, then we can put to rest the scenario of universal disintegration. This strategy leaves the Second Law of Thermodynamics intact but deprives it of cosmological finality, just as the law of gravity is not violated when a person stands up.

Even with all that is unresolved in scientific cosmology, we can regard the universe as friendly in the following ways: It supports life. It is intelligible to a significant degree and provides an environment of dependable facts and causes that we can work with. It gives us the prospect of a friendlier world if we cooperate with one another. And it gives us the choice to believe in a Friend we cannot see and a destiny we cannot prove.

Biology and spiritual openness

It is biology that first brought the idea of evolution to science, an idea that needs clarification because of debates that result from linking evolution to a group of widely varying ideas.

1. *Early life forms were the ancestors of all later life forms.* This idea is called "descent with modification"; many kinds of evidence strongly support this statement.

2. *Natural selection is an important process in evolution.* It is a slow process, a gradual accumulation of numerous small, chance variations

---

29. Paul Davies has reviewed the various scenarios of the far future of the universe that are considered plausible in scientific cosmology. All the scenarios are utterly bleak. See Davies, *Last Three Minutes.* He begins by confessing how speculative these scenarios are, and goes on to tell stories of inexorable, final doom.

that proved beneficial in the struggle for survival. This idea, too, is well supported.

3. *Natural selection is the basic explanation of evolution.* Gaps in the fossil record continue to challenge this statement.

4. *The origin of life on earth is an accident wholly due to physical and chemical processes.* This statement is an unproven hypothesis, and scientists have generally given up trying to build a living organism starting with only water, chemicals, and electricity.

5. *Because of the many similarities between humans and animals, it is a mistake to think that human beings are on a higher level in mind and spirit.* This statement expresses a philosophical view, not a scientific one.

6. *Science is the only reliable source of truth.* This view is scientism, a philosophical view, not anything that science itself could prove.

To lump all these ideas together under the term "evolution" blocks the development of an integral concept of evolution that includes a spiritual side.[30]

Scientific living in the biological realm means caring for our health, for the health of others, and for our ecosystems. Scientific living sets a stern agenda for our age. For example, overuse of social media hampers the development of the brain's capacity to support empathy, complex thinking, and moral decision-making.[31]

Scientific living is healthy living, and biological evolution has provided us with bodies whose health flourishes when the whole person functions in harmony. Vigorous exercise promotes improved cognitive functioning.[32] Allowing the attention to rest quietly on the breath promotes mind-body harmony with a variety of health benefits.[33] Engaging in religious practices is correlated with reduced hypertension, heart disease, cancer, immune

---

30. This list of meanings of the term *evolution* is a variation on one put forth by Plantinga, "Creation and Evolution," 779–89.

31. Small and Vorgan, *iBrain*, chapters 1 and 2.

32. Ratey and Hagerman, *Spark*.

33. Research on the health benefits of mindfulness and breathing can be found on the Harvard, Mayo Clinic, and Georgetown University websites: http://www.health.harvard.edu/blog/mindfulness-meditation-improves-connections-in-the-brain-201104082253 (mentions benefits of mindfulness for high blood pressure, chronic pain, psoriasis, sleep difficulties, anxiety, depression, binge eating, and compromised immune function); http://www.mayo.edu/research/labs/mindful-breathing/overview; http://hr.georgetown.edu/fsap/meditationandmindbodyskills.html.

system troubles, and mortality.[34] Taking fifteen minutes a day for appreciation brings physical benefits.

> A study in 1995 by Dr. Rollin McCraty, director of research for
> the HeartMath Institute in Boulder Creek, California, has found
> that states of appreciation are correlated with a physiological
> state known as resonance (or parasympathetic dominance)—
> where heart, breathing, blood pressure, as well as brain rhythm
> and even the electrical potential of the skin are synchronized.
> Resonance also emerges during deep relaxation and sleep. In a
> state of resonance, says McCraty, the entire body is in a more
> efficient energy state. When we are feeling stressful emotions
> such as anger, frustration, or anxiety, our heart rhythms become
> more erratic. When we are in states of appreciation, gratitude,
> love, and compassion, heart rhythms are coherent and or-
> dered—calming our neurological and endocrine systems.
>
> McCraty measured thirty individuals' brain activity both
> before and during states when they were actively focusing on
> appreciation. He found that heart rhythm and alpha coherence
> significantly increases during periods of appreciation. In an-
> other . . . study, a fifteen-minute focus on appreciation resulted
> in an immediate and significant increase in levels of an immune
> antibody called secretory IgA. Secretory IgA is one of the body's
> primary defenses against invading microbes. After a month of a
> daily, fifteen-minute practice of appreciation, thirty individuals
> had a 100 percent increase in a potent beneficial hormone called
> dehydroepiandrosterone (DHEA), as well as a corresponding 30
> percent reduction in the stress hormone cortisol.[35]

Biological evolution has led to the emergence of human beings who are now
increasingly recognizing that the levels of our being are interconnected.
A healthy body supports, and is supported by, good mental and spiritual
practices.

Neuroscience is amassing evidence that much of our thinking, emotional life, and behavior is highly influenced, if not controlled, by brain
events. Depending on how it is interpreted, this evidence can be useful for
spiritual growth. Consider this experiment. During the peak time of their
practice periods, Christian nuns with at least twenty years of practice in a
contemplative discipline called Centering Prayer and advanced practitioners of Tibetan Buddhist meditation were given brain scans. The results
showed that during profound contemplation or meditation, input is cut off

34. Koenig et al., *Religion and Health*.
35. Post and Neimark, *Why Good Things Happen*, 31.

to a particular region of the brain, the posterior superior parietal lobe. This cutting off of input is called "deafferentation." A wide variety of religious experiences have been found through testing to be associated with some degree of deafferentation. This event in the brain is associated with a lessened sense of dichotomy between self and other, and a lessened sense of the self as localized in space and time.[36] Even in garden-variety experiences of prayer and worship, we relax our customary, highly physical sense of self.

This experiment can be interpreted in very different ways; here are some possibilities. Since neuroscience shows that spiritual experience can be explained by brain events, the results might indicate that human beings are simply hard-wired for spiritual experience. When someone begins to pray or meditate, the mind induces changes in the brain. Whenever the relevant area of the posterior frontal lobe is totally deafferented, the experience of absolute, unitary being is the same, regardless of the subjective interpretations of the individuals involved. Interpretation and experience cannot be separated: the intentions and practices of persons of different religions, plus the grace of God, determine the perceived meaning of any given experience. For example, for the Buddhists, the meditative state was empty of all meaning, whereas religious meaning was part of the experience of the nuns.

This shows us that science by itself does not determine the philosophical significance of its results. Researchers draw on their own philosophical perspectives in designing experiments and reporting results; and science journalism and the interests of publishers and readers introduce additional influences on the way that research is presented. Neuroscience cannot tell the full story of any experience. It can only report on some aspects of what happens under experimental conditions in selected parts of the brain that researchers choose to study when their subjects engage in specific spiritual practices.

Researchers link biological language with language about experience, associating particular parts of the brain with specific functions of consciousness. But science cannot trace a chain of causes that explains even a basic physical function such as the experience of human vision. Neuroscience informs us that light hits the retina in the eye, which sends an electrochemical signal along the optic nerve going to the occipital lobe at the back of the brain—after which "it rises to consciousness." But this last statement refers to experience and thus transcends the language of neuroscience.

Researchers and science journalists sometimes mix neuroscience with confusing speculation about body, mind, and spirit. Sometimes a deliberate

36. For an account of the brain scan research with Christian nuns and Buddhist meditators, see Newberg et al., *Why God Won't Go Away*, chapters 1 and 6.

philosophical choice of reductionism adds to the confusion: a reductionist view of religion claims that God is *nothing but* a projection of the human mind. A reductionist view of psychology says that talking about mental activities is *merely* a way of talking about processes in the brain. A reductionist view of biology sees the language of biology as *just* a convenient shorthand for what physics and chemistry will eventually totally explain. We live at a time when it seems sophisticated to say "in my head" instead of "in my mind"; companies market "smartphones"; and everyone speaks of computer "memory"—all without the slightest sense of treading on philosophical thin ice. The risk is that we may allow the momentum of technological society to corral us into adopting biological materialism as the ultimate interpretation of what consciousness is.

We can interpret the biology of spiritual experience in a way that supports spiritual progress if we remain open to consider the possibility of physical, mental, and spiritual inputs to experience. With that perspective, we can imagine three different types of experience. One type can be thoroughly explained by neuroscience and social science; it would have negligible spiritual content. Another type of experience is purely spiritual; any effects of brain process would play a negligible role in the experience. And a third type of experience carries a mix of inputs; it could have a spiritual core along with a periphery of inputs from mind and body. As we grow, the periphery shrinks and the spiritual content stands out in greater purity, clarity, and distinctness. Given the likelihood that most of our spiritual experiences will have a mix of inputs, we should not assume that they come 100 percent straight from God. But we do not need to speculate on the proportion of inputs involved in a particular experience. Instead, we can do our best to discern its truth, beauty, and goodness, take responsibility for our interpretation, and proceed in humility and joy. As we consider the brain supporting a mind open to spiritual inputs, wonder deepens and mystery remains.[37]

If neuroscience teaches us how we are enmeshed in the deterministic realm of cause and effect, religion, in contrast, teaches liberation. Hinduism offers paths to *moksha*, liberation; Buddha offered a path to enlightenment and *nirvana*. Jesus of Nazareth said, "You shall know the truth, and the truth shall make you free." In order to move from being mostly controlled by

37. To be sure, an individual can be mistaken in identifying an experience as purely spiritual, but to deny the possibility of such experiences shows either a needless skepticism or a lack of experience. Sociologist Margaret M. Poloma balances sympathy with scientific objectivity in a helpful description of Pentecostal and charismatic religious experiences in *Main Street Mystics*. Writing as a participant-observer, she relates moving stories, recognizes dangers, sets forth critical questions, describes behaviors that many people would classify as unspiritual, and gives some empathic interpretations that present a strong case for regarding such experiences as valid.

causes to enjoying increasing spiritual liberty, we can exercise our freedom to choose to walk a spiritual path, a choice that is not caused by the brain. Progressing on that path, we build habits of mind and body that support a higher quality of thinking, feeling, and doing. The spiritual core of our experience increases and the material and psychological periphery shrinks.

Psychology after reductionism

On the psychological level, we participate in evolution by personal growth. As we grow spiritually, we mature our concept of God and increasingly relate to others as family. Psychology in the person of Sigmund Freud put up road blocks to the concept of God as our Father and the teaching that we should love our neighbor as ourselves. Freud found that a child's first image of God tends to come from the child's father. Since the child's relation with the mother is so close biologically, the father is typically the first prominent, genuinely *other* person that the child comes to recognize as such.[38] The young child tends to idealize this other and to project this image in the earliest stage of religious development. But this fact is part of the story, not the heart of it.

If we replace Freud's science-centered account with a spiritually centered one, we may interpret the child's early image of God as Father as a divinely designed, evolutionary scaffolding to be gradually outshone by an increasingly spiritual realization of God's parental love.[39] In this interpretation, the fatherhood of God can be both an evolutionary image arising in the natural mind and also a spiritual truth. In other words, early in life, the Father concept of God is a metaphor based on the child's experience of the earthly father. However, in a spiritually maturing person who continues to relate with God as Father, images from childhood may be left behind.[40] The image of the Creator as an old man with flowing white hair and beard is portrayed in a stunning painting by William Blake, *The Ancient of Days*. Spiritual maturity may be moved by such art; but it can also freely relate without such images.

38. I am indebted to Claire Thurston for this step in the reasoning.

39. De Luca, *Freud and Religious Experience*. See also Rizzuto, *Birth of God*. A more reductionistic view is implied in Fowler, *Stages of Faith*.

40. A spiritually mature concept of God as our Father is not a gendered metaphor projecting a social image of a biological male. The spiritually mature concept is not a metaphor or image at all but rather a realization of relationship. To be sure, any concept will always be short of the mystery of God's infinite and eternal nature. The vast literature on this topic generally affirms the equality of women with men and shows growing recognition of motherly love in God.

Since Freud's day, the sociology of family life and the feminist movement have added complexity to the topic. We are now more ready to recognize that we experience motherly love as well as fatherly love in God. We support each person's freedom to choose the name that expresses his or her experience of relating with God. But after science has spoken, those who wish to relate to God as a son or daughter of a loving Father can in good conscience freely enjoy the spiritual simplicity and power of that relationship. We might even entertain the possibility that the father concept of God will prove to be part of the solution to the troubles of the modern family. The road blocks put up by Freud were built by mixing genuine insight with antireligious philosophy. If we untangle the confusion, then we can slow down, drive around the road blocks, share the insights, and get a better view of the created landscape along the way. Such a disentangling enables scientific living to be part of an integrated experience of living the truth.

Freud provides another example of keen psychological observations mixed with needlessly antireligious philosophy. He challenges the religious idea, found in the Hebrew Bible and the New Testament, "You shall love your neighbor as yourself."[41] While Freud approved of altruism in certain circumstances, he saw the generalized call to "love your neighbor as yourself" as foolish and dangerous. However, if we transplant his critique into the garden of a spiritually centered philosophy, we find a group of useful cautions:

- You need to receive love if you want to give love
- Maintain self-respect
- Do not be driven to become emotionally involved in the life of every person you meet
- Do not neglect your duties as a family member, friend, co-worker, neighbor, and citizen
- With strangers, let trust grow gradually
- Remember that what you can reasonably expect of yourself is less than your ideal of perfection
- Develop a psychologically sound technique for acknowledging and rechanneling your own aggression

When Freud's critique is reformulated in this way, these cautions can help our love to be intelligent and wise.

41. Lev 19:18 and Mark 12:31. The ideas of Freud that I reinterpret come from Wallwork, "Love Thy Neighbor." Freud's cautions about loving everyone are more understandable when we recall that he lived as Jew during the rise of Nazism.

History and hope

On the level of planetary history, we participate in evolution by our contributions to a moral and spiritual renaissance.[42] By the way we live at home, at school, at work, and in our free time, we can bring that better day closer. We live in a time of planetary transition, as an age dominated by materialism and selfishness is destroying itself and a new age is dawning. The vision of a transformed world has been proclaimed by prophets who told of the kingdom of God becoming a practical reality among humankind. That vision of progress was secularized in the eighteenth and nineteenth centuries, and it seemed to be discredited in the twentieth century by world war and other miseries.

From a spiritual perspective, history is like a decathlon, in which the forces of faith and love compete against the forces of rebellion and hatred.[43] In any generation, it is uncertain which team will win; but in the long run, the triumph of faith and love is certain. There are reasons that support this hope, even with the tangle of biological, social, economic, and political problems our generation faces. The religious reason is that God has a destiny for us and will not allow us to destroy the human race; the only question is, how much more misery we will impose upon ourselves before we wake up and cooperate with the divine plan? To break up the tangle of problems, we need a worldwide spiritual awakening. When a critical mass of humanity do wake up, the average level of materialism and selfishness will go down as the level of idealism and generosity rises. Leadership and teamwork will then be empowered to tackle the tangle of problems effectively.

Empirical, historical reasons for hope in a moral and spiritual renaissance have been set forth by Harvard sociologist Pitirim Sorokin, whom we shall meet again in the last chapter.

1. Crises of materialism and selfishness similar to the present crisis have been seen before on a smaller scale; and eventually new leaders have arisen and gained the necessary cooperation.

2. We already see groups of people rejecting false values and disastrous leaders.

42. I use *history* as an umbrella term to include other social sciences such as anthropology, sociology, economics, and political science.

43. A decathlon comprises ten track and field events: 100-meter dash, long jump, shot put, high jump, 400-meter run, 110-meter hurdles, discus throw, pole vault, javelin throw, and 1,500-meter run (women have 100-meter hurdles and a different sequence of events).

3. We already see people turning to the higher way, partly through conscious reasoning and partly because of motivation found in the superconscious realm—that frontier of the human mind where divine spirit injects its creativity, power, and love.

4. Great changes are always assisted by the combined power of impersonal forces and by creative energies coming from a source higher than the conscious mind.

5. Many people, educated and uneducated, are lost and looking for something new.

6. Great moral and religious progress typically occurs during or immediately after crises, as can be seen in ancient civilizations and in Western countries.

7. What has occurred in individuals, groups, and nations may occur on a worldwide scale, and changes that would normally take centuries may instead take decades.[44]

Sorokin was realistic: he saw the need for inspired leaders, but he knew that not everyone could reach a heroic level of altruism; he asked the rank and file to raise their level of altruism by 50 percent.

Participating in evolution, we can cherish high hopes for human destiny and work for historical progress, including a moral and spiritual renaissance. Sooner or later, humankind will turn from an overdose of materialism and self-centeredness to a predominance of spiritual ideals and cooperation, which will remotivate scientific action to replace world war with world peace.

In sum, an integrated concept of evolution embraces a positive attitude to the cosmos; learns from biology the ways of sound health practices and ecological care; promotes a spiritually open interpretation of psychology; and encourages hope for human destiny.

The stability of scientific truth

The truths of science are products gained at the conclusion of a process. The process varies from one science and method to another, but there are family resemblances. Disciplined, critical effort is applied to establish facts with as much care as circumstances require and permit; a search for causes expands understanding; empirical research can correct errors in previous

44. These reasons come from Sorokin, *Reconstruction of Humanity*, 237–41.

research; and the knowledge gained is placed in the overarching framework of cosmic, biological, personal, and historical evolution.

When scientists make claims that go significantly beyond what their research has established, it is understandable that disputes arise; but these should not be allowed to distort the overall picture. There are laws and constants in nature: Gravity holds things together as galaxies whirl in their orbits. Pattern may be discerned. We can establish truths that express these laws and constants because the universe is dependable. The facts of the present are explained by causes from the past, and present facts carry implications for the future. In sum, science discloses the trustworthiness of nature's fidelity to law.

It is commonly said that scientific facts are theory-laden; and this is true in the sense that the meaning of a fact in science relies on a wider context of scientific theory. When the theory changes, the meaning of the fact will change. But it would be a mistake to regard all of science as uncertain and up for grabs. The testimony of philosopher of science Olaf Pedersen restores perspective by reminding us of the stability of scientific truth. He speaks not of theories but of a certain type of statement expressing what he calls primary relations. For example, "The boiling point of alcohol is 78° Celsius at a pressure of one atmosphere, which affirms a relationship between three classes of phenomena—the state of alcohol as a liquid or vapour, its temperature, and the pressure to which it is subjected."

> What I have in mind is primarily that kind of statement which is listed in a work like the well-known *Handbook of Chemistry and Physics* with its thousands of specific gravities, melting points, refractive indices, atomic weights, electrical conductivities, etc.
>
> This work appears from time to time in a new edition which is always more rich and comprehensive than its predecessor. The number of primary statements is ever increasing, and new information of permanent value is obtained all the time. . . . It is simply true in the sense that it would be scientifically impossible to replace it by a contradictory statement.[45]

In the daily practice of most scientists, the flexibility of science due to changes in theory is negligible compared to the stability of well-established facts.[46]

45. Pedersen, "Belief and Science," 127 and 129.

46. The idea of fact has a broad sense and a narrow sense. In this book, it will sometimes be useful to speak, in a summary way, of fact, meaning, and value as the specialties of science, philosophy, and religion, respectively. This way of speaking should not be taken to imply that science lacks meaning or that there are no values inherent in scientific striving. In what sense, then, may science be said to focus on fact? Scientists

The stability of physical fact contrasts with the more varied character of facts established through the social sciences. Research on the unconscious indicates depths in the human being beyond what we can directly observe. Nevertheless, human beings show observable regularities that make social science possible, partly because we are largely material creatures. To be sure, the social sciences also use a variety of methods involving understanding and interpretation of meaning, themes central to the following chapter.

Conclusions

In this universe of awesome stability and dynamism—with its laws and uncertainties, its gradual processes and sudden changes, its beauty and terror—we human beings come on the scene. We discover ways to cope, learn facts the hard way, begin to explore causes, develop science—and our lives begin to change. Whether we are beginners or experts in science, growth in scientific living helps us flourish as largely material creatures in a largely material environment.

Scientific living is the virtue or excellence of being responsible to fact. To love intelligently, to communicate mercifully, to apply justice fairly, we need to understand facts. Scientific living provides a sturdy foundation for

---

typically contrast fact with hypothesis and theory; and, given those distinctions, they are right to resist an oversimplification of their work that conceals the intellectual sophistication of science. Nevertheless, there is another sense in which we may use the term *fact* to describe what science delivers, even in a broad sense. It is a fact, one may say, that there is such-and-such a probability of a particular event occurring. It is a fact that in a given event, a particular causal law accounts for the observed effect. It is a fact that a particular hypothesis has been raised to the status of a theory given its breadth of implication and the strength of supporting evidence. References to hypothesis, causal law, probability, and theory are ways of expressing what science takes to be fact in an intellectually advanced sense—our best attempts to accurately account for the way things are.

In some contexts, where facts are produced by science, we may identify the truths of science with such facts, including facts of great generality. In other contexts, fact and truth are sharply distinguished. Someone may correctly recognize a fact in daily life and wonder what the truth of that fact is.

Sometimes when people speak of a fact and call it a truth, they can be interpreted as presenting the fact as the conclusion of a process of inquiry (informal or scientific) that has indeed given the fact an enhanced truth halo. Or they may be discussing an emotional topic and expressing complete certainty, implying that anyone who takes the trouble to find out will verify what they are asserting. Both of these apparent counterexamples to my terminological proposal may represent a subtle application of the distinction that I am making. Ordinary language uses the terms *truth* and *fact* in a variety of ways; the use of these terms here is designed to clarify some significant distinctions, not to do justice to the various uses of the terms.

living the truth and prepares us to recognize higher meanings and values. Truth, beauty, and goodness all reach into the material realm; so our thinking, feeling, and doing are all enhanced by gaining a good grasp of material fact.

Truth has a spiritual core and a scientific periphery, joined by a philosophical bridge. When these components are coordinated, scientific living aligns with the Creator's laws to participate responsibly in the evolving creation. The spirituality of this philosophy of living is *into and through*, as well as *over and above*. And trust in God as a loving Father transforms our experience of fact, causation, and evolution.

2

From Intuition through
Reason to Wisdom

Socrates and Philosophical Living

In the Louvre hangs a painting traditionally attributed to Rembrandt (1606–1669) and titled *Philosopher in Meditation*. The painting presents an old man, richly illuminated by golden light streaming through the window, in a room dominated by a sturdy and winding staircase leading to the floor above. Transplanting this historical treasure into the garden of our inquiry, we can interpret the scene as suggesting that the philosopher gains wisdom by decades of repeatedly climbing aloft and descending. Since philosophy seeks an integrated comprehension of the full spectrum of human experience, from humble facts to high values, the painting can symbolize for us the experience of insight in the grounded and lofty meditative thinking that is essential to philosophical living.[1]

Philosophical living is about living wisely, combining insights into higher truth with down-to-earth, street-smart sagacity. People gather wisdom from various sources: family, teachers, friends, the lyrics of rock songs, the world's philosophical traditions, Scripture and prayer, and many other aspects of life experience. But when we put a new thought into our basket of wisdom, it may not fit with some of the ideas already there. We allow the inconsistency to fester when we are philosophically lazy. The constructive

---

1. Some scholars hold that this painting was not done by Rembrandt; and some say that it was only after his death that it received its popular title, whose relevance to the painting is disputed. The painting has attracted widespread attention, and various psychological, philosophical, and spiritual interpretations of it can be found. But even if it were the case that this painting is not about a philosopher, it has a depth that invites interpretation, and it can easily be read as representing illumination that comes to meditative receptivity. A philosopher's reflection may be more wise, but it exemplifies a profoundly human capacity that is present in us all.

alternative is to examine the mental tension and either throw out a teaching that is no longer helpful or embark on a process of reinterpretation and revision of our ideas, so that our thinking regains coherence by acquiring a richer complexity.

Sometimes, our wisdom quest grinds to a halt. We try to reach out for wisdom but do not know how. We ask a friend and are not quite satisfied; or prayer leaves us uncertain. We steer clear of the overwhelming resources of philosophy, which has a reputation for being difficult and impractical. But giving up on the quest for wisdom impoverishes our ability to integrate science and spirituality; on our journey into truth, we fly our airplane on two engines instead of three. Neglecting our quality of thinking, we make do with a more surface view. To solve these problems, we need an accessible approach, a sketch of the territory that can provide guidance with a nonsimplistic quality of simplicity.

Philosophical living means living in the light of the wisdom we already have, recognizing the limits of our wisdom, and seeking more wisdom when we realize that we need it. Seeking wisdom cultivates the organizational headquarters of the mind. This cultivation involves philosophical thinking, by which I mean *adventuresome* thinking—making robust affirmations and entertaining critical questions while avoiding the extremes of dogmatism and skepticism. Based on mature concepts, philosophical living grows ever closer to meaningful understandings of facts and values, wiser decisions, and insightfully intuitive spontaneity.

Philosophy is for everyone. Alfred North Whitehead (1861–1947) saw the need for a philosophy of living that would coordinate facts, meanings, and values, and would spread throughout the civilized community.

> Philosophy is not a mere collection of noble sentiments. A deluge of such sentiments does more harm than good. Philosophy is at once general and concrete, critical and appreciative of direct intuition. It is not—or, at least, should not be—a ferocious debate between irritable professors. It is a survey of possibilities and their comparison with actualities. In philosophy, the fact, the theory, the alternatives, and the ideal, are weighted together. Its gifts are insight and foresight, and a sense of the worth of life, in short, that sense of importance which nerves all civilized effort. Mankind can flourish in the lower stages of life with merely barbaric flashes of thought. But when civilization culminates, the absence of a coordinating philosophy of life, spread throughout the community, spells decadence, boredom, and the slackening of effort.[2]

2. Whitehead, *Adventures of Ideas*, 98.

Whitehead's mention of civilization is timely, since Western civilization has chronically struggled to integrate the two great cultural strands of its origin: the holiness and righteousness portrayed in Jewish and Christian religion, and the truth, beauty, and goodness envisioned in Greek culture. That integration can occur by envisioning truth, beauty, and goodness as anchored in the eternal nature of God, and by recognizing the cultural development of these values as part of the divine adventure shared by God and humankind.[3]

If this integration were to occur, the West would have more to give to other civilizations, and it would be better able to recognize and learn from their achievements. In my opinion, learning from the truth, beauty, and goodness that have arisen in other civilizations is essential for the integration to flourish. This solution to this chronic problem of Western civilization makes long-term sense only as a phase in the realization of the potentials of a worldwide civilization.

As a step toward the realization of these ambitious goals, this chapter sets forth an approach to high-quality thinking. It shows a path to wisdom that begins with clarified intuition and reasoning and culminates with philosophical decision-making via interpretation of the meaning of the facts and values that are most relevant to a given situation. After noting how Socrates used this decision strategy in a life-and-death situation, we explore intuition, reasoning, and wise concept formation. We then reflect on the idea of meaning, on the ways that philosophy can cope with mystery, and on the strengths and limits in philosophy's ideas of truth.

From my journey

My philosophical education in meaning began with an ethics course in which we were assigned to write five short papers that cultivated critical thinking, examining ideas by analyzing authors' arguments. Next, in Greek and German philosophy I discovered depth of meaning. Later I took a six-year plunge into Chinese philosophy, which opened me to meaningful

3. Whitehead has paved the way for this integration. Despite a problematic metaphysics, he forged what he called di-polar theism, which recognizes the eternal, *primordial* nature of God (which he reduced to a set of ideas) and also the evolving, relational, *consequent* nature of God, which grows through interaction with every finite "occasion" (Whitehead sees a human not as an enduring being but as a sequence of occasions). The primordial nature of God participates in each decision of our lives by presenting a synthesis of all the ideas relevant to our choice; we feel the synthesis as a lure, which we are free to accept totally, partially, or not at all. The evolving nature of God is a concept that overlaps with the union of truth, beauty, and goodness set forth at the end of this book.

contributions from anywhere. As my interest in harmonious conceptual synthesis grew, I became increasingly dissatisfied with the practice of philosophy as a war zone. In our present culture, conflict of interpretations over the meaning of great concepts is to be expected; and sharp disagreement can be healthy and beneficial. But I began growing toward the goal of integrating critique with appreciative inquiry.

Two experiences made me realize that ideas expressed in very simple words can indicate meanings with cosmic reality. Teaching a seminar on Plato (427–347 BCE) and studying his dialogue the *Parmenides*, I was totally mobilized in a sustained quest for understanding.[4] Plato taught that ideas such as largeness and motion are realities that can be grasped through intellectual insight. One day on the way to school, I got caught up for a moment contemplating the bridge I was driving over, and that triggered a revelatory grasp of *largeness*. A week or so later, while taking a break from work, I was looking blankly out my office window at a group of students passing by on the sidewalk and was suddenly seized by an insight into *motion*. It was terrifying to see a group of persons in such total abstraction from the fact of their humanity. Nevertheless, capacity for grasping universal meanings is part of what makes us human.

Meaning that is intellectually understood and put into practice is a key dimension of human functioning. Meanings are universal in the sense that they may describe an unlimited number of examples. Actions have meaning; therefore we can ask "What if everyone did that?" and philosophers can describe a version of that question as a test of "universalizability." When we pray in the plural, for example, "*Our* Father . . . give *us* . . . " we universalize the prayer; if we have a personal matter to pray about, we can include everyone with the same need, and the experience of the prayer is transformed.

I am grateful to have been able to focus a career on truth, beauty, and goodness, not only in my research and writing, but also in doing experiential projects for growth with classes of students. The combination of study and practice, supplemented by blessings from above, leads to progress in understanding these great concepts. I am thrilled by anticipating the emerging new phase of my career of sharing with and learning from others. As I continue my never-ending inquiry into meanings, I give thanks that intellectual uniformity is not the goal. One of my favorite things about philosophy is that we don't have to agree.

---

4. My guide to the *Parmenides* was Miller Jr., *Plato's Parmenides*. The serious student will find in Miller's book a uniquely clear and detailed account of Plato's mature concept of the forms—an essential chapter in the history of philosophy's concept of meaning.

Socrates' lifelong preparation for his final drama

Imagine the scene: Socrates is in prison, having been duly convicted by the Athenian court; his friend Crito has just arrived to persuade him to escape. Crito has collected enough money to bribe the guard, and friends elsewhere in Greece are ready to receive a beloved seventy-year-old escapee. The hour is fast approaching when the death sentence will be carried out. Should Socrates escape or stay put? The ensuing decision-making process of one of the seminal philosophers in the Western world is a prime example of a philosophical decision made by interpreting the meaning of the relevant facts and values.

To understand why Socrates is in prison, we need some background information. Socrates (469–399 BCE) made a career of pursuing wisdom for himself and his fellow citizens at a time when Athenian citizens, giving way to luxury, abuse of power, and cultural pride, needed to be awakened to the pursuit of understanding and the care of the soul. He sought wisdom from politicians, but they resented his questions; from poets—the defenders of the traditions about the gods—but they could not explain the meaning of their best work; and from craftsmen who, despite their genuine know-how, assumed that their specialty gave them authority to pronounce on other matters as well.

Socrates tried to refute the message conveyed from the revered Delphic oracle, who had declared Socrates the wisest man in Greece. However, unable to find anyone wiser than himself, Socrates concluded that he alone had the wisdom to know where he lacked wisdom. Socrates was wise in the sense of having what the Greeks called a *technē* (skill, art, craft), which implied the ability to do something well that was neither an unexplainable knack nor a mystical gift, but something that could be understood and conveyed to others. But by asking questions of citizens in public places and embarrassing with his refutations those who gave inadequate answers, Socrates accumulated many enemies. To make matters worse, one of his associates betrayed Athens and went over to Sparta during the war between those two adversaries.

After Athens was defeated, Socrates was hauled into court on capital charges of impiety and corrupting the youth. In his courtroom defense, he did his best to explain his career of public, philosophical dialogue, but his accusers could grasp neither his meanings nor his positive intentions. Socrates was skillful in conducting philosophical discussion, but he confessed in court that lacked the wisdom to be certain whether death would be an endless, dreamless sleep or a transition to a heaven, where he could continue his pursuit of wisdom in discussion with great persons who had died. He nevertheless robustly proclaimed his conviction that a good person has nothing to fear in death.

In laying out his proposal for Socrates' escape, the first thing that came to Crito's mind was concern for his own reputation. It was well known that the guards could be bribed—what would people say if he let his friend die in prison when he could have gotten him out? But Socrates redirected Crito from concern about what others would think to the question of what is right and just. Once Crito accepted Socrates' proposal to inquire philosophically about what to do, the core reasoning began. Socrates made statements and posed questions, going forward only if Crito agreed with what he said.

Socrates' reasoning about not escaping from prison

Socrates' analysis had two main parts: a five-step reflection on the meaning of the value relevant to his situation, followed by a discussion of the meaning of the relevant facts. Here we see a great thinker doing the painstaking work of methodical and logical thinking.

First, Socrates expressed the premise for everything that would follow in his reasoning: he anchored the inquiry in a supreme commitment to goodness. He asked whether what matters most is staying alive or *living well*—in accord with goodness. Crito gave a definite answer that to live well is what matters most. This was no vague idealistic gesture, but rather a judgment that the value of goodness is supreme and ranks higher than the value of physical life. On the basis of this shared commitment, the inquiry was able to go forward.

Next, Socrates began to interpret the meaning of goodness. He asked whether living in goodness is the same as living in beauty and justice.[5] For Socrates, beauty was the supreme value next to goodness, and beauty connoted what is admirable as opposed to disgraceful; thus beauty in this situation had ethical implications. Justice was included because it was the specific quality of goodness relevant to the question of whether it is just—right—to break out of prison.[6] Socrates implied that the decision required by goodness was the same as that required by beauty and justice.

5. The term usually translated as "justice," *dikaiosunē*, is also translated as "rightness" and occasionally as "righteousness." It names a human virtue as well as a quality of a law or a code of laws.

6. Other specifics arrayed under goodness include wisdom, courage, self-mastery regarding pleasure, and friendship.

Third, once Socrates and Crito had affirmed their commitment to justice, Socrates posed this question to remind Crito of an implication of that commitment: if we are dedicated to doing what is right and just, may we ever intentionally do what is wrong and unjust? Crito drew the correct conclusion: we must never do wrong.

Fourth, given the agreement that we must never do wrong, Socrates proposed a further conclusion: we must not do wrong in return for wrong done to us. This conclusion, which clearly follows from the preceding agreement, was anything but trivial in that situation, because Socrates was in prison only because of a verdict that was wrong—based on factual errors and distorted interpretations.[7]

Fifth, Socrates asked whether an individual should also refuse to return harm for harm. This may seem like a small step beyond the previous conclusion, but it had a sharp edge of meaning at the time, because it contradicted the popular ethos of ancient Mediterranean society, one of whose leading maxims was to do good in return for good and harm in return for harm.[8] That ethos continued its hold on Crito, despite the fact that he was familiar with Socrates' critique of "repayment thinking" and had agreed with it in the past. Crito's initiative to convince Socrates to break out of prison showed that he was ready to retaliate, to return harm for harm, in accord with the ideas of the unphilosophical majority.

Next, when Crito failed to draw the proper conclusion from Socrates' reasoning, Socrates shifted the focus to the meaning of the facts of his situation. Socrates was a lifelong citizen of Athens whose parents' marriage was certified under the laws of the city. He enjoyed the benefits of growing up and living in the city and never made any effort to bring about change in the laws. Although he could have moved to another city that had a legal code that might have meted out a lesser punishment, or none at all, he chose to stay in Athens.

Socrates interpreted these facts by linking the concept of justice to the philosophical idea of a social contract: if citizens remain in a political community and accept its benefits, they incur a duty to abide by the law. To break out of prison would injure the fabric of law, with its established system of laws, court, and prison, as well as its determinations about which crimes may carry the death penalty. Escaping, then, would violate the citizen's

7. According to Socrates and Plato, judicial punishment of wrongdoers is not wrong, nor is it wrong to defend one's political community by inflicting injury on attackers; it is worse to commit injustice (which degrades the soul) than to suffer injustice. They also held that just punishment is good for the wrongdoer.

8. This historical thesis is set forth in Dihle, *Goldene Regel*; see also "From Greek Reciprocity to Cosmopolitan Idealism," in Wattles, *The Golden Rule*.

implicit agreement to accept the law fabric of the state in which he had chosen to live. Socrates would not return injustice for injustice; he would not retaliate against the unjust judgment of the jury by violating his agreement with the political community.

Socrates' reasoning showed how the meanings of the facts and the meanings of the values in these circumstances were interrelated. When he interpreted justice as the dominant meaning of goodness in his situation, he was guided by the facts of his legal situation. And when he selected and interpreted those facts, he was guided by the concept of justice. Other situations would have led him to interpret goodness in terms of courage, temperance, or friendship.

Toward the end of the dialogue in the *Crito*, Socrates made some ironic statements that appear to advocate slavish obedience to paternalistic government. Such talk was designed to awaken the philosophical reader to inquire more deeply. The irony was clear from his courtroom defense as reported in the *Apology*, where Socrates mentioned two occasions when he refused to obey unjust orders of the authorities. Therefore, we know that he did not hold an authoritarian political philosophy. Socrates' appeal to a particular principle, the principle of justice, is guided by an implicit understanding of what is appropriate to the facts of any given case. Socrates' reasoning in the *Crito* should thus not be read as implying that civil disobedience is always wrong. One should not imagine, for example, that if Socrates had lived during the era of Nazi persecutions and was confronted with a demand to hand over information about the Jews he knew, he would obey. His appeal to a particular principle, the principle of justice, was always guided by an implicit understanding of what is appropriate to the facts of any given case. Socrates appealed to justice in its rigorous implications early in the dialogue with Crito because he had thought through the ethical implications of his situation in prison well before his friend made his offer.

Socrates demonstrated, in a life-and-death situation, the stabilizing influence of an integrated philosophy. He was courageously loyal to goodness, careful in his reasoned examination of the meaning of that value, and insightful in his philosophical interpretation of the facts of the situation.

Socrates on truth, beauty, and goodness

In a concrete way, the *Crito* shows how Socrates participated in goodness. His fundamental insight into the reality of goodness shows up in the commitment that anchors his entire process of reasoning. We can see in his choices the practical value of decades of committed living, shared inquiry, principled decision, and resolute action. Socrates' philosophical living allowed goodness to form his soul. The soul harvest of a lifetime is implicit here.

In various places, Socrates expresses aspects of his understanding of what it means to be a human being. For example, in the *Phaedo* we see Socrates in discussion with friends just before he is to drink the poison decreed by the Athenian jury. As his friends are considering various reasons to believe in the immortality of soul, Socrates explains to them that he is in prison not because of the mechanical arrangement of the body's bones and sinews; considering material factors alone would, in fact, drive him to escape. He helps them to understand that he is about to die because of his soul's purposive decision to do what is best.

At the heart of Socrates' concept of the human being was the conviction that we must rise above a life that is driven primarily by material and emotional concerns, and see through sophistries that confuse and mislead the mind. We are capable of seeking truth, beauty, and goodness, and of living in accord with our best understanding of them. For Socrates, the quest for truth was a rigorously logical search for philosophical knowledge; the search for beauty was a passionate ascent from various levels of beautiful things to beauty itself, which attracts us and leads beyond itself to the good; and the good was the source of the mind's power to know and the source of the meaningful realities that the intellect may understand. It was also the source of physical objects, such as the sun.[9]

For the most part, I shall not list virtues that have already been previously noted. It should be understood that separate virtues are like individual brush strokes of an Italian Renaissance painter; their individuality vanishes in the overall unified impression of the face of a person of noble character. Plato's dialogues show Socrates as exemplifying the following virtues of philosophical living:

- The courage to ask difficult questions of oneself and others
- Humility in acknowledging where one lacks wisdom
- An implicit conviction that if we seek wisdom, we can find it or at least get closer
- A wholehearted and persistent pursuit of wisdom, all the way to insight into truth, beauty, and goodness

9. For Socrates' concept of beauty, see especially his speech in the *Symposium* (199–212); on the Good, see especially the central section of the *Republic*, books VI and VII (507–20).

- The ability to make affirmations free of dogmatism and criticisms free of skepticism

- The courage to live the truth we have found, to stand by great principles no matter what the cost

- Thinking that is independent of conventional opinion

- Skill in analyzing ideas and reasoning

- A passion for engaging others in the quest for wisdom

- The ability to disagree without descending into a battle in which victory matters more than truth[10]

An experiential approach to education in meaning and value

A person can be knowledgeable and brilliant, but wrong; it takes wisdom born of experience to bring forth the fruits supported by intelligence and information. The relation between theory and practice is so intimate that the highest insights arise from the soil of a life devoted to great values. The way that Socrates lived was essential to attaining his high level of wisdom. The implications for philosophical education are clear. Aristotle (384–322 BCE) put it this way.

> A person comes to be just from doing just actions and temperate from doing temperate actions; for no one has the least prospect of becoming good from failing to do them. The many [those who are not philosophical], however, do not do these actions. They take refuge in arguments, thinking that they are doing philosophy, and that this is the way to become excellent people. They are like a sick person who listens attentively to the doctor, but acts on none of his instructions. Such a course of treatment will not improve the state of the sick person's body, nor will the many improve the state of their souls by philosophizing in this way.[11]

In other words, philosophy calls for *doing* what virtue requires. It is not simply about study, discussion, and defending positions by reasoning. It is

10. The core quality in each of the first six of these virtues is delineated in a philosophically excellent way in Roberts and Wood, *Intellectual Virtues*.

11. Aristotle, *Nicomachean Ethics* II.4, 1105b10-19, 22 (modifying the translation of the last four words in the selection). Note that *psyche*, Aristotle's word that is translated "soul," means mind in its range of functions: vital and biological, sensory and animal, and intellectual. Aristotle seems to not affirm individual immortality.

about another kind of growth. A student of mine doing a project on philosophical living came to this understanding in a way that had a strong positive impact on two important relationships in her life.

This young woman was initially intimidated by the assignment, so she started with a question that was simple for her to tackle, what to eat for lunch, which had been discussed in class. Then she was able to begin examining important facts and values in her life, which led her to rethink her values. Then, during a conflict with her boyfriend, she decided that instead of walking out on the relationship, she would go apart by herself for a while and carefully think through the values at stake. She discovered empathy as her core value, at the same time realizing that to overuse empathy when frank discussion was needed was not the right way to handle the situation. Rather than simply announce the results of her inquiry to her boyfriend, she engaged him in the same process that she had just gone through. They talked at length with a new honesty and decided to continue their relationship, agreeing to pay attention to certain recurring difficulties and deal with them in a constructive manner whenever they might arise. In addition, she helped her sister deal with a heavy load of problems, leading the sister to recognize her distorted thinking. In the light of the newfound clarity, the sister was able to come to some important and productive decisions.[12]

If we are ready to take the time to improve our quality of thinking, we do well to consider three components of excellent thinking. The basics, in my view, are intuition, reason, and wisdom; and they are the subjects of the next four sections.

Intuition: the ideal and attainable basis for thinking

In daily life, we have no problem accurately recognizing familiar things, such as an orange on the table. Perception brings instant recognition. We don't need to think about it; we learned about oranges and tables long ago, and now our perception is reliable, so long as we don't have to distinguish a small orange from a tangerine and a tangelo from a distance in poor lighting. We also have no trouble recognizing that 2+2=4, and we know that genocide is wrong. But in situations that are obscure or complex, if we see someone make a hasty judgment, we might raise the question, "How do you know?" That question can launch an inquiry about the powers of the mind and what potentials they hold.

12. Lacking formal permission to share this person's paper, I neither quote nor go into detail nor give the writer's name. Perhaps someday I will be able to remedy that on my weblog, http://UniversalFamily.org.

To improve our quality of thinking, we do well to first appreciate the capacities that we have as human beings to function on material, intellectual, and spiritual levels of reality. Thanks to these capacities, we can function well in everyday life, explore and make discoveries, correct mistakes, achieve insights, and think for ourselves. We can recognize the reality of all three levels of functioning, improve our thinking, sharpen our capacity for intuition, and attain insight. Sometimes we succeed in knowing facts and causes, in knowing what is good and right, and in knowing spiritual values.

We develop these capacities through a growth process that begins with a level of intuition that works well enough for immediate practical purposes, but which may need to be sharpened if it is to reach the level of self-evident insight. For example, science has procedures for taking the mind from perceptual recognition to mathematical physics as a way of establishing fact. Philosophy has its disciplines for exposing sophistry and weeding out error, and spirituality has its ways of seeking truth.

An impulse of mind that is off track might subjectively feel like intuition, but the term *intuition* as I use it does not extend to include such error. True intuition makes cognitive contact with reality. An intuition may lack the excellence of a self-evident truth, but it must be accurate enough for practical use.

Intuitions, like the stars in the sky, come with degrees of *clarity*. The brightest stars in the sky are classified as having first-magnitude brightness; second-magnitude stars are a little fainter, and so on, until we reach fifth-magnitude stars, the faintest ones we can see with the naked eye. First-magnitude intuitions are insights so powerful that their brightness continues to illuminate our understanding as the years go forward. Low-magnitude intuition is our everyday familiarity with things around us. Intuition needs to function in this low-magnitude way, although it is easier to make mistakes and think we have intuition when we don't; moreover, an intuition can be associated with other ideas that are false. As we acquire reasonable practices of cognitive care, we achieve the clarity that each situation demands.

Intuition also has a quality of *simplicity*. Subjectively speaking, we do not know where a particular intuition comes from—that is, whether it summarizes a complex process of prior learning, perhaps triggered by cues of which we are not conscious, or whether it comes as a gift from a higher source. Perhaps it is both: the divinely designed evolutionary process has led the mind to an alignment that is receptive to the gift of insight.[13]

13. The philosophical heritage of this conversation goes back to Aristotle and Descartes. Aristotle wrote of the genesis of the intuitive basis for sound philosophical judgment. The beginnings or foundations (*archai*) of thought, first "principles," cannot be demonstrated; but they do not burst into the mind without preparation, nor are they

Whether we deal with material, intellectual, or spiritual reality, there is a pattern with three elements: intuition, reason, and wisdom. Ideally speaking, we start with intuition, engage reason to draw conclusions, and synthesize multiple intuitions and their lines of reasoning into wisdom. Sometimes this sequence fits our experience: intuition comes into the mind "out of nowhere," and we go from there. But in practice, experience is constantly leading us to update our understanding. And if we set out to cultivate an intuition to the level of insight, it is normal to use reason in the process and to draw on our current wisdom synthesis.[14]

Consider this paragraph from Descartes's *Meditations*. His purpose is to establish an absolutely certain foundation for building a new philosophy, a foundation that the most extreme skepticism cannot shake. He had previously been able to doubt his judgment of seemingly obvious perceptual facts and even his ability to make mathematical judgments. Next he tried to doubt his own existence as he began the series of thoughts that culminate in an updated (1642) version of his famous (1637) "I think, therefore I am."

> Is it then the case that I too do not exist? But doubtless I did exist, if I persuaded myself of something. But there is some deceiver or other who is supremely powerful and supremely sly and who is always deliberately deceiving me. Then too there is no

isolated. They arise from experience as part of a process. Sense perception, retained in the mind, is the origin of memory. Repeated perception and memory leads to what Aristotle called experience. Insight arises through noticing that becomes recognized and asserted in the form of a statement or judgment. Thus identified and expressed, truth comes fully into its own.

René Descartes (1596–1650) set forth an ideal of intuition as a simple and perfect insight. In a teaching akin to that of Buddhism, we are told how to develop intuition: "*We ought to turn the whole force of our minds to the smallest and simplest things, and to stop there for a long time, until we become accustomed to intuiting the truth clearly and distinctly.*" He emphasized two modes of approach to truth: "*Concerning the objects presented to us we should investigate, not what others have thought nor what we ourselves conjecture, but what we can intuit clearly and evidently or deduce with certainty, since scientific knowledge [scientia] is acquired by no other means.*" "By 'intuition' I understand neither the fleeting testimony of the senses nor the deceptive judgment of the imagination with its false constructions, but a conception of a clear and attentive mind, so easy and distinct, that no doubt at all remains about what we understand. . . . Thus everyone can intuit with his mind that he exists, that he is thinking, that a triangle is bounded by only three lines, a sphere by a single surface, and the like. Such things are much more numerous than most people think, because they disdain to turn their minds toward matters so easy." (Rules 9 and 3, in Descartes, *Rules*, 20 and 4–5.)

14. For clarification regarding intuition and self-evidence, I am indebted to Audi, "Intuition and Ethics." He explains how to bring together in one theory two strands of philosophy that work with different meanings of "intuition": in the first strand, intuition is fallible; in the second, it is a synonym for "insight."

doubt that I exist, if he is deceiving me. And let him do his best
at deception, he will never bring it about that I am nothing so
long as I shall think that I am something. Thus, after everything
has been most carefully weighed, it must finally be established
that this pronouncement, "I am, I exist" is necessarily true every
time I utter it or conceive it in my mind.[15]

Notice first the *reasoning* that occurs prior to the confident affirmation of
Descartes's core certitude. Consider next that Descartes is writing in the
tradition of the history of philosophy; Augustine (354–430) had already
written, "Even if I make a mistake, I exist." What Descartes says is part of
an ongoing philosophical conversation. Language is a web of meanings,
embedded in a social history, and thinking usually relies on language as it
strives for insightful intuition. In other words, the quest for truth, even in its
simplest elements, presupposes some background of the best wisdom one
has been able to synthesize from previous intuition and reasoning.

Fortunately, we don't have to climb a cognitive mountain to function
rather well in practice. My wife, Hagiko Ichihara Wattles, has the mind of a
detective. Sharpness is her habit, even in casual situations, so she perceives
things that others overlook. When she wants to know something—for example, when asking for directions at the train station—her concentration
is so focused, her questioning so detailed, her encounter so vigorous, that
she *becomes* the inquiry. At the conclusion, her ready smile and generous
thanks flow spontaneously, but only then. Addressing a practical problem,
such as a wet basement, her imagination brings every tool to bear. She is
never rushed, nor the least anxious. And she is confident in her ability to
figure things out and to construct whatever she needs or, if necessary, to
supervise and discuss strategy with anyone whose help she engages.

Her independence of mind, which defers neither to convention nor
to experts, was developed from childhood, where her environment, a fish-
ing village of 300 persons on a tiny island in Japan, called for toughness
and resourcefulness. Her father trained her to think ahead, beyond what is
expected, demanded, and obvious. And she is strikingly thoughtful when
helping someone in need. Her life testifies that authenticity is an aid to
intuition.

A sign I once saw in front of a church said, "Don't believe everything
you think." Cultivating intuition requires being realistic about how our

---

15. Descartes, *Meditations*, 108. Descartes's quest for absolutely certain intuition
and deduction set up standards that he knew were unrealistically high for daily life. In
the last paragraph of the *Meditations*, he mercifully and humanely acknowledges that
"the need to get things done does not always permit us the leisure for such a careful
inquiry" (141).

mind often judges accurately and often makes mistakes. A study of cognitive strengths and weaknesses by Daniel Kahneman centers on a nuanced and detailed description of the interweaving of intuition and reason—but he uses the term *intuition* to include the possibility that it can be mistaken. He portrays what he calls System 1 and System 2. "System 1 operates automatically and quickly, with little or no effort and no sense of voluntary control." System 1 relies on the association of ideas contained in memory.

System 2 is "the conscious, reasoning self that has beliefs, makes choices, and decides what to think about and what to do. It also generates the effort to focus in a concentrated way. System 1 continuously generates suggestions for System 2: impressions, intuitions, intentions, and feelings. If endorsed by System 2, impressions and intuitions turn into beliefs, and impulses turn into voluntary actions. When all goes smoothly, which is most of the time, System 2 adopts the suggestions of System 1 with little or no modifications. You generally believe your impressions and act on your desires, and that is fine—usually."

System 1 is generally very good at what it does: its models of familiar situations are accurate, its short-term predictions are usually accurate as well, and its initial reactions to challenges are swift and generally appropriate. System 1 has biases, however, systematic errors that it is prone to make in specified circumstances."

In other words, in certain types of situations, System 1 is liable to error; and since we are much better at seeing others' errors than our own, we do well to learn when to take extra cognitive care. Kahneman is prepared to trust expert intuition when the expert has had long experience (the proverbial ten thousand hours) in an arena where it is possible to acquire skill.[16]

Intuition as an answer to skepticism

Recognizing our powers of intuition gives us a bulwark against skepticism in this day when philosophical chaos reigns in the competition between science-centered, humanistic, and spiritually oriented philosophies. Skepticism denies the validity of spiritual experience, the reality of God, and sometimes even the reality of mind.

Some skeptics exploit the fact that we can't endlessly give reasons for what we believe. Sometimes a child asks its parent to explain a natural

16. The quotations about System 1 and System 2, our fallible, everyday analogues of (ideal) intuition and reason, come from Kahneman, *Thinking, Fast and Slow*, 20–21 and 24–25. The reference to "the proverbial 10,000 hours" alludes to the estimate reported by Malcolm Gladwell in his book *Outliers*, a number that has been widely quoted.

phenomenon, and after each answer the child keeps on asking "why?" "Why is the sky blue?" *Because of the way the light goes through the air.* "Why?" *Because little particles in the air bend the light in a certain way.* "Why?" And so it goes . . . . Even a physicist cannot keep giving reasons for reasons forever. There is nothing irrational about not being able to prove your axioms or starting points for thinking. Some things just have to be *seen*. Our capacities for intuition enable us to get started.

If we go to extremes in seeking reasons for reasons, we hinder our intuitive powers. The underground man in *Notes from Underground* by Fyodor Dostoevsky (1821–1881) illustrates the persistent possibility of doubt.

> All straightforward persons and men of action are active just because they are stupid and limited. How can that be explained? This way: as a result of their limitation they take immediate and secondary causes for primary ones, and in that way persuade themselves more quickly and easily than other people do that they have found an infallible basis for their activity, and their minds are at ease and that, you know, is the most important thing. To begin to act, you know, you must first have your mind completely at ease and without a trace of doubt left in it. Well, how am I, for example, to set my mind at rest? Where are the primary causes on which I am to build? Where are my bases? Where am I to get them from? I exercise myself in the process of thinking, and consequently with me every primary cause at once draws after itself another still more primary, and so on to infinity. That is precisely the essence of every sort of consciousness and thinking.[17]

Unlike the underground man, most people do not have unreasonable conditions for trusting the power of reason, and most people do find sufficient bases for thinking and acting.

Philosophy accustoms one to coping in situations where one's ability to keep answering the "why?" question runs out. The intuitive capacities to grasp matter, mind, and spirit function as *assumptions* so basic that their validity cannot be proven. Any attempted proof assumes too much or proves too little. Proofs either use language that presupposes the existence of the realm in question or reduces the realm to something else. For example, to try proving the existence of the material realm by pointing to "this stone here" uses a term, *stone*, that implies its being a material thing in the world. Alternatively, it is possible to appeal to our perceptions of the stone, but we

17. Dostoevsky, *Notes from Underground*, part I, section 5, 15–16.

cannot prove that our coherent perceptions constitute a valid access to a realm outside the mind.

Similarly, in the moral realm the answer to the question "Why be moral?" must be an appeal to intuition. After a number of steps of justification, the ability to keep answering the "why?" question ceases. The person simply has to see, for example, that (other things being equal) it is good to promote happiness, wrong to exacerbate suffering. To justify morality in terms of prudence or pleasure is to abandon the standpoint of morality. Likewise, the reality of God cannot be proven. One can argue for a First Cause or for a self-subsisting Unity; but neither of these ideas is specifically spiritual.

The inability to prove the validity of basic assumptions does not mean that the assumptions are arbitrary, that there is no evidence to motivate them. There is evidence. But if a reductionist calls the validity of the evidence into question, what one can offer in reply is not an argument (except to clear away misunderstandings and attempted refutations) but rather an experience. Is it unreasonable, then, to use unproven assumptions? The very structure of reason requires it. Even an advanced formal system needs to begin with axioms. Nevertheless, it is important to be clear that the philosophy of intuition being discussed here does not take particular propositions as a foundation. Rather, the claim is about capacities that give access to regions of interconnected experiences and beliefs, making possible the adventure of moving from intuition to wisdom.

Each of the three assumptions regarding different levels of reality is a window to experience, as we observe most dramatically in the case of spiritual reality. Those who, debating the existence of God, find the arguments pro and con to be inconclusive, may choose to suspend judgment. But fear of error may conceal fear of truth. If knowing God may be similar to knowing another person, then perhaps most of the relevant evidence comes only to the person who takes the adventuresome step forward.

Someone whose character is formed around integrated living in a multidimensioned reality will hardly find his or her vital spiritual certainty challenged by skepticism. The intuitive dimension of direct religious experience is the kind of proof of the reality of God that we can have, and evidence of its validity can rise to the level of being abundantly, radiantly adequate. Nevertheless, a logically trained person can have an authentic religious experience and wonder later whether it was veridical. The person can come to doubt the experience, analyze it in such a way as to dismember it, and finally reject the sense of reality at its core. I believe that everyone has had spiritual experiences, at least insofar as there is a spiritual dimension to the recognition of value in any fully moral decision. But such experiences are forgotten for various reasons. Some persons totally reject the divine realm of spiritual realities; in that extreme case, the person has cauterized his own spiritual longings, so that the primary spiritual assumption or affirmation loses all appeal.

Those who deliberate whether to refrain from spiritual involvement or to go forward do not face the dilemma of being suspended between two equally attractive piles of evidence and argument; there is some degree of spiritual experience and longing on one side and the abyss on the other. The abyss has its own deep message for us. It is the nothingness over which we live in radical freedom, able say yes or no to our own deepest intuitions. It is our vertigo as we contemplate that nothingness, with which we can choose to identify ourselves. The abyss is the measure of the freedom given to the human mind.[18]

Different cultures throughout history interpret the material universe, the moral domain, and the spiritual world differently; but the capacities for intuition are universal. These powers of intuition are so fundamental that we cannot deny them without contradicting ourselves in practice. Skeptics can deny these capacities but never disprove them.

Radical skepticism rejects the idea of truth, claiming that science (which is in continual flux) is totally revisable, philosophy (where fundamental debates continue without any resolution) is merely a matter of opinion, and religion (with its contradictory claims and tragic blunders) is an illusion. But radical skepticism subverts itself by ignoring some significant points.

First, historical science is needed to establish the fact that scientific ideas change. Second, in order to dismiss philosophy, it is necessary to take a philosophical position and perhaps defend it with philosophical reasoning. Thus, the notion that philosophy is mere opinion implies that it itself merely an opinion, which could be wrong. And finally, the view that religion is an illusion implicitly claims insight that purports to cover every mountaintop of religious experience.[19]

18. I use the term *nothingness* without intending to characterize or comment on Buddhist concepts, experiences, or attainments.

19. Skeptics have argued against the idea of mind as a type of reality; they advocate regarding talk of mind as just talk. For them, there is one reality, the brain, but two ways of describing it, one using biological terms and the other using psychological terms. In my view, spirit is a kind of reality different from mind, just as mind is a kind of reality different from matter. Matter, mind, and spirit are interrelated. How body interacts with mind and how mind interacts with spirit remain classic puzzles, because no seamless explanation connects these realms. In my view, there is a spectrum of material reality, ranging from rocks to neurons; at the high end of the spectrum, matter is responsive to mind. There is a spectrum of mind, ranging from hunger and fear to love and mercy; at the high end of the spectrum, mind is responsive to spirit. And there is a spectrum

Skeptics about beauty deem it purely subjective—"in the eye of the beholder"—and not *also* a value that the Creator both imparts as a quality to what we perceive and correspondingly helps the beholder to feel. But skeptics contradict themselves in practice when they feel contempt (an aesthetic emotion that implicitly claims objectivity) for those who embrace the (allegedly *really ugly*) error of thinking that beauty is real. And skeptics about morality claim that its concepts are mere words used to manipulate, control, and oppress people. These skeptics also contradict themselves in practice, since their critique of oppression is a moral critique; and their confused muddle does not help protect the oppressed. Skepticism may seem brilliant when picking at flaws in dogmatism, but it pales in comparison to the robust appeal of adventuresome thinking, which entertains critical questions while keeping the quest for wisdom open on all levels.

Reason's functions and effective operation

In one way or another, an insight may be put into words; and one or more insights, clearly expressed, provide the ideal premises or starting points from which reason can draw conclusions. Darwin reasoned about the differences between species of finches on neighboring islands and concluded that the differences were caused by biological changes that proved beneficial for reproduction. Socrates reasoned about what was right and concluded that he should not break jail. Spiritual concepts are connected in a spiritual logic that can be variously traced in statements of the mind. Embracing the concept of God as Father, Mother, or Parent leads to the realization that we are family.[20]

In addition to drawing conclusions, reason performs several functions. It cares about consistency and notices contradictions when beliefs are inconsistent. Scientific reason finds ways to test beliefs to see whether they correspond with reality, and works out the symbolic logic used to perform functions such as programming computers. Philosophical reason helps us to say why we accept the beliefs that we do, as well as to sort out truth from error in perspectives that differ from our own and to understand the logic of relations between concepts. When we are deliberating between alternative

---

of spiritual reality that ranges from God's spirit presence within the mind to the infinite Deity. The resulting image shows body and mind coming close enough to interact, though an explanatory gap and a metaphysical difference remain. The same may be said of mind and spirit. Spirit acts in the material realm through the medium of mind.

20. Statements are discussed by philosophers as part of a cluster of closely related ideas including beliefs, propositions, and judgments.

courses of action, philosophical reason exercises judgment in the weighing of the relative significance of pros and cons.

One model of the exercise of reason comes from Thomas Aquinas (1225–1274).[21] When thinking about a particular subject, he took into consideration ideas from ancient and contemporary philosophers and from theologians of different religions. He organized his discussion of topics into a sequence of sharply focused questions. For each question, he created a short article, which began by listing the main objections that his historical and contemporary conversation partners could raise about the answer he was about to defend, and then set forth his own view in a brief, clear, reasoned way. Finally, he showed how to handle the previously stated objections.

If people could form the habit of using an abbreviated version of this procedure prior to entering a debate on a contentious issue, this could transform public discussion from polarized polemics into peaceful progress. It is essential to listen deeply to the perspectives of the groups involved. Fairness requires acknowledging that key premises in each group's position may (perhaps crudely and partially) express a genuine value. In angry debate, opposing sides fail to acknowledge the values cherished by their opponents. True, sometimes a one-sided position finds the insight that slices through all the confusion and goes straight to the right conclusion. But a judicious examination of key ideas from all sides is a more reliable guide to reaching a sound conclusion. In a complex problem, truth cannot be told via one-sidedness; good judgment requires a sense of proportion.

Philosophical training in rational thinking does not ensure that our ideas will be correct, but it does help us spot some types of error. This is serious business, because thinking depends greatly on basic convictions; and in drawing conclusions, any one of us can make big mistakes based on one key premise that is seriously wrong.

Taking a couple of courses on formal logic and critical thinking (informal logic) would improve our ability to protect ourselves from sophistry and participate constructively in group discussion. The study of logic provides a vocabulary for identifying and explaining errors that occur when reasoning—our own or that of others—goes bad, and it helps organize our thoughts in a legitimately persuasive way. It is sad to contemplate the flood of shoddy thinking that pervades public media, which is overloaded with manipulative commercial and political messages. I sometimes entertain the idea that training in logic should be regarded as a requirement for responsible functioning as an adult. It should be widely known that philosophy can be taught at all levels, and that children can begin to develop logical

21. Thomas's *Summa Theologica* is available at http://www.newadvent.org/summa/.

thinking before being trained in formal logic. In France, for example, philosophy is part of secondary education. And one pioneering organization, the Institute for the Advancement of Philosophy for Children, works with active Philosophy for Children centers in more than forty nations, serving preschoolers through high school students.[22]

Wisdom—a synthesis of universal meanings in local facts

Wisdom is an achievement that is beyond particular intuitions and lines of reasoning. Reason can impressively formulate arguments that draw conclusions from premises, but in two ways the result can still be foolish. First, as we have already noted, reasoning from a narrow set of premises carries a risk of one-sidedness and fanaticism. By contrast, wisdom's conclusions are woven from many lines of reasoning, anchored in a broad set of premises. However, while our consideration of perspectives should respect every person equally, not all perspectives are equal.

Brilliant reasoning can also be foolish because premises include words that stand for concepts, and when concepts are inadequate, the conclusions drawn from them may be wrong.

As I use the terms, *concept* is distinguished from *idea*: an idea is solely intellectual, whereas a concept involves all levels of truth—fact, meaning, and value. We can choose which ideas to develop into our major concepts. As we develop a concept, it becomes a hub that attracts relevant ideas into its orbit, and the associations in our mind become more and more integrated. A concept expresses a personal wisdom synthesis. The concepts that are central to our lives are the product of our efforts, perhaps after years of struggle, as we focus on and solve the problems that arise in our circumstances. Struggling with a big problem calls us to grow in intellectual virtues of thinking, spiritual virtues of faith and love, aesthetic virtues of appreciation and creativity, and ethical virtues in what we do and how we do it.

We can acquire ideas as fast as we can read a page; but we do not truly possess a great concept until we have learned to live it. In fact, we don't fully possess it ourselves until we have shared it with others. Since our struggles arise from our particular, personal situation, our concepts have a particular and personal aspect to them. At the same time, our concepts are woven from threads of universal truths; our greatest concepts unite the personal dimension with the universal. And because others share our circumstances

---

22. The Institute for the Advancement of Philosophy for Children (IAPC): http://www.montclair.edu/cehs/academics/centers-and-institutes/iapc/.

in important respects, our concepts may help others who have problems similar to ours.

As our concepts approach fullness, they can be powerfully unified by God's work in our mind. This process of unification can reach a dramatic culmination, as we see in an experience of biochemist Thomas Shotwell, who went to relax in a bar after work one afternoon and sat down beside a bay window overlooking the Mississippi River. In the glow of the setting sun, the river was strikingly illuminated, and he began piecing together the various layers of scientific description that explained the scene—astrophysics, geology, and the physics of flowing water and reflection of light. In the window he noticed the reflection of the dancer on stage, and he thought of the anthropology, biology, psychology, and sociology that helped account for her dancing. As he synthesized the understanding gained by years of scientific study, he suddenly experienced a powerful and blissful unification of cosmic insight.[23]

Excellent thinking on all levels weaves together intuition, reason, and wisdom, carrying us into ever-greater realization of truth.

Meaning and interpretation

Psychiatrist Viktor Frankl observed during his years as a prisoner in Nazi concentration camps that meaning is a vital human need. In those unthinkable conditions, prisoners would nourish themselves on meaning in various ways. Some cherished bits of philosophy, poetry, or music. Although many lost their faith under such conditions, religious life in the camps was very real. And many found strength to keep going from devotion to a loved one in another camp, even though they did not know whether the beloved was still alive. But if a prisoner gave up, let go of what gave his or her life meaning, death would usually come within a few days.[24]

Considering meaning philosophically discloses two aspects. First, meaning is something real that is discovered. That is the way we naturally think of meaning when insight dawns: *Eureka! I have found it!* When we lose faith in our capacity for insight, we descend toward relativism. According to that variety of skepticism, there is no divine standard of truth independent of the human mind, indeed no objective truth at all; and truth becomes "relative to"—reduced to—what an individual or group believes. Relativism undercuts the meaningfulness of discussion and debate. But relativism does

23. Shotwell, "Essay on Beauty."
24. Frankl, *Man's Search for Meaning.*

contain a grain of truth: our capacity for insight is relative to the length of our experience, the breadth of our inquiry, and depth of our engagement.

In its second aspect, meaning is something that we interpret. When we lose sight of this aspect, we tend toward dogmatism: we know that others interpret things differently, but we forget that we, too, are interpreters. Dogmatists suffer a diminished ability to understand and learn from others. It is natural to connect the idea of meaning with interpretation when we are reading something controversial. If we recognize truth as many-sided, it becomes easier to see that differing interpretations may each contain truth. Since meanings are, to a significant degree, socially constructed, to understand something well requires some study of other perspectives.

The two aspects of meaning are connected. When we study perspectives to interpret carefully, we are in search of understanding, insight. We move beyond relativism by affirming a higher standard of truth than mere opinion; and we move beyond dogmatism by recognizing that our personal convictions arise within in a certain social, linguistic, and historical milieu.

The intelligent search for meaning can begin early, as we see in Abraham Lincoln. His stepmother observed that he needed to "understand everything—even to the smallest thing—minutely and exactly. He would . . . repeat it over to himself again and again—some times in one form and then in another and when it was fixed in his mind to suit him he . . . never lost that fact or his understanding of it." "When he came across a passage that struck him, he would write it down on boards if he had no paper and keep it there till he did get paper—then he would re-write it—look at it [and] repeat it."

This early habit of mastering fact and meaning prepared him for later in life when he needed historical and philosophical understanding. Preparing to try a case in court, Lincoln could trace legal opinions back for centuries. "When I have a particular case in hand, I . . . love to dig up the question by the roots and hold it up and dry it before the fires of the mind."[25] To dig a question up by the roots yields historical understanding, which augments philosophical clarity.

Inquiry into meaning leads toward universal insight. When human beings began to ask about the meaning of things, posing the question, "What is it?" they were expanding their mind toward universal humanity. When the ancient Greek philosophers asked what knowledge was, they were not asking about knowledge in Greeks, or in men but not women, but in all humankind. The uneducated slave boy of Plato's *Meno* reasoned his way to the correct answer to a geometrical question and showed thereby that he

25. The quotations are found in Donald, *Lincoln*, 29, 145, and 99.

had the same basic functions of reason that the students in Plato's academy did—an insight that, as Whitehead noted, contributed eventually to the demise of slavery.[26] Even asking the philosophical question about knowledge presupposes that knowledge is somehow one in all knowers, however much we differ. The generality of philosophy's questions tends toward the uniting of humanity—if we gain and share insight.

It is common to see a tension between the ideas of meaning as real and meaning as socially interpreted; a religious view harmonizes both sides within a larger concept.[27] If there is a higher standard of truth, if meanings are anchored in the mind of God, then there is hope for our pursuit of meaning. The presence of God guides our interpretation and leads us patiently and silently toward insight. Thus we are not merely dancing on a sea of colorful and clashing interpretations. Different types of persons might naturally tend to highlight one side or another of a many-sided truth; but if we can come closer to divine understanding, then differing interpretations might never be standardized but they may eventually be coordinated. Without the prospect of harmony, we can only celebrate or resist diversity. With the prospect of harmony, we become more ready to listen for truth in what others say.

Thus, meanings are real, and we discover them in historical, social, and linguistic contexts. Meanings have generality, which makes it possible for people to understand one another; and as we learn by opening ourselves to persons with differing perspectives, we are strengthened in the belief that we share a common humanity. As the first member of the universal society, God may be regarded as the one who gradually helps us weed out error and harmonize our interpretations. God makes possible authoritative insight as well as individual creativity in synthesizing insights into concepts achieved through personal struggle in particular historical circumstances.

It is through language that we express our understanding of meanings; and we live at a thrilling and dangerous time when language is in the blender. Social movements spread intolerance for terms that have acquired

26. Whitehead, *Adventures of Ideas*, 15.

27. What I call *meaning* Plato called *form* (*eidos*), which embraced two notions: (1) the immaterial and intelligible essence of a thing (an object of any sort) and (2) the cause that makes the thing have its structure. Philo of Alexandria, who flourished around 30 CE, created a synthesis of Platonic philosophy and Hebrew theology, which formed the pattern for subsequent centuries of Jewish, Christian, and Islamic philosophy. Philo separated these two functions of form, assigning the causal function to the creative power of God. Building on Philo and Augustine, Aquinas saw forms as "ideas in the mind of God." The quest for meaning then became the quest to approximate, as far as humanly possible, the mind of God, whose eternal and unchanging ideas are implicit in the structuring of everything in our world.

some unwelcome connotations; and linguistic creativity, commercial clev-
erness, social fragmentation, and the decline of education are changing
language so rapidly that it becomes challenging to speak simultaneously to
persons belonging to differing communities. The attempt to please everyone
is laughable, but the option of conforming to currently dominant conven-
tions of expression can also be problematic.

Culture wars are, in a way, struggles over meaning; and when they
generate intolerance for people because of the diverse usage of terms, meaning suffers. Language must change over time, and intelligent criticism helps
us to make those changes thoughtfully and responsibly; thus high-quality
thinking seeks humane expression in a public arena rent by the claims of
opposing groups. Culture wars involving religion obscure divine meaning:
everything is pulled down to the level of the social-political struggle.

If we were to jettison every word whose history reveals associated
abuses, we would disconnect ourselves from the deeper concepts and experiences that some of these words symbolize, and our ability to think, understand, and communicate would be hampered. It is often wiser to keep terms
that refer to something real and important.

The language of conceptual clarity differs from the language of proclamation. A central truth set forth in this new philosophy of living is expressed in the phrase "the universal family"; but in my view the conceptual
core of this phrase is more clearly expressed in terms of the fatherhood of
God and the brotherhood of man. In many circles, we have been taught that
this terminology is sexist, a legacy of religion's complicity with a patriarchal
social order. Should we therefore withdraw all use of such terminology?
After all, a great truth can be expressed in other ways; much of the meaning
in the concept of the family of God can be communicated by speaking of
the parental love of God and the siblinghood or solidarity of humankind.
And people have other reasons for naming God in language that expresses
various concepts. But those who have rejected or are doubtful about the
father concept of God deserve some clarification to remove barriers and
open the way to a new understanding. Here is one woman's perspective on
the matter:

> Many women have problems with the religious use of Father
> language, and the men who love and support them often share
> their concern. But one of the deeper problems underlying the
> reaction to so-called sexist terminology often remains hidden
> or untended to. Speaking from my own experience—which I
> believe is common among women—for most of my life I wanted
> nothing to do with the idea of God as Father because my rela-
> tionship with my own father was so troubled. Of what use would

a "male god" be to me? That would be the last place I would look to find nurture, understanding, unconditional love.

Decades of psychological and meditative therapies and processes to try to "heal the father wound" resulted in almost no change. It took a radical inner revelation in my early fifties of God as Father for the real healing to begin. And we're not talking here about the Old Man in the Sky with a Long Beard, a punitive and scary God that so many little girls have grown up being told they must obey . . . or else! Even though my father was no longer on this earth when I had that revelation, I became aware from a succession of dreams after that a profound healing had taken place between us. And I could see the results in my relationships with men, which became much healthier and more stable after that.

For many seekers of truth—both women and men—the necessary rejection of immature and often damaging notions of God accumulated in childhood has unfortunately slammed the door on a true inquiry into the nature of God as Father. But it's never too late to open that door again. As someone who spent thirty years on an Eastern spiritual path that is not God-centered, I can say that there is no contradiction between the realization of the Absolute and the recognition that one is a son or daughter of a personal God. To me, this is the true vision of East meeting West.[28]

This testimony illustrates the experiential import of a topic that philosophers have begun to discuss in a more personal manner.

In the debate over the alleged sexism of traditional religious language, it has been assumed that the father concept of God is a metaphor, like "God is a rock." In metaphor, the primary meaning is anchored in worldly experience and projected into a context where that meaning does not originally belong. But the Thomistic philosophy of language offers another possibility: the father concept of God may be *analogical*. If God is the prime or ultimate example of what it means to be a father (or parent or mother), then humans are given the opportunity to be parents by analogy; we reflect the divine pattern. The analogical use of language allows us to uphold the concept of the personality of God while preserving the truth that what it means for God to be a personality is different from what it means for us as human beings.

28. These observations were made by my editor Elianne Obadia, author of a forthcoming book on the healing of the father wound through the realization and ongoing experience of God as Father. Her outlook reflects an expanded concept of God as an Impersonal Absolute, a transcendent Divine Other, and the inner divine counterpart of our human nature.

Thus we both honor the mystery of God and discover ourselves more fully in relation with him.[29]

My favorite question is, "What does it mean to you (or what would it mean to you) to be a son (or daughter) of God?" The beautiful variety of answers to this question encourages me that, whatever the interpretation, whatever the language, the concept of the family of God will abide.

Mystery and personality

Philosophy interprets meanings, but mystery goes beyond what we find meaningful, what we can comprehend. A philosophy of living remains open to that which transcends philosophy, as we see in a section from one of the Confucian classics, *The Doctrine of the Mean*.

> The Way of the superior person functions everywhere and yet is hidden. Men and women of simple intelligence can share its knowledge; and yet in its utmost reaches, there is something which even the sage does not know. Men and women of simple intelligence can put it into practice; and yet in its utmost reaches there is something which even the sage is not able to put into practice.[30]

This passage, as I interpret it, speaks of a way that is not a human artifact; it is a cosmic way (*tao*) marked by simplicity and depth that can be known and lived, albeit imperfectly, by human beings. This way gathers people into a

---

29. In *The Golden Rule* I discussed this problem of language as follows.

> Concerning the practice of reforming language to make explicit the essential truth of the equality of women with men, though I have migrated from the complacent habits of an earlier generation, I do make occasional use of the phrase, "the brotherhood of man." A couple of times I use "the siblinghood of humankind," a phrase with the necessary familial connotations that may become standard in the next generation. I do not banish the older phrase, which elicits intuitive understanding and much favorable recognition around the world. When explaining the texts of other authors, I do not hesitate to reproduce their terminology, whatever its conscious or unconscious associations with sexism may have been, though I avoid "languageism"—taking an author's terminology as sufficient ground for accusation. English is in rapid flux, and it takes an extra measure of good will for communication to be successful in the environment of contemporary sensitivities. (10)

30. *The Doctrine of the Mean* 12, 100 (replacing "man" with "person").

common humanity: not everyone is a sage, but the way is one, and we dwell together in its mystery.[31]

Every personality is a mystery; we can never completely understand even those we know best. A physician could describe the body, a psychologist the mind, and a theologian the soul, but their descriptions cannot define the person we know and love. In the beloved there is something unique and indefinable. When the grandmother says to the grandchild, "My, how you've grown!" she does two things: observes change and recognizes continuity. The word "you" refers to what is constant through change. Body and mind change; character grows; yet she identifies the child as the same one she knew earlier. Year after year, we go through changes, yet we are the same person.

Wisdom does not try to reduce mystery to something explainable, but neither does it fall into permanent silence in the face of mystery. For example, there are some things that we can say about personality. An adequate philosophical concept of the person had to await the tradition of personalism, which upholds the primacy of persons and tends to regard human beings as including body, mind, and soul. In addition to these components, it recognizes that unique, indefinable, and unchanging mystery in all of us; personalist Nikolai Berdaiev (1874–1948) called it personality. He associated several characteristics in his concept of personality:[32]

- Each personality is unique

- Personality is mysterious, never fully predictable or comprehensible

- Personality is "the unchanging in change, unity in the manifold"

- Personality has free will

- Personality is beyond everything worldly that can be treated as an object by biology or the human sciences

31. The idea of the one way will of course be variously interpreted by different religions and by differing perspectives within those religions.

32. The term *personality* is used not only to name the unanalyzable constant in persons; it is also used to name the entire mind-body-soul system that is coordinated by the free will of personality. The way that Berdaiev used this term does not fit either common usage or the theories of psychology—for example, the theory that defines personality in terms of five variables; once a person has developed his or her degree of each variable, there is little chance of much change. The variables can be expressed through questions. How extraverted or introverted is the person (including traits such as outgoing, talkative, energetic, and assertive)? How agreeable (including sympathetic, kind, affectionate, compassionate, and loving)? How conscientious (including organized and thorough)? How neurotic (e.g., tense, moody, and anxious) or emotionally stable? How open to experience (including being intellectual, insightful, imaginative, and having broad interests)? This summary follows that of University of Oregon psychology professor Sanjay Shrivastava at http://pages.uoregon.edu/sanjay/bigfive.html.

- Personality transcends itself by relating to God, to other people, to supreme values, and to the inner depths of the world

- Personality has the potential for victory beyond merely belonging to a particular hereditary or social group—success in effort and conflict, triumph over slavery, mastery of self and world

- Personality includes reason but is not governed by reason

- Personality is not the soul

- Personality encompasses spirit, soul, and body. "Personality, which is not a sum of parts, acts always as a whole . . . on the way to perfectly accomplished unity and wholeness."[33]

Religiously speaking, we encounter mystery above all when we try to fathom the infinite and eternal God, who surpasses all value that we can comprehend. God chooses to be a Father, to relate with other persons.[34] Personalism has tended to conceive of God as being, first and foremost, a person of truth, beauty, goodness, and love.[35] Every relationship of personalities is marked by mystery.

The inscrutable arrival of wisdom is expressed in this poem of Emily Dickinson:

> The Crickets sang
> And set the Sun
> And Workmen finished one by one
> Their Seam the Day upon.
>
> The low Grass loaded with the Dew
> The Twilight stood, as Strangers do

---

33. Berdyaev, *Slavery and Freedom* 5, 6, and 25. These ideas of his are developed in Rolnick, *Person, Grace, and God*. For this book, I have chosen to follow the spelling used by most scholars, "Nikolai Berdaiev."

34. For some people, the concept of personality is anthropomorphic—bound up with partiality and imperfection; so they have tried to get beyond the concept of God as a person. We might agree that a personal God would transcend our highest concept of personality, and also that God may have impersonal aspects, just as human persons have impersonal energies coursing through them. But if personalism is right, then the concept of an infinite and divine personality is not incoherent; and human beings made in the image of God are theomorphic. On this view, when we try to think of ultimate reality as utterly impersonal, and if we strive to become like that, we end up thinking and trying to become something less than personal.

35. For an introduction to personalism, see Bengtsson, *Worldview of Personalism*. On the themes of truth, beauty, and goodness, see 37–38, 47, 52–54, 260, 286–87, 337–38, and 357.

With Hat in Hand, polite and new
To stay as if, or go.

A Vastness, as a Neighbor, came,
A Wisdom without Face, or Name,
A Peace as Hemispheres at Home
And so the Night became.[36]

The image of crickets putting down the sun injects a playful tone, opening our mind to novelty. The image of workmen putting a seam upon the day suggests that the day was in pieces, in need of being put together. A seam is "a junction made by sewing the edge of two pieces, or widths of cloth, leather, etc."[37] The work of composing the day as a completed unity required the contribution of all the workmen.

And then wisdom arrives. Duality, hemispheres, may still be distinguished, but there is no tension, for the hemispheres fit together perfectly. The poet breaks the customary association of wisdom with light. To find wisdom as vastness, as a neighbor, and as peace and harmony—this requires that we do our work. To neglect that work leaves us with fragmentation; the sensitive mind feels isolated, if not threatened. But when wisdom arrives, fragmentation is dissolved, and philosophical living becomes another mode of being at home in the universe. Wisdom is not itself a person, has no face or name, but it comes as a neighbor, something deeply akin to our mind. The discovery that we can seek, find, and befriend wisdom is philosophy's contribution to the list of ways in which the universe is friendly.

The coherence of philosophical truth

In order to speak of truth justifiably, we need some way to sort out truth from error. Philosophy has developed a few main theories of truth, each with implications for how to do that sorting. Each of these ideas is important to the whole picture, and each has limits. Thus the ideas do not add up to a rigorous system that can guarantee intellectual success. Rather, what we gain from drawing on them all is a dynamic, progressive, satisfying (but never final) integration. Human knowing is never absolute; when we have an insight, we can never totally prove it. If truth is not static, then recognizing these limits helps us participate in the adventure called living the truth.

36. The poem has no title, only a number, 1104, as presented in Dickinson, *Complete Poems*, 498.

37. For the definition of "seam, n." I used *The Oxford English Dictionary*.

The first idea of truth is factual correctness or, more broadly, the *correspondence* of a belief or statement with reality. Is it stormy or calm outside now? Is there only one door in this room or more than one? Have a look. Considered in its generality, this line of thought leads to the correspondence theory of truth, whose main insight is that reality is the criterion in terms of which any statement is true or false. In other words, the concepts of truth and reality are inherently connected.[38] A limitation of the correspondence theory of truth is that sometimes there is no way to compare a statement with the reality that it claims to express. For example, if there is a basic framework for human thinking that includes some of the capacities for intuition that we have discussed, we cannot step outside of that framework to compare it with reality to see whether our framework is correct.

A second idea essential to an adequate account of truth is truth as *coherence*.[39] Are the concepts of this thinker consistent? Is this statement or action consistent with the ideals of truth, beauty, and goodness that the speaker claims to represent? We often accept new ideas merely because they fit easily with our beliefs and desires. Coherence is a mark of truth, but it is not sufficient to make something true. Coherence in a narrow sense is satisfied if our ideas cohere with each other, but any system of ideas is in trouble if our thinking is one-sided or built around a premise that is false. Loyalty to a false premise conserves coherence but proliferates error.

A third idea deepens the first: truth is the *manifestation or disclosure of the real*. Disclosure may be direct or indirect, sudden or gradual. Inquiry prepares us to recognize disclosure but does not produce it. The human mind interprets but does not fabricate disclosure. The limits of the idea of truth as disclosure are that disclosure is always partial; in a many-sided reality, not every side can be shown simultaneously. Furthermore, interpretation may be distorted by cultural and personal factors.

This review of ideas of truth does not leave us mired in skeptical paralysis, since each idea contributes something essential to progress in truth; taken together, they help us exercise intellectual responsibility. Good thinking is accurate regarding fact, free of contradictions in its reasoning, and receptive to disclosure.

---

38. Other theories of truth presuppose a realist, or correspondence, theory of truth, according to Alston, *Realist Conception of Truth*.

39. Since I use the term *coherence* here not only to name a major theory of truth but also in the title of this section to summarize the overall character of philosophical truth, I need to clarify. I interpret the correspondence theory as saying that true statements are those that cohere with reality; an analogous remark applies to the following theory of truth as disclosure.

Conclusions

If we persist in the quest to understand a meaning, sooner or later our questions become philosophical. And when we carry the inquiry still further to realize the practical implications of our findings, we begin philosophical living, which seeks wisdom, acts on what it finds, and lives meaningfully. Philosophical living takes the time needed for the work of sharpening our capacities for intuition, reasoning appreciatively and critically, and maturing key concepts. It forms meaningful connections between fact and value, matter and spirit, science and religion.

Wisdom has a contemplative side, as symbolized by illumination in Rembrandt's *Philosopher in Meditation*, and by the settling of evening in Emily Dickinson's poem. The search for wisdom leads ultimately to its source. God is not only the Creator of the universe and its laws, and not only the loving Father known through revelation and experience, but also the God of mind and meaning, inquiry and insight, reason and wisdom.

At its height, wisdom embraces truth, beauty, and goodness as qualities anchored in the eternal nature of God. These values evolve in time as we actualize them—and to do this is to participate in the divine life.

3

Faith's Voyage to the Center of Truth

Jesus of Nazareth and Spiritual Living

I LOOK OUT MY bedroom window in the morning and see the sunrise—but not directly, for my window opens to the north. Behind our backyard, I see tall trees, lots of them. The tallest ones catch the light first. In the canopy, I see where the bright rays of sunlight are pouring in. The shorter trees will catch theirs before long.

This scene symbolizes the dawning of a new day of spiritual living in our world: some people absorb and reflect the light before others. To prepare for, and contribute to, this dawning, we need to glimpse some of the light coming in and enhance our own spiritual experience.

Of course, we can allow our participation to be delayed by uncertainties, but divine truth gives assurance that heals paralysis and empowers progress.

"How soon will the spiritual awakening gain the upper hand in our world?"

"I don't know."

"Will a person like me really be able to pray and worship and commune and serve at a new level?"

"Yes."

"Will God really look after me if I undertake transformative change?"

"Absolutely, but not necessarily in the manner that you may have in mind. What you can look forward to is that your fear of what God's will may require of you will be replaced with trust in God's gentleness and goodness."

"How can I satisfy the material demands of living if I pursue the fulfillment of my spiritual longings?"

"True spiritual guidance is inherently balanced and wise, and it helps you accomplish whatever you must do to fulfill your material responsibilities."

"Am I ready to allocate the time needed for spiritual growth?"

This chapter cannot answer all these questions, but it offers much to support the transformation of anxiety associated with uncertainty into faith. The following pages present a fresh vision of meaning and value in the teachings of Jesus of Nazareth, whose way of living is accessible to us all, whether or not we belong to a particular religion. To point the way to frontiers of spiritual experience, the following basics are described: the receptive and active phases of faith; God's presence within; our search for wisdom in prayer; and spirit-led worship. And the concluding concept of truth offers a way to coordinate scientific and philosophical truths with spiritual truth.

Working with these basics fosters spiritual experience. Alone and of themselves, religious beliefs, social feelings of belonging, and prescribed actions do not bring us to the center of truth. Something more has to be present—for example, when prayer brings a fresh realization, worship becomes sublime, or we really enjoy doing something for others. Nothing dramatic or mystical is necessary; garden variety experiences can accomplish the essential function of helping us realize and practice the truths of the universal family.

From my journey

My journey in God has been marked by countless religious experiences, innumerable wanderings off the path, and gradual growth. Having come of age spiritually during the rise of feminism, I emerged only gradually from a sense of conflict about my religious language. Although my name for God is "Father," I also use other names—Your Oneness, Father-Mother God, Parent, Source, Spirit, Master of the Universe, I AM, and amigo. I also have a philosophical name for him: the self-focalization of infinity.[1] Only today,

1. Calling God "Your Oneness" modifies the appellation "Your Highness" to denote the unity of God. "The self-focalization of infinity" is a name for God that I fashioned in order to reply to Martin Heidegger's critique that God has typically been thought of as merely *a being* rather than something greater (such as Being or the Ground of Being). But the truth of God's infinity has long been clear. The Apostle Paul said, "In him we live and move and have our being" (Acts 17:28). In order for God to enter into relationship with finite creatures, he focalizes himself.

before I put the finishing touches on this book and send it to the publisher, was I given thorough spiritual liberation from the hard-edge drive to assert the fatherhood of God.

Most days, I take an hour or more for my number one relationship. Although I usually spend too much time thinking, new realizations land, and usually I move toward communion and worship. Each day that I persist, I discover a new reason—a trampoline, if you will—for worship. Every morning I wake to some sense of my ever-changing situation. For example, having read news magazines before going to bed one night, I awoke the next morning to a sense of geopolitical danger. At first, a thin layer of fear overshadowed my mind. But then, turning to prayer, I found courage in the God who does triumph and will triumph in all things. I contemplated the plague of cowardice and division that keeps our world from dealing with its problems, and I became ready to go through everything with everyone as a citizen of this world. I identified in solidarity with the persons who directly confront aggression on a daily basis, and I identified in love with their enemies.

Emerging from that renewal, I felt strong and alive. The meaningful sweep of that meditation provided the perfect platform for the morning worship. Entering that sacred space as a radiant soul, I became able after a while to let go and allow the worship to be led by the indwelling spirit. Next, it was time to have some breakfast, interact with the comical cat and the ineffable wife, and then settle down to create a brand new version of this section of this chapter.

Selected facts of the life of Jesus of Nazareth

Jesus' mission made its way amid the religious and political realities of the time and place into which he was born. Shortly before the beginning of Jesus' career as a public teacher, his cousin, John the Baptist, inflamed the countryside with his preaching, whose main message was, "Repent, for the kingdom of heaven is at hand."[2] To a majority of Jews at that time, the

---

As a trinitarian deeply involved in my inner dialogue with Islam, I regard God as so great that he can encompass three persons. The unity of God is not a mathematical oneness; on that intellectual level we would properly say that three cannot be one since they do not have all the same predicates. I conceive the unity of God as higher, personal. I believe that followers of Jesus can join with other monotheists in saying that we worship only God ("There is no God but God"); and we can recognize Moses, Mohammad, Guru Nanak, and others as prophets. And friendship with persons outside one's own religion can become a revelatory spiritual experience.

2. Matt 3:2. In this book, I use the New Revised Standard Version unless otherwise

coming of the kingdom meant the coming of the Messiah ("Christ" in Greek, God's "anointed" one), who would lead an army to overturn Roman rule, restore the older monarchy—"the throne of David"—and establish Jerusalem as the center from which God's justice and peace would become effective among the nations. But Jesus took a different path.

He taught a new concept of the kingdom, one that was free of military and political overtones. During the first period of his ministry in Galilee, Jesus functioned primarily as a teacher and healer, proclaiming his new vision of the kingdom of God. He preferred family terms when speaking of the new social order. And he presented God not as a king or judge but as a loving and merciful Father. The liberating simplicity of his message and his powerful appeal aroused antagonism in the religious leaders, whose opposition to him grew increasingly hostile.

The hour would soon come when, as Jesus put it, the good shepherd would lay down his life in defense of his flock.[3] But while he was still active in public ministry, Jesus taught widely and answered questions from those who were sincere and those who schemed against him. He was able to get his message across in many ways—indirectly through a parable, for example, or by turning a trick question on the questioner, or by keeping silent when he perceived that his words would not penetrate stubborn hearts and minds.

As the attacks against him increased, Jesus took the offensive and escalated his response. His denunciations of the hypocrisy of his enemies were fearless and vivid.[4] Yet for a final confrontation with the religious rulers in Jerusalem, he entered the city riding a donkey to symbolize his peaceful intent.[5]

Jesus' defense of his followers demonstrated the wisdom and superiority of his spiritual way over all the material force and intellectual arguments his opponents could muster. He "cleansed" the Temple, overturning the tables of the money changers (who were charging unfair rates to exchange money into the coin in which the Temple tax had to be paid) and opening the animal pens containing the ritually perfect animals that were sold at high prices for the noisy, bloody sacrifices associated with the Temple rituals of that day.[6] In this revolutionary and ethically elegant act, no person was injured, no money stolen, no property destroyed. But the business was disrupted.

noted, and in this verse, I use the second reading (not the kingdom "has come near").

3. John 10:1–18.
4. Luke 20 and Matt 23.
5. See Zech 9:9 and context.
6. John 1:13–16; Matt 21:12.

Jesus' poise was evident during his last supper with the apostles, when he knew that he was about to be betrayed, arrested, tried, and crucified: "Peace I leave with you; my peace I give to you. I do not give to you as the world gives. Do not let your hearts be troubled, and do not let them be afraid." He repeatedly encouraged, "Be of good cheer."[7]

For all the happiness and peace that he brought, Jesus did not promise that his way would lead to prosperity, success, and freedom from serious difficulties. His struggle in Gethsemane is a reminder of what a grievous test even a spiritually advanced person may have to go through.[8] Having done everything possible for his followers, he turned to prepare himself for what he would soon have to endure. He asked Peter, James, and John to stay awake with him during this time of anguish, but repeatedly he had to rouse his friends from sleep. He prayed that this "cup" be removed if it were the Father's will, and his prayer was answered with a renewal of his strength and poise.

During the agony of the cross, Jesus said, "My God, my God, why have you forsaken me?"[9] These words have given some the impression that Jesus felt spiritually abandoned, but there is another possible interpretation. These are the very words that begin Psalm 22, a poem that begins in desperation and ends in triumph. The speaker is a man pursued by his enemies, who have encircled him and seek his death. He prays to God for deliverance and receives it, and he gives thanks and rejoices greatly.

Sometimes the victory and rejoicing come after death.[10] But no matter what one believes about life after death, it is clear that Jesus' last hours show a victorious way to die. In his lifetime, he went through the full human experience, attentive to the needs of others, always submitting to the Father's will and, at the end, praying to God to forgive the soldiers whose duty it was to carry out the crucifixion. His last words were spoken in a strong voice: "Father, it is finished. Into your hands I commend my spirit." Seeing how nobly Jesus died, the Roman centurion who supervised the execution came to believe in him.[11]

7. John 14:27 and 16:33 (Revised Standard Version); cf. Matt 9:2, 9:22, 14:27, Mark 10:49, and Acts 23:11.

8. Luke 22:39–44.

9. Matt 27:46.

10. Matt 27:45.

11. Luke 23:46 and Matt 27:54.

Jesus' many-sided concepts of the kingdom and the universal family of God

Jesus did not teach the kingdom concept as a system of meanings that would focus attention on intellectual interpretation at the expense of the lesson needed most by the individual or group he was addressing. He used the term *kingdom* with different meanings in various situations to present the meaning most appropriate for the occasion.

Jesus portrayed the kingdom of heaven as a dynamic spiritual reality uniting many contrasts: present and future, inner and outer, a personal experience and a destiny for the planet, a link between heaven and earth, a joyous celebration, and a commitment that may cost the believer's life.

- The kingdom of God is at hand—now[12]

- The kingdom is also in the future. Jesus prayed, "Our Father, who is in heaven, hallowed be your name. Your kingdom come. Your will be done on earth as it is in heaven."[13]

- The kingdom is within you—the Father is not only the God of heaven; he is also close so that we can experience him[14]

- The kingdom is outer as well, something a person can join; it is like a net that gathers many fish, some of which will eventually be thrown out. All are welcomed into it, but some who enter give up along the way[15]

- The kingdom begins like a tiny seed of faith that grows into a mature tree, where the birds of the air come and make their nests in its branches[16]

- The kingdom is the reign or rule of God linking heaven and earth, the will of God in the mind and heart of the believer.[17] Jesus' total

12. Mark 1:15.

13. Matt 6:9–13.

14. Luke 17:21. The NRSV translates "The kingdom of heaven is *among* you" and puts "within you" as an alternate. Although "among you" conveys a truth—that the kingdom is also a social group—it makes less sense in context, in which Jesus is telling his hearers not to look for the kingdom as something that can be observed or to think that they have found it here or there. The Greek word in question, *entos*, can have either meaning.

15. Matt 13:47–48.

16. Ibid 13:31–32.

17. Matt 6:10 and 22:37.

commitment was to the Father's will.[18] Thus it is no surprise that at one point, Jesus defined his family as "whoever does the will of my Father in heaven"[19]

Anyone seeking entrance into the kingdom with the faith of a child is welcomed in. Jesus said, "Ask, and it will be given you; search, and you will find; knock, and the door will be opened for you." "You will know the truth, and the truth will make you free."[20]

Jesus' language of family relationships also contains multiple meanings. His preaching of the kingdom of God expressed his own spiritual experience of being part of the universal family. For Jesus, the kingdom of God was the family of those who accept in faith their status as God's sons and daughters. By relating to God as a son or daughter, we find God as our Father.

On the one hand, Jesus invited his hearers to *become* sons and daughters of God, teaching that we become his children by faith. On the other hand, Jesus' way of loving all people proclaims an inclusive message of family: we are *already* the children of God, no matter what we believe or don't believe—and thus we are all brothers and sisters as well.[21] We can come to God with a child's trust and dependence that opens the door to the spiritual experience of living in the family of God. By his life, Jesus revealed the fatherhood of God and the brotherhood of man, and called his followers to continue that revelation.

Jesus often spoke in parables—simple comparisons or stories that typically make one main point by means of an analogy between the kingdom of God and everyday things, events, or people—and many of these also reflected the theme of God's family. But Jesus' most direct expression of the fatherhood of God and the brotherhood of man comes at the most striking time: the high point of Jesus' conflict with the religious leaders.

Open antagonism between Jesus and many of the leaders had been going on for some time before Jesus gave his final talk in the Temple to a crowd of friends and enemies. Along with his blistering denunciations of the murderous hypocrisy of the religious leaders, Jesus told them that "you

18. Jesus expressed strong antagonism toward actions that rebelled against the Father's will. For the high point of Jesus' critique, see Matt 23; Jesus understood that sin is destructive to the person (Mark 6:14–23).

19. Matt 12:46.

20. Matt 7:7 and John 8:32.

21. Matt 23:8–9. Albrecht Ritschl, Adolf von Harnack, Walter Rauschenbusch, and the social gospel movement made the breakthrough to the recognition of Jesus' gospel of the kingdom as the Fatherhood of God and the brotherhood of man.

are all brothers" and "you all have one Father."[22] Jesus appealed to them in terms of elemental truths.[23] It is noteworthy that Jesus' affirmation of their humanity as members of the universal family occurred in the midst of a life-and-death conflict that would normally overshadow that truth.[24]

Jesus himself lived as a brother to everyone. In the Sermon on the Mount, he warned against being angry with a brother and urged reconciliation.[25] Consider the scope of the term "brother" here and whether it is spiritually acceptable to be angry with nonbelievers. If not, then we should interpret this as a teaching about the universal family of God.[26]

Although the Hebrew Scriptures clearly command the love of the neighbor, the issue of whom to regard as a neighbor was a debated question. Jesus' parable of the Good Samaritan emphasizes that we do not have to belong to the religious in-group to be an outstanding example of love. A man on the road from Jericho to Jerusalem is beaten, robbed, and left half-dead; he is ignored by one member after another of the religious elite before a Samaritan comes along (the Samaritans were looked down upon by Jews because of their unorthodox beliefs and practices). This Samaritan put the injured man on his own animal, took him to an inn, and paid for his care.[27] Jesus told this parable to challenge prejudice and show the extent to which love is willing to go in service to a stranger.

22. Matt 23:8-9. To emphasize a point made earlier, the quality of relationship should not be sacrificed to language: those who have problems with the Father concept of God should choose the name that they find best expresses their relationship with God.

23. *Adelphoi*, the word translated as "brothers," carries no implication regarding gender; "siblings" would capture the meaning. The NRSV puts "brothers" in a note and uses "students" instead; the RSV uses "brethren."

24. The powerful truth of the universal family runs through the Hebrew Scriptures. The book of Genesis represents God as saying "Let us make humankind in our image." (1:26). That we are *all* created in the image of God is the deepest factor that grounds our common humanity. The Holiness Code of Leviticus (chaps. 19–26) teaches love for the stranger, in many cases a non-Jew: "The alien who resides with you shall be as the citizen among you; and you shall love the alien as yourself, for you were aliens in the land of Egypt: I am the Lord your God" (Lev 19:34). The book of Job shows the logic of Job's integrity: "If I have rejected the cause of my male or female slaves, when they brought a complaint against me; what then shall I do when God rises up? . . . Did not he who made me in the womb make them?" (Job 31:13–15). The prophet Malachi protested wrongdoing: "Have we not all one Father? Has not one God created us?" (Mal 2:10). Many other religions have teachings that overlap with these.

25. Matt 5:21–24.

26. References are given in chapter 1, note 40, to books that update Freud's critique of the Father concept of God.

27. Luke 10:29–37.

Jesus' acceptance of all kinds of people is evident in his readiness to party with those of lax morals; he identified with the hungry, the thirsty, the one in need of clothing, the sick, the poor, the prisoner, and the stranger; he reached out to the lost and extended forgiveness to penitent sinners; and he taught that a truly great person is one who serves everyone.[28]

Jesus' spirituality was relational. The kingdom is a web of relationships. The gospel—the good news or glad tidings—proclaims the primal truths of personality relationships. Their beautiful ethical implications Jesus summed up in the twofold command: "You shall love the Lord your God with all your heart, and with all your soul, and with all your mind, and with all your strength" and "you shall love your neighbor as yourself."[29] That teaching in its simplicity makes most sense in the light of the gospel of the universal family.

The gospel message as presented by Peter and Paul centered on the divine and risen Christ. But a fresh presentation of Jesus' original message of the family of God could go places where that traditional message cannot go and do things that it cannot do. Such a message could promote receptivity to the higher truths of the universal family without upstaging the gospel movement to which Jesus devoted his public career as a teacher.

Jesus' happiness in the family of God

Because so much attention has been placed on the tragic closing chapter of Jesus' life, it has been easy to overlook the liberating joy and happiness of his life and teachings. Happiness pervades Jesus' religion of spiritual experience. "Happiness" is variously defined, but for Jesus, true happiness is spiritual.

Jesus expressed in his beatitudes the wisdom and happiness of this way of living. The beatitudes proclaim the joy of divine assurance: the certainty of welcome into the family of God in the present, and confidence in the

---

28. For Jesus' readiness to party with outcasts, see Matt 9:10–13 and 11:19; for Jesus' identification with the hungry, the thirsty, the one in need of clothing, the sick, the poor, the prisoner, and the stranger, see Matt 25:35–40 and Mark 12:41–44; and Luke 14:13; for selected stories of healings and exorcisms, see Mark 1:23–2:17; 5; 10:33–37; Matt 5:3–12; 11:5 and 28; 15:30–31; 17:14–18; Luke 6:1–4 and 35; 7:36–48; for forgiveness for one who is lost and then found or for a penitent sinner, see Luke 7:36–48; 15; 19:1–10; 23:32–47; and for the teaching that greatness implies serving everyone, Mark 10:42–45.

29. Mark 12:30–31. These commandments come from the Hebrew Scriptures, Deut 6:4, and Lev 19:18.

eventual harvest of our efforts to grow in righteousness and to live in accord with divine wisdom.

> Happy are the poor in spirit, for theirs is the kingdom of heaven.
>
> Happy are those who mourn, for they will be comforted.
>
> Happy are the meek, for they will inherit the earth.
>
> Happy are those who hunger and thirst for righteousness, for they will be filled.
>
> Happy are the merciful, for they will receive mercy.
>
> Happy are the pure in heart, for they will see God.
>
> Happy are the peacemakers, for they will be called children of God.
>
> Happy are those who are persecuted for righteousness sake, for theirs is the kingdom of heaven.
>
> Happy are you when people revile you and persecute you and utter all kinds of evil against you falsely on my account. Rejoice and be glad, for your reward is great in heaven, for in the same way they persecuted the prophets who were before you.[30]

The first beatitude is the gateway to the others. *Those who are poor in spirit* as they seek entrance to the kingdom are the ones who seek in a way that is humble, sincere, and open.[31] To them Jesus gave assurance: *yours is the kingdom of heaven.* Once persons receive that welcome with open arms and realize that they are accepted as sons and daughters in the family of God, they become ready to trust the promises for the future given in the other beatitudes.

When a believer *mourns* for a loss, the mourner comes to realize God's comforting embrace.

In Jesus' teaching, *the meek* does not refer to timid people who habitually defer to those who are aggressive. Spiritual meekness opens one to the will of God—the ultimate happiness highway. Jesus expresses his farseeing vision of the future kingdom: for the meek to inherit the earth means that in the end, the good guys win.

When *striving for righteousness* reaches the level of hunger and thirst, one gets a taste of the God's eventual fulfillment of that desire. He is the

30. Matt 5:3–12, substituting "happy" for "blessed."

31. Jesus taught in the language of Aramaic, in which the way to say "poor in spirit" means "humble."

one who imparts righteousness as a gift, as a happy first installment on the perfection that is our destiny. Kingdom believers can rejoice now in this gift, which marks an important stage in a process not yet completed.

There is a happiness that comes to those who can let go of judgmental attitudes and *practice the ways of forgiveness* toward others: they are able to experience God's mercy.

Those who are pure in heart are happy because they are assured of seeing God in the next life. They also enjoy a foretaste of future happiness since they experience divine truth, beauty, and goodness in this life.

Peacemakers gain happiness in their work for understanding and reconciliation.

Persons who suffer verbal abuse, persecution, and even death for following the new way are promised a heavenly reward and encouraged to rejoice greatly.

When such truths of spiritual experience are felt in the soul, the beauty of truth shines forth, and we recognize it with joy. Jesus highlighted joy in many of his parables. "The kingdom of heaven is like treasure hidden in a field, which someone found and hid; then in his joy he goes and sells all that he has and buys that field."[32] Jesus' parables also include three lost-and-found stories,[33] all of which tell of the exceptional joy when the person who had been lost is returned to the circuit of loving community.[34] Great rejoicing reveals the tremendous value of the individual.

32. Matt 13:44.

33. Luke 15 contains these three parables. According to Tatum, *In Quest of Jesus*, a parable in the teaching of Jesus makes a comparison—sometimes through a narrative that uses an expanded simile or metaphor—between "commonplace things, events, and persons" and the higher reality of the kingdom of God. A parable "tends to make one point," unlike an allegory, which "makes many points" (193–94).

34. The first story tells of a sheep that wanders off from the flock. The shepherd goes out to find the sheep, and when he finds it rejoices and calls to friends and neighbors to rejoice with him. Jesus speaks of joy among the angels when one who has been lost is found. The next story tells of a woman who carefully and thoroughly searches for a lost coin until she finds it, and rejoices. The third story tells of the younger of two sons, who asks to receive his inheritance and then goes off with the money and lives in reckless immorality. When the consequences of his foolishness land him in misery, the prodigal son decides to return and ask his father for forgiveness. His father sees him coming, greets him with rejoicing, and throws a party to celebrate his return. The diligent and reliable older brother refuses to join the merriment and protests against the lavish reception, so his father explains that it is right to celebrate when someone who was lost is found, when someone who was dead comes back to life.

Jesus' down-to-earth understanding of fact

By the time he was ready to begin his public career as a teacher, Jesus had a habitual, down-to-earth, and realistic sense of fact. Most of his observations relate to human psychology and the society of his place and time. The cosmological theme of the friendly universe shows up a couple of times, as well as realism about the facts of political power, an extraordinarily keen interpretation of Scripture, and encouragement to use religious and historical understanding to interpret current events.[35] Those who know the goodness of Jesus' good news become more able to face bad news honestly and constructively.

Jesus on life after death

The more we come to know God, the more naturally we look forward to continuing the friendship after this life. But we lack insight into the beyond, so we wonder: Is there is something after death? If so, is what happens the same for all? If not, what opens the door to everlasting life?

The human mind desires a criterion that would provide certainty about the afterlife; but Jesus' teachings do not satisfy that desire. The righteous God of love and mercy cannot be represented with a one-size-fits-all formula. Jesus offered guidance, encouragement, and sometimes warning, saying different things to people at different stages on their journey. As I interpret

35. Jesus made various psychological observations: a person can focus on a small fault in another person while being blinded by a huge fault of his own (Matt 7:3); some people who seem like prophets are charlatans in disguise (Matt 7:6); people will respond very diversely to the message of the kingdom due to factors beyond the control of the messengers (Matt 13:3–9); evil in the heart corrupts our thoughts and actions (Matt 15:18–20); his enemies fell into numerous hypocritical behaviors (Matt 23); some people hang on fearfully to the truth as it was given to them, while others work productively and creatively with what they have (Matt 25:14–31).

Jesus made sociological observations: a group that is torn by divisiveness cannot endure (Mark 3:24); because his messengers were being sent into a hostile environment, they needed to be wise and take care not to inflame the situation by, for example, offering advanced spiritual teaching to people who could not profit from it and would react aggressively (Matt 7:6 and 10:16–28, and John 16:18).

Jesus made further observations that could be classified as relevant to other disciplines: he acknowledged the need to live with the fact of political power and distinguished the political from the spiritual realm (Matt 22:17); he showed evidence of extraordinarily careful study of the Scriptures (Luke 20:37–38); he encouraged people to interpret current events in a perspective that combined history and religion (Matt 16:1–3); he gave advice about how to conduct a fair grievance procedure (Matt 18:15–17); and he gave indications of a just and friendly universe (Luke 12:22, Matt 5:45 and 6:25–34).

Jesus, what is essential for being in the family of God is living faith; and living faith is growing faith.[36] The lack of a fixed criterion should not make us anxious, however; assurance comes from within loving relationship.

An expert in religious law asked Jesus, "What must I do to inherit eternal life?" In response, Jesus asked what answer the man would give. The lawyer answered by drawing on two verses from the Hebrew Scriptures: "You shall love the Lord your God with all your heart and with all your soul and with all your strength and with all your mind; and your neighbor as yourself." For Jesus, these two commandments expressed our whole duty; and he assured the lawyer that his reply was sufficient: "Do this and you will live."[37] Jesus thus gave a promise of eternal life without any condition about believing in him.[38]

Jesus said little about heaven. Perhaps he did not want to corrupt faith by speaking frequently or in detail of the rewards of faith; but he did refer to the Father in heaven, the kingdom of heaven, the angels' heavenly joy, and to the many "mansions" or places in the Father's house. He spoke of heaven as a place where the will of God is done.[39] One thing stands out in these teachings: heaven is *wonderful*, and many people in his time and place believed in some sort of heaven and wanted to make sure they were going

36. Paul's teaching in Galatians 3 is an influential expression of salvation by faith.

37. Luke 10:25-28; the lawyer quotes from Deut 6:4 and Lev 19:18.

38. Though everyone needs faith to embrace God's invitation to life after death, it might be helpful to consider more deeply what this actually means. In defining the requirements for salvation, many Christians appeal to the following statement, made by Jesus to his apostles on the night before his crucifixion: "I am the way, the truth, and the life. No one comes to the Father except by me" (John 14:6). This teaching is often interpreted to mean that every person must come to believe in Jesus during this life on earth in order to be saved. But this overlooks some of Jesus' own teachings on the matter. Thus another interpretation is possible: that a living faith in God is sufficient for salvation, and we have the opportunity to discover higher truth about Jesus after this life.

This interpretation makes John 14:6 consistent with other sayings in which Jesus makes no reference to faith in himself when he tells the lawyer what is sufficient for salvation (Luke 10:25-28), tells Zacchaeus that his generous repentance has brought him salvation (Luke 19:1-10), tells the rich young ruler what is required in his case for eternal life (Mark 10:17-27; Matt 19:16-22; Luke 18:18-23), and assures his hearers in the Sermon on the Mount that the kingdom of heaven belongs to the poor in spirit (Matt 5:3). To treat the complexities of this topic adequately is beyond the scope of this book. The important point is that we have evidence that Jesus on several occasions addressed the topic of salvation without indicating that faith in him was necessary.

39. Matt 6:9-10; 26:29; Luke 15:3-7; John 14.2. For further indications about heaven—indeed multiple heavens—see Deut 10.14; Neh 9.6; Ps 148.4 (cf. 1 Kgs 8.27; and 2 Chron 2.6 and 6.18); 2 Cor 12:2-4; Heb 10:34; 11:10 and 16; and Rev 4. I regard the many heavens as places where we continue our growth toward perfection, which is finally complete only in Paradise.

there. Furthermore, faith involves love and trust, and no true Parent would dismiss a sincere and growing child who wants to stay in relation.

If a person does not go to heaven, then what? The popular idea of hell pictures a place of everlasting torture, but the New Testament word translated as "hell" is *Gehenna*, which refers to a valley near Jerusalem where garbage was burned; it may also symbolize the "second death," the destruction of a soul that has finally rejected the chance to go forward with God.[40]

Those on their way to everlasting life go to heaven. Children grow up to be like their parents; and we can grow to become like God. Jesus said, "Be you perfect, even as your Father in heaven is perfect."[41] Many people reject perfection as a meaningful goal because of its association with moralistic or legalistic standards; but Jesus' call to perfection expresses his great faith in the capacity of human beings to be transformed; and his parables of growth make it clear that spiritual growth is a gradual process.[42] His call to perfection, his invitation to become like God, implies a stunning promise: the person who stays with the program will, through divine aid, attain that goal.

In the course of his life, Jesus developed a character that unified spiritual virtues with other strengths. The unhurried simplicity of his balanced character reflected the nature of God. The virtues that we find in his life include the following:

- Firm groundedness in a sharp awareness of fact

- Wisdom derived ultimately from prayer

- Wholehearted faith in truth coupled with loyalty to supreme values

- Total trust in God and complete dedication to his will

- Love for God with all the powers of body, mind, and soul, and a love for other human beings as oneself

- Majestic poise rooted in an authentic, authoritative, and charismatic personality

- Capacity to respond with gentleness or power as the occasion demanded

40. Matt 10:28; Rev 20:14 and 21:8. The truths of the family of God are eternal truths, but a person can falsify them in his or her own case by rejecting them day by day, year by year, until finally the person comes to reject them eternally. God is love, and love does not force free will to receive love. The divine Parent is willing to allow the rebellious child to destroy itself, while welcoming into the ongoing adventure the sons and daughters who choose the way of life. See Pinnock, "Conditional View" and "Annihilationism."

41. Matt 5:48.

42. Matt 13:1–32.

- Artistic and original teaching methods, with great sensitivity to the receptivity of his listeners

- A great ease in being at home in nature, observant of nature, and using images from nature in teaching

- Ability to sustain joy even amidst difficulties

- Faithful endurance of the worst afflictions

Jesus' life and teachings demonstrated core spiritual truths recognized in many religions: the goodness and love of the one Creator God, the presence of the divine spirit within us, experiencing God in prayer and worship, the liberation and joy of the life of faith, meaning that helps us go through suffering, and commitment to treat others with respect and compassion, and humankind as a family. Even the happy mystery of the fatherhood of God has been recognized in many religions.[43]

Today, the recognition of the universal family is expanding. In addition to experiencing divinely fatherly love, with its greater emphasis on purpose, creative design, and will, we experience divinely motherly love, with its greater emphasis on personal, responsive, expressive, merciful, encompassing, hands-on nurturing qualities. These varieties in the expression of divine love should not lead back to the polytheism transcended by Jews, Muslims, and others. The more we live the truths of the universal family, the more the truth of the unity of God becomes a reality in our experience. In my view, that unity is expanded, not broken, by this testimony from nineteenth-century preacher Rebecca Jackson. "I saw that night, for the first time, a Mother in the Deity. This indeed was a new scene, a new doctrine to me. But I knowed when I got it, and I was obedient to the heavenly vision. . . . And was I not glad when I found that I had a Mother! And that night She gave me a tongue to tell it! The spirit of weeping was upon me, and it fell on all the assembly. And though they never heard it before, I was made

---

43. We find expressions of the fatherhood of God in the Hebrew Scriptures, from Moses (Deut 32:7) to Malachi (Mal 2:10). In Confucianism, the most valued text by Chang Tsai (Zhang Zai) (1020–1077 C.E.) begins with these words: "Heaven is my father and earth is my mother. . . ." (Chan, *Source Book*, 497). The thirteenth-century Japanese Buddhist prophet Nichiren wrote in his *Dedication to the Lotus*, "Our hearts ache and our sleeves are wet [with tears], until we see face to face the tender figure of the One, who says to us, 'I am thy Father'" (349). The most dynamic late–twentieth-century expression of faith in the fatherhood of God, the brotherhood of man, and the indwelling spirit of God has been the thousands of *Swadhyaya* ("Self-study") villages that thrive mostly in western India, in response to the leadership of Hindu teacher Pandurang Shastri Arthavale, who in 1957 started a movement of communities effectively devoted to worship, study, and social service (http://swadhyay.org).

able by Her Holy Spirit of Wisdom to make it so plain that a child could understand it."[44]

To cultivate our experience of such truths, we can deepen our practice of the spiritual living basics described here: faith, centering, friendship with God, prayer, and worship.

Faith's receptive and active sides

To find the truths of science, we must experiment; to find the truths of philosophy, we must interpret meanings; to find the truths of spiritual experience, we need faith. To begin to develop a person-to-Person relationship with God, all we need is the faith of a beginner's willingness to reach out and open the door to the God who reaches out to us by knocking respectfully, patiently, and lovingly.

But it can take quite a journey before we are prepared for that simplicity, as is shown in this report by a Muslim student. Her seeking to find God had been ardent and persistent—anguished at times—and then her soul found full satisfaction.

> When I decided to set out on my journey of spirituality through regular meditation, I had already been told that I would experience many wonderful things. I heard also that the path to eternity was not supposed to be smooth at all times and that I was going to be faced with difficulties along the way. In my heart, I accepted the truth of these words and was eagerly ready to embrace the changes I was going to experience. However, at that moment, I never expected the breeze of change to come along so quickly, as if it had been waiting at my door all this time, longing to come in and blow on my life.
>
> Righteousness, as I have come to know it in the past few weeks of my spiritual experience, is the natural consequence of sincere and heart-filled meditation on the presence of God.

---

44. Johnson, *She Who Is*, 170. Some thinkers have proposed that women should develop a concept of a female deity to worship, as men worship a male deity. Although I can empathize with the idea, I regard male and female as biological categories that may be misleading if projected into the spiritual realm. The larger truth is that both men and women can express divinely fatherly love and divinely motherly mercy. The one God has been portrayed as having both kinds of quality. "As a mother comforts her child, so I will comfort you" (Isa 66:13). Moreover, Jesus compared himself to a mother hen, and one of his kingdom parables features a woman searching for a lost coin (Luke 15:8-10; see also Matt 13:33). When we know the God of mercy and love as an undivided spirit presence, these problems lose their sharp edge. Linear thinking and static concepts block progress in the experience of mystery.

> During the past weeks, I experienced the most joyful moment of
> my whole life, the moment of liberation. The moment I became
> aware of the spirit of God, or "the gift of the spirit" within me, I
> was set free from the chains of prejudice, ignorance, and doubt,
> and I entered a new phase of my life. To set my spirit free was
> the single drop that satisfied my thirsty soul and the key that
> opened my heart to the work of God. What immediately fol-
> lowed from that was my sincere submission to the will of God
> and his purpose for me. I have realized that being righteous is to
> let the spirit take over and guide my actions . . . .[45]

Faith has a receptive phase and an active phase. Receptivity recognizes that
faith is a gift from God: his indwelling spirit enables our mind to intuitively
register spiritual truth when it comes along; and truth itself is a gift. But it is
up to us to embrace faith and act on it. We act on faith as we enter the heart
of what it means to live the truth: to develop our spiritual experience and
friendship with God and live as a member in the universal family by doing
God's will.

The two phases of faith are intimately connected. I used to welcome
the occasional vivid spiritual experience and wish that I could prolong it
forever. It was like getting a brand-new, bright yellow, fuzzy, bouncy tennis
ball. Now I regard spiritual experience as a part of an ongoing conversation,
an interactive relationship, like the back and forth in tennis. It is my job to
keep the ball in play. Looking at it this way, I began responding to spiritual
experiences by reflecting on my experience to find a clue in it that I could
follow by making some decision for the will of God. Then I would look
for an opportunity to put that decision into practice. My active responses
have enabled the ball to come back into my court more frequently.[46] And
spiritual experience need not be dramatic to initiate such a process; it may
be subtle, like a whisper, or simply bring a special quality of calm.

Faith is not the same as a belief. Faith is our spiritual access to truth, to
the spirit, to God. A belief (when it is correct) expresses our understanding
of a truth. Faith is one; beliefs are multiple. Truth is one; truths are many.
When someone accuses a person of being mistaken in claiming to have
"the truth with a capital T," what is meant is that a particular belief is being incorrectly raised to the supreme and divine level of truth itself. Truths

---

45. The student chose that her name should not be mentioned.

46. Psychologist Abraham Maslow classified people as being either peakers or
non-peakers: some have peak experiences at least every few days, while others only
rarely. But "non-peakers" begin having peak experiences much more often once they
learn to recognize them.

can be stated as beliefs; but truth—living truth—is not anything we could construct, for example, by adding up beliefs.[47]

Belief that God exists is not the same as faith in God; and knowing *about* God is not the same as *knowing* God. The distinction between faith and belief does not imply that there is anything wrong with belief, for beliefs may be true. There is no problem in having beliefs unless they usurp the place of truth. And the relations between belief and truth may be friendly. It is natural to express the truths that dawn in spiritual experience as beliefs. Once expressed, a word of truth may be passed on to another mind. Once planted in the mind, belief can blossom into faith like a time-release vitamin, as the meanings of truth are pondered and put into action.

A thought may get planted in the mind when a particular phrase or sentence stands out as we are thinking or reading or listening to someone talk about spiritual things. It speaks to our situation; it strikes home with conviction; intuitively, it has a flavor or spirit of truth. This experience is traditionally called illumination. It need not be intense; no light flashes in the mind.[48] But we experience truth with greater conviction.

Illumination is the womb in which faith in God is born. Illumination is something that God does—the intuitive conviction of the spirit reality of God is not our own work.[49] In that moment of grace, of childlike, intuitive openness, we become receptive to divine truth, which becomes so clearly apparent that we have no doubt or hesitation about what we have received. No abyss separates subject from object. Thus we can say that faith is a gift, infused in the mind by God.

47. Centuries ago, the word *belief* did refer to a relation of love and trust. However, by the early twentieth century, the term had come to refer to an act of the intellect. In other words, religious believers themselves reduced the concept of saving faith to a set of propositions that a person had to believe to be saved. See Smith, *Faith and Belief*.

48. In spiritual experience, we are not particularly aware of the mind. Sometimes we can still distinguish our consciousness from God; at other times God is so immediately present that we lose all awareness of self. For this distinction see Alston, *Perceiving God*, 20–24.

49. To be sure, in many experiences, resistance partly obscures childlike openness; moreover, the social environment influences our early ideas of God. Working in phenomenology, the philosophical discipline that rigorously describes structures of experience, I developed several of the ideas advanced in this chapter in my "Phenomenology of Religious Experience": https://sites.google.com/a/kent.edu/jwattles/home/publications/husserl-on-religious-experience.

Spiritual centering

God is the center of everything, and spiritual centering means, above all, centering on God. His presence within us establishes a nucleus that makes it meaningful to speak of centering as also an inner process. A number of spiritual paths teach a practice of centering. One way to begin to center ourselves is to move from the mind into the soul. We do this by stepping back from being caught up in the mind's immediate concerns, its passing thoughts and emotions. We take time to allow ourselves to abide in and as our true and deeper self. The soul is deeper than the mind; the soul is the true self. The soul expresses itself in the book of Psalms, from the depths of agony to the heights of celebration.

Flashes of lust, anger, and pity are material emotions of the mind; but love, genuinely righteous indignation, and compassion are feelings of the soul.[50] However, in my opinion, if we make significant decisions based on material emotions, they may become part of who we really are, our soul.[51] When we follow a spiritual path, that soul, or deeper self, grows; and we contribute to that growth by the decisions we make, the attitudes we express, and the character we develop in cooperation with the spirit of God. In this way, the soul can move from being lost, through seeking, to connected; from hurt through healing to radiant; from torn through reconciled to unified; from rebellious through obedient to wholehearted.

The ultimate goal of inward centering is to realize the indwelling presence of God. Countless persons have discovered an inner source of energy, power, wisdom, insight, peace, love, joy, creativity, purpose, and guidance. Despite differences in vocabulary, concept, context, and practice, many religions recognize what is called the indwelling spirit of God.[52] Hinduism speaks of the *atman*, the (eternal, spirit) self. Buddhism calls it Buddha-nature. Judaism speaks of the spirit in man, "the candle of the Lord." Jesus proclaimed, "The kingdom of God is within you." The Qur'an says, "We

50. All emotions have their evolutionary function, so nothing about emotions being material makes them unfortunate. Oxytocin stimulates a kindness that may fall short of love at its greatest, but the world could use a lot more of that kindness. A fuller account of the brain's role might show that higher feelings have less limbic and more neocortical support compared with material emotions.

51. The soul is contrasted with the old self, the tissue of mental habits destined for transformation.

52. Some spiritual experiences are not recognized as divine gifts; Thomas Shotwell, whose realization of cosmic beauty was described in chapter 2, never acknowledged the Creator. Mindfulness fosters a harmony of mind and body that allows the indwelling spirit to bless us with beautiful experiences, though many practitioners simply give credit to mindfulness.

created man. We know the promptings of his soul, and are closer to him than his jugular vein."[53] Knowing the inner life deeply, the Chinese philosopher Mencius (Mengzi) (371–289 BCE) summarized a spiritual path centered on the *tao* (the way). "A noble man steeps himself in the Way because he wishes to find it in himself. When he finds it in himself, he will be at ease in it; when he is at ease in it, he can draw deeply upon it; when he can draw deeply upon it, he finds its source wherever he turns."[54] Guru Nanak, the founder of Sikhism, wrote, "Behold the Lord within yourself"; "Thou art concealed within"; "Thy light shines in every heart."[55] It is encouraging to see harmony on such a basic truth.[56]

We recognize soul and spirit from within the conscious mind, and we do so fallibly. Taking a pragmatic attitude to our use of language, we can regard our experience and language as that of beginners, human beings with imperfect discernment and a long way to go. If we use these terms to express our interpretations, the truth of our beliefs may be humanly measured by the way they seem to help our growth. We can also see intellectual uncertainty as part of the Creator's provision for our growth. If we cannot nail down answers to some religious questions, then in the quest for God, we must reach beyond the limits of our mind and dare to venture. We grow through trial and error and are rewarded for our efforts.[57] Sometimes the reward is a spiritual experience that needs no pragmatic interpretation since it brings insightful intuition.

Friendship with God

The God who dwells within us relates to us as Parent and Friend.[58] Most spiritual and religious persons would welcome a closer friendship with God.[59] God's very greatness is expressed in his reaching forth to us in friend-

53. See the Bhagavad Gita 2.18-25, 6.47, 9.29, and 18.61; the Mahaparinirvana Sutra; Prov 20:27; Luke 17:21; and the Qur'an 50.16.

54. Mencius, *Mencius*, 4B14.

55. Guru Nanak quoted in McLeod, "Teachings of Guru Nanak," 174–75.

56. Of the books I know, none gives a more sustained, varied, and inspiring call to continuous communion with the indwelling spirit of God than Strong, *Scattered Brotherhood*.

57. The philosophy of language here is akin to the pragmatism of William James in *The Varieties of Religious Experience*.

58. In God, persons experience Motherly love as well as Fatherly love. This frontier is explored in Johnson, *She Who Is*, and McFague, *Models of God*.

59. The concept of God is central not only for Jews, Christians, and Muslims but also for Zoroastrians, Sikhs, and Bahá'ís. In addition, many Hindus are more

ship. This realization is expressed in the oldest of the Hindu Scriptures, the Rig Veda: "All the friends rejoice for their Glorious Friend at the end of the journey, reaching fulfillment, for he brings nourishment, and removes their guilt, and he is prepared to act courageously."[60] Sufism, the mystical branch of Islam, refers to God as the Friend.

Both human and divine friendships develop from an initial meeting. As we move beyond formalities, awkwardness, and a clumsy kind of respect, we begin to talk openly and naturally, sharing ideas, feelings, and questions about life. We take time to listen, understand, and respond. We do things together. As time goes on, we feel comfortable falling into silence together. We come to the point where we can communicate with even a slight gesture or expression.

The difference between friendship with God and friendship with humans is that we almost never actually hear God speak. But even sharing thoughts and feelings with God is a striking improvement over the ordinary habit of conducting the inner life as if we were alone. When we are ready to send some communicative pulse from our side to God, we can use words or a wordless gesture of soul. But the answer is rarely anything we can hear, such as a string of words coming into the mind; instead the response is from God's spirit to our soul: a gift of truth, beauty, and goodness.[61]

In spiritual experience, truth, beauty, and goodness are more than ideas; they are divine values. In spiritual experience, we find truth, beauty, and goodness as qualities of God, who is the maximum of these values and is their source. Value is what we long for or strive for when it is absent; and value is what we enjoy and celebrate when it is present. Genuine values, when we embrace them, bring us closer to God and thereby integrate the different aspects of our being while also coordinating us with one another.

monotheistic than polytheistic, and Mahayana Buddhists in the Pure Land tradition hold a concept of Amitabha or Amida Buddha comparable in many respects to a belief in God. Just as theistic religions recognize spiritual experience that is not specifically personal, religions that are not primarily oriented to a personal deity make room for personal spiritual relating. See Berger, ed., *Other Side of God*. Responding to earlier studies in comparative religion that overemphasized similarities, many later twentieth-century studies in comparative religion tended to overemphasize differences.

60. Rig-Veda, X.71, in Le Mée, ed., *Rig-Veda*, 148.

61. God can and does speak verbally from within in self-evident revelation, utterly distinct from any thought that the mind addresses to itself. The challenge is to be humble as we interpret experiences that are less clearly divine. We want to avoid the pitfall of mistaking products of the human mind for divine communication; for example, the human mind can sometimes address us with commands or "speak" in the second-person singular, and we might take that to mean we are hearing from a divine source.

Spiritual experience takes us to the heart of the values we find outside the specifically religious sphere—for example, when we are appreciating a well-built house, a lovely garden, or a skillfully written essay. An insightful expression is true, but truth itself is the spiritual value that is present in intellectual excellence. A thoughtfully designed flower garden is beautiful, but beauty itself is the value that illuminates the experience of that garden. A sturdy house is good, but goodness itself is the living, spiritual reality that shines in a full appreciation of the construction of the house.

A more thorough prayer process

I had a dog that I would take on walks through the woods. When he came to a fork in the trail, he would bound ahead toward whatever attracted him at the moment. It would have been out of character for him to stop, turn around, sit down, give me that happy smile, and wait for me to indicate which way to go.[62]

When we come to a fork in our trail, we can take time to pray. Patiently turning to God opens us to spiritual experience that completes philosophy's quest for wisdom. God wants to give us the wisdom we need, and we can receive it by sincerely opening ourselves to him in prayer. Most of the time, prayer for divine wisdom is a simple matter. Many people ask and promptly experience what feels like an answer. But these quick requests need to be interspersed with longer times for prayer. When there is need and time for a thorough prayer process, we do not content ourselves with a quick glance above to see what may immediately come to mind.

Prayer is an education in cooperating with God. This implies being responsible for our side of the relationship. It would not be right to ask God to do our homework for us or clean up our mess. God does these things *with* us, adding to what we can do in countless ways but without doing our duty or taking away the privilege of doing our utmost. At the height, we mobilize our powers of heart and mind in our best study, reflection, and effort.

But what we want to see actualized might not be as good as what God has in mind. So we entrust everything into his hands. We let go of attachment to our favorite ideas and urgent desires in order to open ourselves to something greater. This profound expression of trust allows us to receive a fresh gift of divine truth, beauty, and goodness. Indeed, if we do not slow down and allow the momentum of heart and mind to be stilled, our

---

62. In the Cuicatec language of Oaxaca, Mexico, the word for "worship" means "wagging one's tail before God." Sadly, I have lost my reference for this fact.

decision may not be truly free, and our ability to discern the will of God may be greatly reduced.[63]

Prayer allows the hungry heart to express itself and to be transformed. Prayer processes desire; we honestly express our feelings and then let God change them. In the light of that transformation, we naturally become happy and grateful, and thanksgiving carries us like an updraft that birds catch as they circle higher. When thanksgiving or appreciation rise to their maximal height, they become worship.

Ascending to the heights of worship

Worship involves a variety of practices, when we are part of a group or alone. Worship has one set of meanings as a group practice and a different set when done alone. Here worship refers to our highest, most complete, and most direct relating to God. When we make a request for ourselves or for others, we are praying; but there is a spontaneous response to God that rises above prayer. Worship can even ascend beyond what we can put into words. In worship, we fulfill the Psalmist's invitation: "Taste and see that the Lord is good."[64]

On one occasion, Jesus conversed with a Samaritan woman who asked whether worship should be on Mount Gerizim, where the Samaritans would go, or in Jerusalem, the center of Jewish worship. Jesus' reply set aside the question of location and went straight to the essential: "God is spirit, and those who worship him must worship in spirit and truth."[65] This teaching comes without illustration or commentary. It speaks with a generality that addresses us all; its invigorating simplicity leads us like a wilderness guide into the high country of our primary relationship.

The mind knows something of the truth of God. The spirit uplifts the mind and refreshes the soul. At its peak, worship is not altogether something that we do; ultimately, it transpires within us. We need the spirit to take worship to the summit. As we consent to this leading, we cooperate in something beyond our comprehension and trust the spirit to shepherd our highest person-to-Person experience.[66]

63. The brain commonly prepares the motor process for carrying out an action a fraction of a second before the conscious decision. A brief summary of this finding by Benjamin Libet is found in Shusterman, *Body Consciousness*, 197–98.

64. Ps 34:8.

65. John 4:24.

66. The initiative of the spirit in prayer has long been recognized: "The mysterious impulse which drives [the truly and deeply religious person] to prayer is the revelation of the indwelling God at work in the deepest places of his soul" (Heiler, *Prayer*, 108).

The simplicity and complexity of truth

Just as we can have a sturdy grasp of fact without science and a keen sense of meaning without philosophy, we can experience value without spiritual experience. But if values at their height are divine realities, qualities of God, then our most true, beautiful, and good experiences of value will be spiritual.

Sometimes we think of truth as including the truths of fact and meaning as well as value; and the term *cosmic truth* can symbolize that comprehensive concept. I have previously characterized truth as having a spiritual core, a scientific periphery, and a philosophical bridge between them. But now I want to modulate the concept of truth into a higher key. Truth has a simplicity that we know most radiantly in spiritual living. We meet truth in spiritual experience and recognize it as divine. Although truth implicitly contains all truths, it is not merely a collection or even a synthesis. It has its own living nature.[67] Seers in different times and places have experienced this. Consider this story from Taoist philosopher Chuang Tzu (Zhuangzi).

> Cook Ting was cutting up an ox for Lord Wen-hui. At every touch of his hand, every heave of his shoulder, every move of his feet, every thrust of his knee, zip! zoop! He slithered the knife along with a zing, and all was in perfect rhythm, as though he were performing the dance of the Mulberry Grove or keeping time to the Ching-shou music.
>
> "Ah, this is marvelous!" said Lord Wen-hui. "Imagine skill reaching such heights!"
>
> Cook Ting laid down his knife and replied, "What I care about is the Way, which goes beyond skill. When I first began cutting up oxen, all I could see was the ox itself. After three years I no longer saw the whole ox. And now—now I go at it by spirit and don't look with my eyes. Perception and understanding have come to a stop and spirit moves where it wants. I go along with the natural makeup, strike in the big hollows, guide the knife through the big openings, and follow things as they are. So I never touch the smallest ligament or tendon, much less a main joint.

The Book of Common Prayer characterizes adoration as "the lifting up of the heart and mind to God, asking nothing but to enjoy God's presence"; and praise is "not to obtain anything, but because God's Being draws praise from us" (Church Publishing, 857). On the whole, Eastern religions have given greater emphasis to the difference between the highest spiritual practices and those based on human desire or need.

67. The religion of the spirit stands above science, philosophy, and art; and it is available to persons regardless of these cultural achievements. Philosophy should not try to domesticate or control the spirit by presenting advanced culture as a prerequisite to transformation.

"A good cook changes his knife once a year, because he cuts. A mediocre cook changes his knife once a month—because he hacks. I've had this knife of mine for nineteen years and I've cut up thousands of oxen with it, and yet the blade is as good as though it had just come from the grindstone. There are spaces between the joints, and the blade of the knife has really no thickness. If you insert what has no thickness into such spaces, then there's plenty of room, more than enough for the blade to play about in. That's why after nineteen years the blade of my knife is still as good as when it first came from the grindstone.

"However, whenever I come to a complicated place, I size up the difficulties, tell myself to watch out and be careful, keep my eyes on what I'm doing, work very slowly, and move the knife with the greatest subtlety, until, flop! the whole thing comes apart like a clod of earth crumbling to the ground. I would stand there holding the knife and look all around me, completely satisfied and reluctant to move on, and then I wipe off the knife and put it away."

"Excellent!" said Lord Wen-hui. "I have heard the words of Cook Ting and learned how to care for life!"[68]

This story has surreal touches (the knife with no thickness that never gets dull), indicating that it is not to be taken literally; rather the story is about how to care for life. Life is something like cutting up an ox: a large task, involving work for others, requiring tools and skill, and offering the possibility for three levels of growth.

If we transplant this story into the garden of our inquiry, we can interpret as follows.[69] We begin caring for life on the level of perceptual fact, advance to intellectual understanding, philosophical reflection, and then ascend not merely to ideas about spiritual realities but also to spiritual realization and relating. The way the ox (life) looks when we are living mainly on the material level is different from the way it looks when reflective thinking has matured; and the intellectual level is quite different from the spiritual level of relating. A person who lives mainly on the spiritual level continues to engage in problem solving that requires renewed focusing on material

68. Chuang Tzu, "Caring for Life," 46–47.

69. I do not claim that Chuang Tzu's concepts of mind and spirit are the same as mine; but the fact of cultural difference does not erase the possibility—even the likelihood—that the experiences that come to expression in our writings have a common human core and that to some degree our concepts overlap. I think that if I were to learn Chinese and devote myself to the study of Chuang's thought, I would have a heightened sense of the differences between his garden of concepts and mine, and I would enjoy seeing my own thinking progress through the dialogue of scholarly interpretation.

and intellectual concerns; but the spiritual way of doing so differs from an immature way of doing the same things in its freedom from egocentric pressuring. The story of Cook Ting tells of rising step by step to the integrated experience of living the truth.

A recipe for spiritual intuition

It makes no sense to talk about truth unless there are ways to distinguish truth from error. The spiritual domain does not give the kind of evidence and the kind of certainty of truth that science does; but it does offer a tremendous adventure of growth in discernment.

Suppose we want to sharpen our capacity for spiritual intuition in a situation in which we are seeking the will of God. This recipe symbolizes how to do that. Although it is never wise to absolutize any human judgment—indeed, we do well to open ourselves for divine revelation to bring in a brand new perspective—thoroughness in our preparation can forestall numerous errors throughout the process and add maturity to our discernment.

- Begin with a large bowl fashioned of receptivity
- Pour in a cup of awareness concerning the factual situation about which you are inquiring
- Add two precisely measured teaspoons of scientific perspective
- Blend in two heaping tablespoons of considered philosophical reflection
- Toss in a dash of good-humored relaxation
- Mix everything together with sincerity and trust
- Warm on low heat the meaningful mixture in the grateful listening pan for long enough to melt the impulse to get a quick "answer" to prayer
- Taste the truth, beauty, and goodness flavor before serving

We also enhance our spiritual discernment by the happy discipline of back-and-forth relating with the God of perfect goodness and love. Simply trusting that God is all-knowing and wants to help us along the way makes a big difference. Decades of devoted living improve discernment; the more we grow, the more quickly we become aware when we get off track as we sense spiritual support being withdrawn for a decision or undertaking that is not in alignment with God's will. By the same token, getting to know him is like approaching a bakery: our nose confirms that we are going in the right direction.

We also discerningly seek out new truth. During the California Gold Rush of 1848–55, it became common to say, "Gold is where you find it." Sometimes a prospector would look where he thought he had a good chance to make a strike and find none, while another would stumble across gold in what seemed an unlikely spot. Similarly, truth is where you find it. You never know where the next helpful insight may come from.

Finally, we must cheerfully acknowledge that our discernment is imperfect and must grow over time.[70] We can relax into the humble recognition that most of our high-value experiences result from a mix of biological, psychological, and spiritual inputs, factors that may either support or distort experience. Fortunately, we do not have to reach definitive conclusions about the source of any given experience; if the subconscious mind gives rise to fresh energies and useful ideas, we welcome them.

Three theories of spiritual truth

A full concept of spiritual and religious truth includes three ideas or theories, each of which makes important contributions and has limitations. If we work wisely with all three, the results will be dynamic, satisfying, and progressive.

First, *divine truth is intuitively recognized.* It has a certain flavor, an aroma or spirit that strikes the hearer as insightful, authoritative, resonant with our deepest knowing. Limitations to the idea of a spiritual intuition of truth are that people disagree about what is intuitively true; and we may be hasty in claiming insight. But wholehearted and persistent striving validates the assurance "Seek and you will find."

Next, *we only comprehend truth by living it.* When it is lived, truth carries its own authority. Even so, truth moves like the wind and cannot be fixed and pinned down. It is by grace and through our sincere commitment to God that we gain a quality of living that enables us to make choices and act faithfully according to the truths we are able to discern. The limitations

70. Traditional tests of the validity of allegedly spiritual experience can be helpful, but none of these furnishes an absolute criterion: error can affect reason, tradition, and the consensus of authorities. Scripture, sometimes inspired, poses problems, too. Even the most conservative position must still be ready to confess perplexity: "God said it, but what does he mean?" Gandhi wrote, "My belief in the Hindu scriptures does not require me to accept every word and every verse as divinely inspired. . . . I decline to be bound by any interpretation, however learned it may be, if it is repugnant to reason or moral sense." Gandhi, *All Men Are Brothers*, 61.

to this idea are that our lives may be full and satisfying partly because of our beliefs and practices and partly in spite of them. And many people whose lives may seem inspired and who are sincerely committed to living the truth can disagree substantially with others about what is true.

Finally, *truth comes as revelation from a superhuman source*. People claim to find revelation in their own or others' inner convictions, visions, or inspiration for what they say or write; a person regarded as an incarnation of a divine being; or a book in whole or in part. Without revelation, the human mind could not know spiritual realities, but questions can be raised about a revelation's sources and content.

- Does the allegedly superhuman source of the revelation really exist?
- Did the revelatory event actually occur?
- What roles did the recipient's physical condition and cultural background play in shaping the revelatory experience?
- What kinds of power do people consciously or unconsciously exercise by reporting their revelatory experiences?
- How fully and accurately did the recipient(s) communicate the experience?
- Has the original record been altered?
- What is the relevance of a revelation that occurred at another place and time for our own situation here and now?

Revelation uses the language and ways of thinking appropriate to the receiving culture; in that sense, divine truth has already been adapted to the human mind. Since many claims to revealed truth are inconsistent with each other, we still need to exercise scientific, philosophical, and spiritual responsibility in discerning which claims are valid and in interpreting for our ever-changing circumstances the meaning of what has been revealed.

This review of ideas of truth does not leave us mired in skeptical quicksand, since each idea contributes something essential to our progress in truth. The limits of these ideas do not force our faith in truth to be tentative or hypothetical, for persistent faith yields radiant assurance in our progressing experience of God. We can take care to be accurate regarding fact, consistent in our concepts, receptive to disclosure, responsive to the spirit of truth, discerning with regard to revelation, and authentic in living the best we know today, which enables us to know more tomorrow. It is God's plan that we grow into the fullness of humanity; and growth requires that we reach today beyond the bounds of yesterday's certainty. If we had a set of absolute criteria that the human intellect could apply without fail, there would be no adventure, no transformation, no stretching ourselves to live the divine life and allow God to live through us.

In the quest for God and divine truth, right belief helps faith grow into truth, but more important than beliefs are *sincerity, wholeheartedness, and persistence*. We do not need a perfect set of beliefs or 20/20 discernment. Faith trusts that wholehearted sincerity is sufficient for the adventure of being led into an ever-increasing realization of truth.

The life of truth

Truth engages us in its dynamism because truth itself is alive. Like a living cell, it needs both stability and flexibility. Our bone cells have a preponderance of firmness, while the neurons of the brain have a marvelous plasticity. Each type of cell needs both qualities in the proportions required by its function. Similarly, science tends to stabilize our grasp of reality, while truth known through spiritual experience liberates us with its flexibility.

To understand the life of truth, we must recognize its sturdy reliability: the seeker can return again and again to what is true. Truth is eternal reality as known on high and revealed below, pondered in the mind, realized in the soul. Though we continue to find new meaning and value in a truth, we never have to reject it. Truth abides. But truth does not hold its smile, posing for the picture that will enable it to be mechanically reproduced and circulated in digital format on the World Wide Web, conveyed to multitudes in a moment's time. The reliability of truth does not mean that we can get inspiration on demand; and yesterday's illuminated insight may not shine brightly for us today; even the words of a favorite passage of Scripture may look dead on the page—until the spirit moves. Any insight we glean may not come to life again until, in the silence of waiting or in the midst of action, a fresh dawning occurs.

Truth comes as revelation; it comes as intuition; it haunts us as an ideal that scientific research and philosophical examination can approach but never totally grasp. Whatever our limitations of experience, discernment, and interpretation, however, we can sense the aroma or spirit of truth; it is a gift, a ladder extended to us from eternity, enabling us as creatures of time to understand what we can as beginners on the cosmic journey.

Truth is not an intellectual snob. It adapts to the level of intelligence and education of the creature. Flexibly, truth submits to our interpretation. Above all, the life of truth shines in its adaptable quality. Like the light on a miner's helmet, truth illuminates ever-changing circumstances in response to our degree of receptivity. The truth that we needed yesterday may not be the one that we need today.

In all these ways, truth is more a *who* than a *what*. "Truth" is one of the names of God. And truth—divine truth, living truth—is the door to eternal life. Tasting the divine life enables us to delight in that promise and its long-term implications. Attracted by the flavor of truth, we recognize when the spirit of truth is leading us forward. The beauty of truth moves our feeling, and the relevance of truth to our practical situation directs us in the ways of goodness. Truth touches with insight, empowers, guides, brings assurance.

Conclusions

In Chuang Tzu's story, Cook Ting achieved a skill level at which he no longer struggled to coordinate the complexities of his craft; he attained an all-pervading simplicity. His success may be compared to that of a pianist working to learn a complex and difficult passage of music. She slowly and repeatedly goes over the passage, analyzing it and acquiring habits in her hands; and as she gradually masters the passage, her focus on the details is subordinated to her performance of the passage in its expressive wholeness. Similarly, our labor on the various strata of truth gradually leads to a quality of life with a rich simplicity.

All the complexity of truth that we cope with, and more, is contained in the God of love; the more fully we live in harmony with all truths, the more closely we live in accord with the indwelling spirit. In that sense, spiritual living encompasses living the truth. That integration is what Jesus demonstrated.

The idea of living the truth does not presuppose a lofty and fixed ideal, a mountain that we must painfully ascend before we can experience truth's liberating joy. With simple steps of faith and trust, invigorated by the spirit of God, a beginner can know the experience of living the truth. Difficulties of various sorts arise even for persons of advanced spirituality; we do not simply sail intuitively through a sea of difficulties. The moments when we correct our errors are part of the journey, and sometimes we just have to stop and wait for the spirit to show us a better way. Cook Ting sometimes had to slow down and take great care. Jesus sometimes had to pray.

Once we break through to find truth, we cannot build a bunker around it and defend our territory. We have to move, either forward or backward. Truth leads us forward. As we follow it in the best way we know, we embrace the adventure of stretching beyond ourselves for divine insight and companionship. Increasingly, we realize what it is to be part of a universal family, get in better touch with divine spirit, and pray and worship with greater depth. These elemental spiritual experiences are our primary source of insight into truth, beauty, and goodness.

Part II. Walking in Beauty

4

Invisible Harmonies in the Visible

John Muir and Living amid the Beauties of Nature

SOMETIMES WHEN WE READ about science, philosophy, or even spirituality, the experience is more or less flat. But at other times we are moved, and a note of positive feeling accompanies our understanding: "That's a really cool proof" . . . "How those plants conserve water to stay alive in the desert is awesome" . . . "The way Black Elk added humor to the ritual he created was amazing." The isolated intellect can recognize truth with little feeling, but when we realize it deeply, we feel the beauty of truth. Positive feeling is our way of registering the realization of beauty.

Truth can fill mind and soul to the brim and become a way of living. In their different ways, Darwin, Socrates, and Jesus knew the thrill of seeking, finding, living, and helping others find truth. Similarly, we can walk in beauty by enjoying, more or less continually, the beauty of truth, the beauty of goodness, and the beauties of nature and the arts. The robust positive feelings that accompany living the truth are the ideal introduction to walking in beauty.

Since truth is beautiful, its beauty is one of the ways that we recognize it; but our aesthetic, feel-good responses are not an infallible guide to beauty. We may feel a great satisfaction when we attain what we think is a solution to a big problem, while in fact what we take for insight is only a subjective harmony among ideas of our own that do not yet have enough reality in them. So, as lovers of divine value, we need to cultivate the soil for our aesthetic discernment to grow.

"Walking in beauty" is a concept that runs through many native American cultures and has been recently associated especially with the Navaho concept of *hózhó*, which embraces the peace, harmony, and beauty that come from the integration of person, community, land, cosmos, and

Deity. When things are out of joint, it is necessary to restore *hózhó* through artistic ritual. Such restoration does not fix unavoidable and difficult conditions; rather it enables participants to face squarely what they must go through. The process of walking in beauty is voiced in this Navaho prayer.

> With beauty before me, I walk
> With beauty behind me, I walk
> With beauty above me, I walk
> With beauty below me, I walk
> From the east beauty has been restored
> From the south beauty has been restored
> From the west beauty has been restored
> From the north beauty has been restored
> From the zenith of the sky beauty has been restored
> From the nadir of the earth beauty has been restored
> From all around me beauty has been restored.[1]

This prayer-poem symbolizes the drama of beauty—actual and potential. Walking in beauty involves, first, being receptive to actual beauty and, second, being creative in actualizing potentials for beauty. Accordingly, each of the two chapters devoted to beauty—this one and the one following—focuses on one of these phases of walking in beauty: living amid the beauties of nature, and artistic living.

Beauty is real or actual in the wider cosmos (above us) and on the earth (below us, and in the east, south, west, and north). Once we find cosmic beauty surrounding us, we can find it within us, and then go on to express it. To walk in beauty restores beauty in the one who does so, and that person becomes a center from which beauty refreshes others. Asking about this concept from my Shawnee colleague in philosophy Thomas Norton-Smith, I received this reply: "You will understand it by living it."

But most of us would have trouble responding to a call to walk in beauty, and not just because of its cultural strangeness. We spend much of our time with an overall attitude that leans in a negative direction. Even if we intellectually believe that life is basically good, the way that we go through our daily activities often conveys a quite different stance. We feel hurried, stressed out, or besieged; we may be driven by fear of failure or compulsive, competitive ambition. Most of us could be better grounded in our bodies and on the earth, with a deeper connection to beauty in the wider universe.

---

1. Martin, *Way of the Human*, 24–25.

I think we all need guidance and grace in order for beauty to increasingly pervade our attitude and activities.

We can deepen our exploration of beauty with lessons on feeling from psychology and glimpses into an integrated experience of beauty in nature. This chapter departs from the pattern of presenting the virtues of an exemplary human life, followed by a sketch of concepts and principles. Here glimpses of John Muir's life and writings illustrate a sequence of levels of aesthetic experience. As we shall discover, the life of John Muir demonstrates a wholeheartedness that unites the many layers of that experience: scientifically informed perception, artistically cultivated empathy, intellectual insight into the harmony of contrasts, philosophical reflection, and a realization of beauty as divine.

From my journey

I have found it a great social icebreaker to ask people about their favorite places in nature; these are often places where they feel safe and enjoy getting away from people to commune. My own walk in beauty has been enhanced by playing with pets, collecting rocks, riding horseback on pack trips in the mountains, visiting botanical gardens, savoring wind, snow, and starry skies, swimming in lakes, canoeing on rivers, and contemplating oceans. I open my window in the morning or look out in the evening and take in the common and thrilling scene, often experiencing a sunrise or sunset as the turning of the earth in its silent, smooth, mighty, irresistible yet calming course.

It helps to remember that my body is a part of nature. When I occasionally preached at the Matilda Brown Home for retired women in Oakland, California, I would sometimes tell these women in their seventies and eighties and nineties that the number one purpose of the body is to support a mind that can host the presence of God. Natural beauty can profoundly affect the emotional life. When I become frustrated by my imperfections or others', I know that distortions of self, others, and society are not destiny. One way to regain peace is to look out my bedroom window at the sky and trees and grass, or to do a bit of conscious breathing, or remember myself and others as being embodied in a realm where evolution moves in rhythms that contrast with irregular human reactions. For all the stresses that bear upon it today, nature still manages to remain a place of communion where we can return to find perspective.

After staying on Bali for a week in a region with no running water, and being aware of the ecological need to conserve water, I know that taking a shower is a privilege that I do not want to abuse, and I enjoy that water most completely when I experience it as a gift from the universe. When I am living at my best, I enjoy pleasures as a phase of divine communion.

Lessons on feeling from psychology

When beauty touches us, it awakens our aesthetic response, ranging from calmness, contentment, and satisfaction to delight, rejoicing, and awe: these experiences register our recognition of universal beauty. Responses to beauty—present, remembered, or anticipated—are implicit in the most common positive emotions: joy, gratitude, serenity, interest, hope, pride (paired with humility), amusement, inspiration, awe, and love. As long as positive emotions arise from perceptions that are in tune with reality or from actions that are good, the emotions not only feel good at the moment but also are essential for our well-being. There is a common tendency to cut short our own positive emotions before they have a chance to fulfill their mission in us. Instead, we need to allow them to blossom fully: when positive emotions begin to dawn, we can take the time to allow them to come forth abundantly, to permeate, uplift, open, and strengthen us.[2]

There is a wide-ranging lesson to be derived from beauty's correlation with varieties of positive emotion or aesthetic response. A correlation exists between types of experiences and types of objects: vision sees the visible, hearing hears the audible, and, in general, perception perceives the perceivable.[3] Knowing knows what is intelligible; valuing appreciates value.[4]

In the philosophy put forth in this book, the most important correlations are that fulfilled thinking connects with truth, feeling with beauty, and doing with goodness. To expand our concept of beauty, we can think about

2. This list of positive emotions and the lessons about their function and flourishing come from a popular book by a leading psychologist: Fredrickson, *Positivity*. I regard her discovery about the need to allow positive emotions to blossom fully as one of the most important aids to worshipful living. This book describes a "tipping point": in order to achieve a life that has an overall positive emotional quality to it, we need to attain at least a 3:1 ratio of positive to negative emotion (taking duration and intensity into account). Fredrickson uses the word "emotion" to cover the entire spectrum of relevant experiences, although, as a scientist, she does not explore differences between (1) secular material and social emotions and (2) feelings of soul. Presumably, a positive emotion that begins in a simple, everyday way, if given the chance to blossom fully, could encompass the range from material to spiritual.

3. Phenomenological studies of perception describe structures that are common to all five senses.

4. Such correlations between the conscious act and its object were explored by phenomenology as pioneered by Edmund Husserl (1859–1938).

various positive feelings and their correlates: gratitude correlates with gifts that we have received; hope correlates with what we expect to enjoy in the future; interest correlates with new discoveries to be made. I expand my concept of joy by regarding positive emotions as varieties of joy, just as I regard their appealing correlates as varieties of beauty.

Walking in beauty heightens the resonance between beauty in our surroundings and beauty within; and this resonance enhances vitality. Vitality is associated with energy, enthusiasm, zest, and vigor. As psychologists describe it, vitality involves the entire personality, embracing several kinds of value: biological, psychological, social, philosophical, and spiritual. Vitality expresses physical health and stamina as well as mental well-being; it includes being decisive and effective in getting things done; and it is an indicator of personal and social integration. Since it owes so much to genetic inheritance, vitality is not a typical virtue. But self-cultivation and personal growth can sustain and enhance natural and acquired vitality, which seems to be a result of balanced energies. Tension, stress, and conflict depress vitality. Researchers have noted another aspect of vitality with great implications for the value priorities of our culture.[5] Vitality is linked with happiness (in the classic sense of full functioning and self-actualization) rather than pleasure (in the sense of momentary self-gratification). The pursuit of pleasure can compromise vitality and interfere with true happiness.[6] A paragon of positive emotion and vitality is John Muir.

Total mobilization of body, mind, and soul

John Muir (1838–1914) came with family at the age of eleven from Scotland to the United States. After working on family farms and taking a few science courses at the University of Wisconsin, he set out on foot to travel to Louisiana, where he took a boat to San Francisco, and then he walked the 165 miles to Yosemite. He had long sought a soul-satisfying realization of divine beauty in nature, and there his quest finally found fulfillment. Eventually, he was led into action to share and protect what had nourished him so deeply. He would crystallize his observations, adventures, ecstasies, and concerns in articles and books that aroused appreciation for nature and mobilized

5. Tillich observed in *The Courage to Be* that it is a major error to give top priority to values of vitality such as strength and willpower.

Heightened vitality would also affect body image—how a person sees or pictures herself, believes others see her, and feels about her body and in her body.

6. This paragraph summarizes Bernstein and Ryan, "Vitality," in Peterson and Seligman, *Character Strengths and Virtues*.

national support for protecting wilderness in line with the aims of the Sierra Club, which he founded and led for the benefit of future generations of all species.[7]

A philosophical analysis of Muir's writings can distinguish layers in his many-dimensioned engagement with divine beauty in nature, but the dominant characteristic of Muir's experience is that these layers are more than integrated; they are unified. Muir exemplifies the principle of total personality involvement. All his powers of body, mind, and soul were harmoniously activated. His appreciation of the beauties of nature flourished as a result of character traits evident early in life.

> When I was a boy in Scotland I was fond of everything that was wild, and all my life I've been growing fonder and fonder of wild places and wild creatures. Fortunately around my native town of Dunbar, by the stormy North Sea, there was no lack of wildness, though most of the land lay in smooth cultivation. With red-blooded playmates, wild as myself, I loved to wander in the fields to hear the birds sing, and along the seashore to gaze and wonder at the shells and seaweeds, eels and crabs in the pools among the rocks when the tide was low; and best of all to watch the waves in awful storms thundering on the black headlands and craggy ruins of the old Dunbar Castle when the sea and the sky, the waves and the clouds, were mingled together as one. We never thought of playing truant, but after I was five or six years old I ran away to the seashore or the fields almost every Saturday, and every day in the school vacations except Sundays, though solemnly warned that I must play at home in the garden and back yard, lest I should learn to think bad thoughts and say bad words. All in vain. In spite of the sure sore punishments that followed like shadows, the natural inherited wildness in our blood ran true on its glorious course as invincible and unstoppable as stars.[8]

Note several qualities that Muir would display throughout his life: an embrace of nature as a whole combined with a delight in detail, autonomy balanced with social companionship, resilience undeterred by pain and punishment, persistent flight from the restrictions of the domestic circle, and all-consuming enthusiasm. He embraced all the moods of nature. Storms he welcomed as displays of high energy and drama, and he habitually placed

---

7. Most of what I include here by and about Muir is part of my article "John Muir as Guide."

8. Muir, *My Boyhood and Youth*, 1–2.

himself in their midst with relish. Muir's wholeheartedness united material, intellectual, and spiritual aspects of his aesthetic experience.

Keen perception

Although the aspects of experience fused in Muir's aesthetic appreciation of nature do not fit into a simple linear sequence, there is an obvious place to start. Perception—delighting in fine detail and in sweeping vistas—is the gateway to the beauties of nature. Visual perception is most prominent, and color alone may convey ineffable beauty, as Muir finds, for example, in the pure white of the flower of the rare *Calypso borealis* orchid.[9] Here we have beauty on the most elementary level: that which pleases upon being seen. Muir delighted in soundscapes too, in waterfalls, birdsong, and wind in the trees.

> After listening to it in all kinds of winds, night and day, season after season, I think I could approximate to my position on the mountain by this pine music alone. If you would catch the tone of separate needles, climb a tree in breezy weather. Every needle is carefully tempered and gives forth no uncertain sound, each standing out with no interference excepting during heavy gales; then you may detect the click of one needle upon another, readily distinguishable from the free wind-like hum.[10]

These details illustrate the height of concentrated and patient attention in perception.

Perception is not restricted to individual sense organs but is also an affair of the total body—taking it all in. "Drinking this champagne water is pure pleasure, so is breathing the living air, and every movement of limbs is pleasure, while the whole body seems to feel beauty when exposed to it as it feels the camp-fire or sunshine, entering not by the eyes alone, but equally through all one's flesh like radiant heat, making a passionate ecstatic pleasure-glow not explainable. One's body then seems homogeneous throughout, sound as a crystal."[11] Muir's recipe for awakening vitality can remind sedentary modern workers that the nervous system is not limited to the brain but extends through the entire body.

9. Badè, *Life and Letters*, 71.
10. Muir, *Yosemite*, 105.
11. Muir, *Summer in the Sierra*, 174–75.

It takes time to bring perception to its fullness. In a book with topographical and other maps, Muir gave instructions for a walk from Yosemite Valley to the head of the Nevada Fall.

> Linger here an hour or two, for not only have you glorious views of the wonderful fall, but of its wild, leaping, exulting rapids and greater than all, the stupendous scenery into the heart of which the white passionate river goes wildly thundering, surpassing everything of its kind in the world. After an unmeasured hour or so of this glory, all your body aglow, nerve currents flashing through you never before felt, go to the top of the Liberty Cap, only a glad saunter now that your legs as well as head and heart are awake and rejoicing with everything.[12]

Here we see the kinesthetic and more generally "somaesthetic" (feeling of the body) dimension of the invigorated experience of nature.[13]

Muir's writings also show perception as *ordinary-practical* when they narrate the human interactions of a trip, as *scientific* when they record observations of trees and glaciers, and as *aesthetic* when expressing the glories of what he had seen, heard, felt, and lived.

Scientific learning

Muir's lifelong plunge into nature was largely as a naturalist. After his few courses in botany and geology, he continued to read and to make observations, becoming a leading authority on glaciers. Perceptual delight naturally deepens into scientific inquiry, and scientific knowledge adds an important dimension to the fullness of aesthetic experience. He wrote, "How interesting everything is! Every rock, mountain, stream, plant, lake, lawn, forest, garden, bird, beast, insect seems to call and invite us to come and learn something of its history and relationship."[14]

When we open ourselves to nature, we allow such interest to arise spontaneously.

Artistically cultivated imagination

Though deprived of school and normal access to books, Muir discovered at fifteen a strong desire for learning, and he studied whatever he could find,

12. Muir, *Yosemite*, 198.
13. I owe the term "somaesthetic" to Shusterman, *Body Consciousness*.
14. Muir, *Yosemite*, 322.

including books on mathematics and the poetry of Shakespeare and Milton. His prodigious memory enabled him to learn much of the Bible and other texts by heart. He particularly recommended a passage from Milton's *Paradise Lost* (also a favorite of the young Darwin), where in book 5 we see Adam and Eve regain peace of mind by giving voice to their adoration. The first lines of the hymn proclaim the invisible, all-powerful God, the "Parent of good" who transcends the creation and is beyond thought and language, but who may nevertheless be "dimly seen" in nature. The basic universal structure of creation shows God to be wondrously beautiful ("fair").

Artistically stimulated imagination is a crucial layer of Muir's delight in nature. Muir used metaphors from painting, music, poetry, sculpture, and architecture to express the artistry he celebrated. He was molded by poetry that conveyed to him the music and meter and meaning of the boundless grandeur of God, filling infinite space and every aspect of the physical creation.

Muir was glad to lead artists to picturesque scenes, and many of his exultant descriptions focus on them. Although his perception was grounded in a fine knowledge of *what* he was seeing, hearing, and feeling, he could focus on size, shape, color, movement, and sound as formal properties, enjoyed more or less independently of the things whose qualities they are. Sensuous abstraction, divested of the sense of *what* underlies the color or sound, is illustrated in Muir's celebration of the "snow banners" emerging after a snowstorm in the mountains.[15] "The peaks . . . are then decorated with resplendent banners, some of them more than a mile long, shining, streaming, waving with solemn exuberant enthusiasm as if celebrating some surpassingly glorious event."[16] "They are twenty miles away, but you would not wish them nearer, for every feature is distinct, and the whole wonderful show is seen in its right proportions, like a painting on the sky."[17] Here the description takes flight from mountains and snow, using imagination to animate sensuous abstractions, which play a more prominent role in the arts.

15. The term "sensuous abstraction" I owe to Samuel Todes. The concept is found in Martin Heidegger: "We hear the door shut in the house and never hear acoustical sensations or even mere sounds. In order to hear a bare sound we have to listen-away [*weghören*] from things, divert our ear from them, i.e., listen abstractly." Heidegger, "Work of Art," 152.

16. Muir, *Yosemite*, 70.

17. Ibid., 74.

Empathy for the expressiveness of nature

Muir's empathy for all life began with identifying with the *mind* of the creatures whose intentions and moods he came to know.

> We worked with [oxen], sympathized with them in their rest and toil and play, and thus learned to know them far better than we should had we been only trained scientific naturalists. We soon learned that each ox and cow and calf had individual character. . . . The humanity we found in [oxen] came partly through the expression of their eyes when tired, their tones of voice when hungry and calling for food, their patient plodding and pulling in hot weather, their long-drawn-out sighing breath when exhausted and suffering like ourselves, and their enjoyment of rest with the same grateful looks as ours. We recognized their kinship also by their yawning like ourselves when sleepy and evidently enjoying the same peculiar pleasure at the roots of their jaws; by the way they stretched themselves in the morning after a good rest; by learning languages,—Scotch, English, Irish, French, Dutch,—a smattering of each as required in the faithful service they so willingly, wisely rendered; by their intelligent, alert curiosity, manifested in listening to strange sounds; their love of play; the attachments they made; and their mourning, long continued, when a companion was killed.[18]

Muir had a tremendous capacity for identifying in feeling with people, animals, and nature generally. We have seen him write of "wild, leaping, exulting rapids," a "passionate river," and "snow banners waving with solemn exuberant enthusiasm." All these phrases exhibit his sense of the expressiveness in nature.

Some people attribute this way of experiencing to imagination. If an Indian healer from Latin America is quoted on National Public Radio as saying that the earth is groaning and struggling during this time of environmental abuse, the average listener is expected to hear him sympathetically, as speaking not from poetic imagination but from deepened sensitivity— empathy. And, if and insofar as nature actually is expressive, we might better speak of empathy rather than imagination. At the very least, we can say that both empathy and imagination affect perceptual life, and both of them bridge perception and spiritual faith. When perception is abstracted from the fullness of experience, it does not convey expressiveness.

Muir's empathy extended to embrace plant life and even the physical elements. But some of the expressiveness in which Muir delighted strikes

18. Muir, *My Boyhood and Youth*, 92–93.

the modern reader as simply a product of imagination. For example, Muir describes a glacier as like an oak tree in its "gnarled swelling base and wide-spreading branches."[19] But metaphor has been a normal tool of scientific description and should not be dismissed as a component of aesthetic experience.[20] Muir uses metaphor to describe what he saw atop Alaska's Glenora Peak. "As I lingered, gazing on the vast show, luminous shadowy clouds seemed to increase in glory of color and motion, now fondling the highest peaks with infinite tenderness of touch, now hovering above them like eagles over their nests."[21] Here exquisite, imaginative, and playful sensitivity merges with a thorough identification with the processes of nature.

Intellectual discovery of harmony

The most pivotal and most neglected layer of experience in a full and integrated experience of beauty in nature is the intellectual discovery of harmony. Muir's lifelong quest to discover harmony began at the University of Wisconsin when he was challenged by a fellow student to find the unity and variety in the Creator's handiwork and "to examine plants to learn the harmony of their relations." Muir responded with his entire being. "This fine lesson charmed me and sent me flying to the woods and meadows in wild enthusiasm. Like everybody else I was always fond of flowers, attracted by their external beauty and purity. Now my eyes were opened to their inner beauty, all alike revealing glorious traces of the thoughts of God, and leading on and on into the infinite cosmos."[22]

Muir's evocations of harmony typically bring contrasting phenomena together, as in this description of Yosemite Valley with its granite walls and waterfalls: "rocky strength and permanence combined with beauty of plants frail and fine and evanescent; water descending in thunder, and the same water gliding through meadows and groves in gentlest beauty."[23] These descriptions provide a model for those who wish to develop their aesthetic appreciation of the environment.

19. Muir, *Yosemite*, 188.

20. For a historical argument that metaphor should not be dismissed as merely fanciful and unscientific, see Foucault, *Order of Things,* chapter 2. The metaphorical style of scientific description remains much in evidence in the travel writings of William Bartram (1739–1823), one of the Philadelphia naturalists.

21. Muir, *Travels in Alaska*, 96.

22. Muir, *My Boyhood and Youth*, 282.

23. Muir, *Summer in the Sierra*, 279.

Muir observed many types of harmony, from simple to complex, easy to difficult, and small scale to cosmic. The simplest harmony he notes is the shape of a five-petaled flower, something one might customarily perceive in a summary way. A slightly more advanced harmony is found in a group of mosses with their "tones of yellow shading finely into each other."[24] Here the contrasts are mediated by continuous variation. He uses the term "harmony" to refer to an underlying unity, such as a shared geologic history found in a group of mountains or islands.

Four types of harmony are not immediately apparent. They are found in a scene where the initial impression indicates no intelligible order, in a tree that does not fit one's typical notion of beauty, in a canyon that at first just seems strange and almost scary, and in a unity of contrasting geological processes. Muir also observes that the basic aesthetic tendency to focus on a particular harmony can be overwhelmed by the magnitude and majesty of a scene.

It took Muir two weeks of patient observation and geological reflection before he gained insight into the harmony implicit in a mountain range, which at first glance was unintelligible:

> Generally, when looking for the first time from an all-embracing standpoint like [the top of Mount Ritter in Yosemite], the inexperienced observer is oppressed by the incomprehensible grandeur, variety, and abundance of the mountains rising shoulder to shoulder beyond the reach of vision; and it is only after they have been studied one by one, long and lovingly, that their far-reaching harmonies become manifest. Then, penetrate the wilderness where you may, the main telling features, to which all the surrounding topography is subordinate, are quickly perceived, and the most complicated clusters of peaks stand revealed harmoniously correlated and fashioned like works of art—eloquent monuments of the ancient ice-rivers that brought them into relief from the general mass of the range. The canyons, some of them a mile deep, mazing wildly through the mighty host of mountains, however lawless and ungovernable at first sight they appear, are at length recognized as the necessary effects of causes which followed each other in harmonious sequence—Nature's poems carved on tables of stone—the simplest and most emphatic of her glacial compositions.[25]

24. Muir, *Travels in Alaska*, 62.

25. Muir, *Mountains of California*, 68–69. Note the references to "ancient ice-rivers" and "glacial compositions": it was Muir, the amateur, who persuaded the scientists of the role of glaciers in sculpting Yosemite.

This is a story of the aesthetic reward for a persistent effort to discover causes, an effort based upon a faith in the lawful workings of a majestic cosmos.

The next difficult harmony is found in the typical regularities of a tree that seems at first simply huge and irregular:

> The perfect specimens [of sequoias] not burned or broken are singularly regular and symmetrical, though not at all conventional, showing infinite variety in general unity and harmony; the noble shafts with rich purplish brown fluted bark, free of limbs for one hundred and fifty feet or so, ornamented here and there with leafy rosettes; main branches of the oldest trees very large, crooked and rugged, zigzagging stiffly outward seemingly lawless, yet unexpectedly stopping just at the right distance from the trunk and dissolving in dense bossy masses of branchlets, thus making a regular though greatly varied outline,—a cylinder of leafy, outbulging spray masses, terminating in a noble dome, that may be recognized while yet far off upheaved against the sky above the dark bed of pines and firs and spruces, the king of all conifers, not only in size but in sublime majesty of behavior and port.[26]

One quickly senses the complexity of an object described with such detail. A great sequoia, which is so tall that its unity cannot be appreciated from up close, is a challenge to aesthetic perception due to features that Muir acknowledges; yet he weaves his noticing of what is crooked, zigzagging, stiff, and seemingly lawless into a portrait of nobility.

Some scenes are strange, uncanny, if not frightening. In Yellowstone there is a canyon "twenty miles long and a thousand feet deep,—a weird unearthly-looking gorge of jagged, fantastic architecture and most brilliantly colored." Despite the impression of its strangeness, "[t]he lovely Linnaea borealis hangs her twin bells over the brink of the cliffs, forests and gardens extend their treasures in smiling confidence on either side, nuts and berries ripen well whatever may be going on below; blind fears vanish, and the grand gorge seems a kindly, beautiful part of the general harmony, full of peace and joy and good will."[27] Here small-scale beauties, set in contrast with their background, trigger a sense of cosmic harmony.

A final sense of harmony manifests on many levels. Just as Muir sought harmonies on a large scale spatially, he also sought them on a large scale

26. Muir, *Summer in the Sierra*, 350; "port" refers to demeanor, and a "boss" is "a protuberance or swelling on the body of an animal or plant" (*Oxford English Dictionary Online*).

27. Muir, *Our National Parks*, 49–50.

temporally. His implicit teleological faith about the evolutionary destiny of nature and persons enabled him to place in a wider time perspective that which transiently manifests as ugly. In a first example, Muir gives a profile of Yellowstone's past.

> While this [glacial] ice-work was going on, the slumbering volcanic fires were boiling the subterranean waters, and with curious chemistry decomposing the rocks, making beauty in the darkness; these forces, seemingly antagonistic, working harmoniously together.[28]

> We see Nature working with enthusiasm like a man, blowing her volcanic forges like a blacksmith blowing his smithy fires, shoving glaciers over the landscapes like a carpenter shoving his planes, clearing, ploughing, harrowing, irrigating, planting, and sowing broadcast like a farmer and gardener, doing rough work and fine work, planting sequoias and pines, rosebushes and daisies; working in gems, filling every crack and hollow with them; distilling fine essences; painting plants and shells, clouds, mountains, all the earth and heavens, like an artist,—ever working toward beauty higher and higher.[29]

Truths about geological and botanical evolution give rise to observations that lead us to delight in aesthetic evolution. Each of these discovered harmonies Muir describes with cosmic overtones, suggesting analogies that encourage faith and add perspective to daily life.

In an extreme case, the necessary conditions for discovering harmony are absent, because no contrast emerges; no object distinguishes itself, no figure arises against a background. In the following scene, no one phenomenon stands out in the totality of what can be seen. Rather, the experience here is the very balance of the whole, where no part upstages the general impression.

> It is easier to feel than to realize, or in any way explain Yosemite grandeur. The magnitudes of the rocks and trees and streams are so delicately harmonized they are mostly hidden. Sheer precipices three thousand feet high are fringed with tall trees growing close like grass on the brow of a lowland hill, and extending along the feet of these precipices a ribbon of meadow a mile wide and seven or eight long, that seems like a strip a farmer might mow in less than a day. Waterfalls, five hundred to one or two thousand feet high, are so subordinated to the mighty

28. Muir, *Our National Parks*, 65.
29. Ibid., 74.

cliffs over which they pour that they seem like wisps of smoke, gentle as floating clouds, though their voices fill the valley and make the rocks tremble. The mountains, too, along the eastern sky . . . and the succession of smooth rounded waves between, swelling higher, higher, with dark woods in their hollows, serene in massive exuberant bulk and beauty, tend yet more to hide the grandeur of the Yosemite temple and make it appear as a subdued subordinate feature of the vast harmonious landscape. Thus every attempt to appreciate any one feature is beaten down by the overwhelming influence of all the others.[30]

The majestic vastness of the whole puts even grand things in their places.

The mind's intellectual discovery of harmony is crucial to the transition from the physical to the spiritual levels of aesthetic experience.[31] A perceptually attentive, scientifically informed, empathic, and imaginative noticing of attractive features is not yet a realization of beauty in its fullness. The second phase of the transition is philosophical.

Philosophical reflection

Notwithstanding his readings in Henry David Thoreau, Muir's lack of philosophical education and ignorance of other historical and cultural perspectives provide ample opening for his ideas to be criticized and supplemented. Nevertheless, he thoughtfully integrated various tensions in his experience and his culture. In particular, he arguably did well on the relations between the beautiful, the sublime, and the picturesque.

Muir wrote in an age when the concepts of the beautiful and the sublime were in flux. They were sometimes sharply distinguished, with beauty associated with intelligible order and delightful proportion, and sublimity characterized in terms of awesome vastness and power that terrified as much as attracted. Sometimes the beautiful and the sublime were brought together closely, with sublimity being a particularly lofty kind of beauty.[32] Muir, influenced by poets of the seventeenth and eighteenth centuries, straddled both ways of relating the terms, but even when he associates the

30. Muir, *Summer in the Sierra*, 175–76.

31. There is another kind of harmony, which I call ontological complementarity. "Ontological" refers to different levels of being: for example, when I see a plant growing in a curved indentation in a rock in a stream, and when I learn that the weathering of that rock produces precisely the chemical elements needed by the plant, I see complementarity between inanimate and animate levels of being. I further expand the picture to include other levels of being: the mind of the observer and the spirit of the Creator.

32. See Nicolson, *Mountain Gloom and Glory*.

terms closely, he shows sensitivity to their shades of difference. "The scenery of the ocean, however sublime in vast expanse, seems far less beautiful to us dry-shod animals than that of the land seen only in comparatively small patches; but when we contemplate the whole globe as one great dewdrop, striped and dotted with continents and islands, flying through space and other stars all singing and shining together as one, the whole universe appears as an infinite storm of beauty."[33]

Muir is willing to speak of "sublime mountain beauty."[34] He was in Yosemite for an earthquake, a "wild beauty-making business."[35] "The Eagle Rock on the south wall, about a half a mile up the Valley, gave way and I saw it falling in thousands of the great boulders I had so long been studying, pouring to the Valley floor in a free curve luminous from friction, making a terribly sublime spectacle—an arc of glowing, passionate fire, fifteen hundred feet span, as true in form and as serene in beauty as a rainbow in the midst of the stupendous, roaring rock-storm."[36] Religiously, the heights of the sublime elicit awe before the mystery of God, who is beyond beauty and always has more beauty to reveal. After telling how the grandeur seen from an Alaskan fiord is beyond words to convey, Muir confessed, "Still more impotent are words in telling the peculiar awe one experiences in entering these mansions of the icy North, notwithstanding it is only the natural effect of appreciable manifestations of the presence of God."[37]

It was not only literary sensitivity and extraordinary awareness of the nuances of experience that enabled Muir to clarify the relations of beauty and sublimity. One reason for his untutored achievement was his freedom from fear, which was commonly regarded as an ingredient in the sublime. "Wild beauty," a contradiction in terms for some, became a meaningful phrase in his aesthetic vocabulary.

Associating beauty with sublimity preserves beauty from being reduced to the category of the picturesque. The picturesque is that charm of a scene, more or less framed in comparative isolation from its surroundings, which invites the painterly eye and hand to render it in art. Muir noted that many a mountain landscape is not "separable . . . into artistic bits capable of being made into warm, sympathetic, lovable pictures with appreciable

33. Muir, *Travels in Alaska*, 5.

34. Muir, *Summer in the Sierra*, 153; for contrasts between beauty and sublimity see 208 and 295.

35. Muir, *Yosemite*, 82.

36. Ibid., 79.

37. Muir, *Travels in Alaska*, 64.

humanity in them."[38] Muir celebrated wildness over artificial norms of civilized order, and he recognized that the beauties of nature commonly exceed what can be framed.

Appreciation of beauty as divine

Muir's concrete description often had no need of words such as "beauty," or "divine," or "God"; but such language is frequent enough to indicate a pervasive dimension in his aesthetic experience. Muir's expressions of delight in nature—the dominant emotion of his life—convey one thought above all: beauty is divine. He was a man in love with the Creator, and his spirituality was religious, liberated, and good-humored.

Muir's quest as a young man was to find God in nature, and that quest was fulfilled in Yosemite during the summer of 1869. "Looking back through the stillness and romantic enchanting beauty and peace of the camp grove, this June seems the greatest of all the months of my life, the most truly, divinely free, boundless like eternity, immortal. Everything in it seems equally divine—one smooth, pure, wild glow of Heaven's love, never to be blotted or blurred by anything past or to come."[39] Muir summed up a July day filled to the brim: "A fruitful day, without measured beginning or ending. A terrestrial eternity. A gift of good God."[40] Beauty is portrayed as possessing some of the qualities of God: "In my life of lonely wanderings I was pushed and pulled on and on through everything by unwavering never-ending love of God's earth plans and works, and eternal, immortal, all embracing Beauty . . . ."[41] "One bird, a thrush, embroidered the silence with cheery notes, making the solitude familiar and sweet, while the solemn monotone of the stream sifting through the woods seemed like the very voice of God, humanized, terrestrialized, and entering one's heart as to a home prepared for it."[42]

Beauty is not God, but the relations between the two are intimate. For Muir, God is the Creator, the source of beauty, whose thoughts are discovered in the harmonies that unite contrasts. We have previously seen Muir's report that the pursuit of harmony led from external beauty to inner beauty and thence to the thoughts of God and the cosmos.

38. Muir, *Mountains of California*, 49.
39. Muir, *Summer in the Sierra*, 90.
40. Ibid., 178.
41. Badè, *Muir's Life and Letters*, 349.
42. Muir, *Travels in Alaska*, 61.

Muir connected physical and spiritual levels in describing the dance of sunlight on a waterfall as "the most divinely beautiful mass of rejoicing yellow light I ever beheld."[43] Here the distance between distinguishable sides, "subjective" rejoicing and "objective" light, falls away. Muir's feeling of expressiveness in nature should not be too quickly dismissed as imaginative projection. If the physical creation is the work of an expressive Creator, then our efforts to empathize with natural phenomena may somehow reflect the feelings of God, even as knowing the laws of nature may count as human-level recognition of the thoughts of God. If God is on the other side of the phenomenon, so to speak, and if God is (in some analogous sense) rejoicing in the delight of the creature, then if Muir feels rejoicing "in" the yellow light, is it possible that his wild openness enabled him to gain an insight that a cautious mind would block? From a theistic perspective, an aesthetics that places all its weight on objective properties or on the response of the subject does not do justice to the Creator's contributions to both sides of the equation.

On the other hand, we should not allow Muir's eloquence to silence our critical reflection. A sober assessment of how often we fail to understand the thoughts and feelings of other people, let alone those of animals or God, may lead us to reassess Muir's uncritical confidence in voicing the expressiveness of things. Nevertheless, challenges to our capacity for empathy invite us to understand better; they do not force us to conclude that there are no feelings at all in animals and no feelings in God analogous to our own. When we detect a divine, artistic touch in creation, we may legitimately allow ourselves to give voice to what we feel. But we do well to remember that our interpretations help create our religious experience.

Another critique of Muir comes from contemporary environmental aesthetics, which is more sober, not given to untrammeled romantic enthusiasm for natural beauty, due to the haunting awareness of pollution. In reply, it is important to note that Muir sounded his notes of high eloquence so often partly to motivate his audience to pressure politicians to protect wilderness lands. He despised what he regarded as the spoiling of Yosemite by ranchers who grazed their sheep there. He felt the growing encroachment of civilization and experienced profound disappointment over political defeat after investing much of the last years of his life in an unsuccessful effort to win the battle to save part of the Yosemite complex, Hetch Hetchy Valley, from being dammed to make a reservoir.[44] Today's path to wholehearted

43. Muir, *Yosemite*, 34.

44. For all his heroism and vigorous exhortation, Muir compassionately acknowledged the mystery of suffering beyond what human wisdom can fathom. Replying to a letter from a grieving friend, he wrote, "My heart aches about Janet—one of the sad, sad, sore cases that no human wisdom can explain. We can only look on the other side

aesthetic celebration expands on Muir's, relying on a reinforced vision of evolution in which humankind eventually learns to live harmoniously on earth. Reasons to believe in a friendly universe and a high planetary destiny for humankind are scattered throughout these chapters, and all these encouraging considerations support renewed rejoicing.

Muir was no theologian, but his experience suggests that the mission of beauty is, in part, to help overcome a sense of separation between the physical and the spiritual. Faith opens the door to experiencing beauty in nature as divine. The physical is fact. Harmony is thought, idea. Beauty is spiritual value, a quality of God, a relationship with creation initiated by God. Perceived and expressed separately, they may seem unlikely ingredients in a united experience. But if human experience is an arena where nature, human mind, and divine spirit are accelerated into relation, then beauty is a reality dynamically linking Creator and creature. Beauty is dipolar: one pole is the source, the eternal nature of God, and the other pole is the obvious or obscure harmony in ever-changing nature.[45] Muir's religious life enabled him to rise from the recognition of harmony to spiritual experience. In the wilderness, his communion with God seems to have been continuous.

The conclusion suggested by John Muir's life and writing is that we have the capacity to intuitively recognize the harmony of integrated material, intellectual, and spiritual reality. What we see before us and appreciate intellectually is physical harmony; what we feel in the soul is beauty coming from the Creator. Wholehearted engagement of all the levels of the personality enables us to unify these components of experience, and the intuition of beauty courses through our being.

The feeling that most directly expresses our holistic intuition of beauty is joy. Muir discovered part of what it means to be human: "I think that one of the *properties* of that compound which we call man is that when exposed to the rays of mountain beauty it glows with *joy*."[46]

The virtues we see in John Muir that promote sensitivity to the beauties of nature fall into two groups. The background virtues call us to provision the mind with relevant scientific knowledge and familiarity with the arts, to cultivate empathy with diverse types of creatures, to foster creative and sensitive imagination, to befriend the Creator, and to care responsibly for nature. Then there are the virtues specific to environmental aesthetics:

---

through tears and grief and pain and see that pleasure surpasses the pain, good the evil, and that, after all, Divine love is the sublime boss of the universe." Badè, *Life and Letters*, 307–8.

45. On this point, my "dipolar" analysis of beauty follows the theism of Alfred North Whitehead.

46. Cohen, *Pathless Way*, 39.

- Vitality

- Positive emotion

- Eagerness to discover harmony on all levels

- Wholeheartedness that unifies experience on material, intellectual, and spiritual levels

- Willingness to take time to explore and savor the beauties of nature

- A feeling for divine beauty

Searching for beauty as well as for beauties

One student of mine accepted the challenge to discover beauty itself, not merely things that had beauty; she persisted and wrote the story of her breakthrough. Born with only 30 percent of normal hearing, Andrea Mc-Ghee discovered nature as a realm as of solace.[47] She diligently visited several places of natural beauty and found occasions to describe the layers of beauty noted in a version of my article on Muir. As she approached beauty itself, free of religious pressure, she began to be liberated as she "dusted off the many layers of personal protection that I had always used to insulate my soul from the fear of failure." One day when she was alone on a grassy hill, in gentle sunlight, with a faint breeze on her face, her emotions began to intensify.

> I almost wish I could hear on the right side of me. I feel I am missing something. This mystery is filling my veins. I cannot take this pressure. I wonder, what is this? I cannot go further. My impairment has refrained from going any further. I need to let loose. I need to try this again. . . . I had been waiting during this entire experience for an opportunity to connect with the spiritual. I came ready to conquer my adversity head on. Ever since I was little, I have been fascinated with the idea that fear is just a state of mind. This was my time to shine. Nothing was going to stand in the way of my latest milestone. It was now or never. . . . I had played out this scenario in my head, week after week, for the past four weeks. There was no turning back now.
>
> As I geared myself up to climb to the top of my emotions, I felt a rush of adrenaline pump through my body and a drip at my forehead. My body jolted. This was all about me. All of a sudden, I felt a mind-numbing torture come over my body,

47. Andrea McGhee was a student in aesthetics at Kent State University in the fall of 2011, and her paper is used by permission.

and I no longer had any control. The twisting and turning of my emotions, at what seemed like 120 mph, passed through my peachy-pink face. Then a water drop from up above hit my eye, and I snapped back into reality. I was gasping for air and just could not catch my breath. My mouth pressed firmly together, my tears pooling around my mouth and nose, mingling with cool, crisp air. I wanted to escape from what was holding me back. I just kept telling myself, "Everything is going to be OK. I just need to focus."

Then something strange happened. A calming voice repeatedly replied, "You are all right now. You can get through this. Whatever you need, I am here to help." But, I did not see anyone. When I finally emerged from my thoughts, I slowly concluded where the voice had come from. It had come from within. I was eagerly awaiting this happy ending. As I looked around, I was proud. I had waited for this moment to arrive, but never thought in a million years that I would feel so liberated. I had dug down deep to find my true self. All that was needed was to keep trying until I let myself open up. It was a challenge at first, since I did not understand the process. But, finally, this day, it hit me, after four weeks of enjoying the realm of the natural environment. Beauty within oneself allows one to dawn and grow. I allowed the spirit to dawn, and my soul, my true inner self, came out.

Conclusions

As truth guides thinking by appealing to the intellect, beauty attracts the heart through feeling. We can explore natural beauty by scientifically informed perception, artistically cultivated empathy, intellectual insight into the harmony of contrasts, philosophical awareness, and realization of beauty as divine—all brought into intuitive unity by wholeheartedness. We are part of nature; our bodies are continuous with our surroundings. When we enjoy this continuity, positive emotions enhance our vitality. Gradually, we learn to walk in beauty, and it dawns on us that doing so is a phase of becoming like God.

5

Crafting Experiences,
Crafting Your Life

Johann Sebastian Bach and Artistic Living

IN 2008, I ATTENDED a play based on Lewis Carroll's *Alice's Adventures in Wonderland* and *Through the Looking Glass*. Watching *Alice* was my first experience with these stories; I had never read the books, and all I knew is that they were written mainly for children.[1] The play changed my thinking about two important concepts. It presented meaninglessness and madness in much that is socially accepted as meaningful and sane; and it showed meaningfulness and sanity in much that would be socially regarded as meaningless and mad. After exiting the artificial space of the theater, I could no longer take conventional notions of these concepts at face value. That a work of performance art could point the way beyond intolerant oppositions and into such sophisticated awareness in the space of a couple of delight-fully entertaining hours is indeed a cultural achievement.

Many people's definition of art is limited to what is usually referred to as the fine arts; but I propose that there is an artistic way of doing anything whatsoever. Once our concept of art expands to embrace everything done with gracious effectiveness, we can include in it the industrial arts, medical arts, and so on. At their best, the arts lead us into artistic living. Skillful use of time and space, handling material things well, managing a process efficiently—all these become forms of art. Art then becomes adverbial, a matter of *how* something is done or the *quality* of an action.

1. *Alice*, written and directed by Matthew Earnest, was presented in July 2008 at Porthouse Theater, Boston Mills, Ohio. Act I was based on *Alice in Wonderland*, and act II on *Through the Looking Glass*. Later, when I read the books, I realized that my analysis of the play did not altogether fit what I found in the books; but the point in this paragraph is essential to my argument.

Artistic living completes the experience of walking in beauty. We take in beauty wherever we find it . . . in spiritual experience, nature, the arts—anywhere. We return the gift of beauty consciously and unconsciously as we craft experiences. No one wholly creates his or her own or anyone else's experience; but artists craft possibilities for other people's experience, and we can shape our own more artistically.

At their best, the arts educate our feeling in ways that stay in touch with thinking and doing. The appeal of a great painting, for example, does not come simply from sensory and emotional attractions, even in association with spiritual ideals; the intellect is engaged as well. One basic connection between thinking and feeling—as neuroscience, psychology, and personal experience attest—is that our feeling about someone's actions, for example, is based on our view of the facts of what that person has done. When we appreciate a painting, we do not merely use it as a stimulus for subjective reactions with no regard for how well they may track with the dynamics of the work itself.

Our perceptual, interpretive, and evaluative processes are cultivated by truly fine art. Consider Rembrandt's *Philosopher in Meditation,* described in chapter 2. The painting draws us into its world perceptually at first, eliciting certain emotions. We see an old man with a beard sitting in a chair next to a window; the warm light that illuminates him from outside invites us to feel warmth. Taking time to experience more fully, we notice details and reflect on relationships between aspects of the painting. We observe the prominent winding staircase and other details; we consider the relation of the incoming light to the domestic scene. Meaning begins to emerge.

The high art of the painting is to lead us from our initial response into some discernment of the thought that is embodied in the work. Contemplating its meaning, our realization expands and a certain enjoyment comes over us, and we become more fully human. But when we are considering symbols in the arts, with their various conscious and unconscious meanings, we need to avoid narrow interpretations; hastily "transplanting into one's own garden" can truncate the receptive process of listening within the world as delineated in the work. I believe that when we deeply enjoy a work of art and can humbly join our opinion, knowledge, and insight with others', we emerge with a broader understanding and an enhanced capacity for living in community.

An experience of a work that activates, gratifies, challenges, and harmonizes the dimensions of our being can strengthen us to live in a new way. On a large scale, God and the universe pour inner and outer beauty into perceptive souls; and artistic living takes in beauty's nourishing joy and helps build a nest of emotional harmony so that we can process the ugliness, danger, agony, and grief that are also part of our life journey. Artistic living thus actualizes high value potentials and adds to others' enjoyment.

Several virtues that make for artistic excellence are evident in the great composer and musician Johann Sebastian Bach. The short review of his life in this chapter will illuminate the basics of artistic living, helping us to tackle the challenge of turning our lives into works of art by learning to appreciate with greater discernment, evolve emotional harmony from experiences of what is ugly, and unite intelligent design with liberated performance in daily activities. Later in the chapter, we probe examples of fine art that ennoble the soul, and finish with some reflections on beauty.

From my journey

I have had many fine opportunities to develop my interests in the arts, including my early years with an excellent piano teacher, hundreds of hours in great art museums of Europe and North America, and the poetry readings at Kent State University's distinguished Wick Poetry Center. But being an "arts person" does not make one's life artistic. When I am not walking in beauty, stuck in my old self, various symptoms remind me to reconnect: my room and office get messy. I'm not getting outside or taking time to play guitar and sing. Time for inner communion is truncated. Social emotions get tight, and excessive intellectual discipline throttles relaxation and the humor that depends on it. I work too much and neglect practical things that need doing.

Tackling a front-burner issue—one that lies beyond the scope of my strengths—I had needed motivation to clean up my office and my room; but one morning I got myself into gear and spent most of the day picking up and organizing. It made a big difference—not enough to complete the task but enough to make me feel much better. My space feels a little more like something an architect would design, and I feel more liberated to be creative and enjoy what I am doing.

An experience that graced a meditation and yoga retreat provided my greatest inspiration for artistic living. Occasionally composers or religious people report hearing the music of the spheres; and once I heard cosmic harmony as a complete chord encompassing the full range of pitches from bass to treble. The lower tones descended below my range of hearing, and the higher tones ascended above it. For a few seconds, I was nothing but an open area within infinite musical space through whom, below whom, and above whom poured forth these incomparable tones. This revelation symbolizes my ideal of harmony and the divinity that I aspire to communicate.

Bach's talent, humility, and cultivation of skill

Johann Sebastian Bach (1658–1750) came from an unusually musical family. His grandfather was a town musician, and each of his three sons was a musician; all of them had three sons, each of whom was a musician. If there was ever a clan that prepared a person genetically and culturally for music, this was it. Bach's extended family included town musicians, cantors, organists, and composers, as well as a court musician and an instrument maker.

Cultivation in the arts brings with it an awareness of degrees of excellence. As a choirmaster, Bach had to assess prospective members, and we have his evaluation of two dozen boys. Eleven of them he appraised as having "no musical accomplishments"; the others were ranked in terms of the strength and quality of the voice and their proficiency as fine, good, mediocre, indifferent, or slight.[2]

Bach had elitist moments in his attitude to other musicians with whom he had to work, but he could also express humility. One of his sons wrote that he was "anything but proud of his qualities and never let anyone feel his superiority."[3] One person who knew him reported that when asked how he had become such a master at composition, he would reply, "I was obliged to be industrious; whoever is equally industrious will succeed equally well."[4]

From childhood, Sebastian's life was punctuated by the deaths of those close to him. At age six, he had an eighteen-year-old brother die; when he was nine, his mother died and then his father. After his first wife died, he married again, and had thirteen more children, only six of whom survived into adulthood. He wrote music with emotional depth to accompany biblical texts portraying scenes of great agony and loss; the sincerity in that music must owe something to his own experience.[5]

Making the most of one's gift takes long immersion to acquire the needed skills. From early childhood, Bach was surrounded by good music. Indeed, music *was* his life. Simply by growing up in the home of a town piper, he would have shared his home with two or three persons who, like his brother, were apprentices to his father. Activities in the daily life of the Bach home consisted, according to Christoph Wolff, "not merely of teaching, practicing, rehearsing, and performing, but also of collecting and copying

2. David and Mendel, eds., *Bach Reader*, 116–18.

3. Wolff, *Bach*, 180.

4. Descartes and Einstein made statements similar to this one, quoted from ibid., 50.

5. Jones, *Creative Development*, 9. Dealing with agony, great music portrays a harmonious resolution; but the authenticity of the resolution cannot exceed the authenticity of the agony.

music, repairing and maintaining musical instruments, and other endeavors related to an extended music-business establishment."[6] Sebastian would have learned how copying, studying, composing, and performing reinforce one another. When the clan would gather, they would sing together—first some piece of religious music and then various popular, comical, and sometimes crude songs.

Great achievement requires great striving, and one measure of a person's aspiration is willingness to travel. To listen to and study with other organists, Bach *walked* to cities thirty miles, 200 miles, and 250 miles away. The young and ambitious Bach made himself a master of a wide array of contemporary styles, which he would integrate with the traditional elements of his craft. He was a craftsman in the classical sense, which implies the ability to pass on knowledge and technical pointers to cultivate understanding and skill. As a teacher with responsibility for the progress of his students, Bach wrote books for learners, with compositions of gradually increasing difficulty both in technique and in musical complexity. Countless piano students today study his two- and three-part inventions; another classic for students and professionals is his *Well-Tempered Clavier*, with preludes and fugues for each of the twenty-four major and minor keys.

Bach's intellectual art

The intellectual character of Bach's music is something that listeners immediately sense. Consider his idea of harmony. Some people associate the idea of harmony with a tepid peace that suppresses difference, a static unity without dynamism. However, for Bach, harmony resulted from interaction between "consonances and dissonances" and "between music reflecting the glory of God (who ordered everything by number, measure, and weight) and music reflecting and serving the nature of man for the renewal of spirit, mind, and soul."[7] Johann Abraham Birnbaum, one of Bach's foremost advocates, formulated Bach's concept of the nature of music in these words:

> The true amenity of music consists in the connection and alternation of consonances and dissonances without hurt to the harmony. The nature of music demands this. The various passions, especially the dark ones, cannot be expressed with fidelity to Nature without this alternation. One would be doing violence to the rules of composition accepted everywhere if one wished to slight it. Indeed, the well-founded opinion of a musical ear

6. Wolff, *Bach*, 23.
7. Ibid., 310.

that does not follow the vulgar taste values such alternation, and rejects the insipid little ditties that consist of nothing but consonances as something of which one very soon becomes tired.[8]

Harmony is clearly not a bland notion here but the unification of essential tension. This concept of harmony has application far beyond classical music.[9]

The place of thinking in the arts is often neglected. Bach admonished, "An hour of practice with the mind is worth two hours merely with the fingers alone."[10] The intellectual character of Bach's compositions can be perceived in their intricate design. Some of this art he adapted from others whose skills he came to understand through his prodigious studies. From Antonio Vivaldi, Bach learned a combination of virtues: "simplicity (implying a broad spectrum from purity, clarity, and correctness to graceful and natural elegance) and complexity (implying intellectual analysis, sophisticated elaboration, and rational control)."[11] Learning from others and adding structure of his own, Bach gave his music a special order, coherence, and proportion.[12]

Bach's balance of religion and humor

Abundant evidence exists that Bach's dominant motivation as a composer was religious. In his Bible he wrote, "With devotional music, God is always present in his grace."[13] For his religious music, he wrote abbreviations for "Jesus, help" or "To God alone be the glory" at the top of his scores; even in introducing a secular book of keyboard exercises, he wrote, "In the name

8. Ibid., 431.

9. The tension between nature and the ideal provided the dynamic for a kindred musical goal. Birnbaum explains how to resolve the tension artistically: "The essential aims of true art are to imitate Nature, and, where necessary, to aid it. If art imitates Nature, then indisputably the natural element must everywhere shine through in works of art. . . . . Now, the greater the art is—that is, the more industriously and painstakingly it works at the improvement of Nature—the more brilliantly shines the beauty thus brought into being" (ibid., 466). Nature provides much to "imitate" or represent in art, but nature itself is not a panorama of perfection.

10. The quotation comes from an assignment book and practice record that I was given as a young piano student.

11. Wolff, *Bach*, 173.

12. The terms are *Ordnung, Zusammenhang, Verhältnis*, which Wolff translates by multiple terms: "order/organization," "coherence/connection/continuity," and "proportion/relation/correlation." These terms were used by Bach's first biographer, Johann Nicolaus Forkel, cited in ibid., 171.

13. Ibid., 139.

of Jesus." He defined the aim of the theory of harmony as "to produce a well-sounding harmony to the glory of God and the permissible delight of the spirit."[14]

For all his religious devotion, we see balance in Bach in several ways. Commenting on his method of composition, Bach's son Carl Philipp Emanuel Bach observed that "the approach taken by his father never reflected the tensed-up, arduous, and compulsive attitude of a fanatic but served, instead, to provide him with fun and, often, a playful intellectual pastime . . . ."[15] Such balance is essential to artistic living. Bach was trained in Lutheran theology, but in the text for his *B Minor Mass* he omitted points that fueled theological controversy and emphasized themes that expressed life's depths.[16]

Bach's sense of humor is evident in the *Coffee Cantata*, composed for performance by Bach's Collegium at a Leipzig coffeehouse.[17] Coffee houses were the rage in Europe, and coffee was praised by Enlightenment enthusiasts for its powers of restoring reason after indulgence in wine. The text presents a playful dialogue between a scolding father and his daughter, who passionately likes drinking coffee, which she says is "sweeter than a thousand kisses." The father warns her that she will find no husband until she renounces coffee, and she secretly vows that she will marry no one without a contract that she can make coffee as often as she likes. In the end, the male chauvinism of the father is defeated by three generations of women— daughter, mother, and grandmother—each one loyal to coffee.

Bach's achievements in aesthetic virtues were won, as usual, through a life marked by struggles, sometimes due to the consequences of his own imperfections. The following are significant qualities that enabled his musical gifts to flourish:

- Appreciation of diverse excellences in others' artistic achievements

- Realism about differences in talent

- Humility about one's own gifts and accomplishments

- Intelligent design evident in one's creative work, combined with a sense of the higher significance of harmony

14. Grout, *History of Western Music*, 387.

15. Wolff, *Bach*, 469.

16. Pelikan, *Fools for Christ*, 163. The term "existential reinterpretation" refers to a tradition of biblical interpretation emphasizing profound meanings of human existence that can be found in Bible stories, which need not be taken literally but rather may be cherished because of their insight into the depths of human living.

17. Another example of Bach at play is the *Peasant Cantata*, BWV 212, *Mer hahn en neue Oberkeet* (Cantata Burlesque). Here a duet in dialect portrays rural life from the low end of society with its drinking and lovemaking (despite the Reverend's anger).

- Diligence in developing and exercising skills
- Excellence as a performer and teacher
- Capacity for expressing emotional and spiritual depth
- A balancing sense of humor

Fortunately, we can also learn about artistic living from persons who do not have the degree of excellence implied by the term "virtue." Some people show a childlike humility, a delight in the journey, and faith their ultimate achievement as they trust themselves to divine guidance. They show how the journey to artistic living can itself be artistic, despite all the uncertainty, mistakes, confusion, resistance, tentative steps, and fleeting successes. When we are living truth, beauty, and goodness to our maximum, excellence may be a long way off, but we have the thrill of doing our best.

The great challenge of artistic living

The following cluster of four sections shows how to tackle a great challenge posed by two attractive but seemingly utopian ideals. The first ideal—that a person's life can become a total work of art—was championed during the late nineteenth and early twentieth centuries by the arts and crafts movement. Artisans responded to the benumbing effects of mass production by creating handcrafted artifacts for daily living. The movement spread the idea that labor could be joyous and devoted to producing something beautiful in a spirit of cooperation. People from across the political spectrum also had a vision of progressive architecture that would transform homes and the built environment generally into an integrated, encompassing artwork.[18]

The second ideal is called being "in the zone," known to researchers as *flow*. In the paradigm case, an athlete or mountain climber—one of high skill—faces a steep challenge, right at the level that calls forth his or her best. "The main dimensions of flow—intense involvement, deep concentration, clarity of goals and feedback, loss of a sense of time, lack of self-consciousness and transcendence of a sense of self, leading to an autotelic, that is, intrinsically rewarding experience—are recognized in more or less the same form by people the world over."[19] The goals are clear and feedback is immediate, so the person can continually adjust to change. It is an experience of effortless action. Mihaly Csikszentmihalyi, the leading researcher

18. See Kaplan, "Design for the Modern World."
19. Csikszentmihalyi, "Future of Flow," 365.

and theorist of this phenomenon, envisions more than feats of unsustainable excellence: he envisions the flourishing of entire cultures.

> The relative rarity of flow experiences is due, by definition, to the fact that in everyday life the opportunities for action are seldom evenly matched with our abilities to act. . . . Often what prompts the development of a civilization is not a change in objective conditions, but a conceptual reorganization that allows a group of people to recognize challenges where they did not see any before. For instance, the great awakening of Islam in the seventh century or the transformation of Japan in the last two centuries are more easily explained in terms of a reconceptualization of what was possible, rather than in terms of changes in the external possibilities. Such reconceptualizations, according to Toynbee, were the task of "creative minorities" within each culture. . . . The Occitan culture is . . . an example of that rare adaptation, a way of life that absorbs all the energies of its members in an enjoyable, fulfilling interaction. Work is just as enjoyable as leisure, and leisure is as meaningfully related to the rest of life as work is. Great regrets, unfulfilled desires, or chronic discontent might be present in each person's individual life, but they are not built into the fabric of goals and means that the community provides.[20]

A glimpse of historical highlights with its intimations of potentials still to be actualized invites a person to dream and dare to set out toward the destination of artistic living.[21] The great challenge is to develop flow not only in times of peak exertion but also in the rest of life. The flow of artistic living comes to pervade our entire lives one day, one project, one course of action, and one experience at a time.

Discerning appreciation

At their best, the arts inspire receptive persons to a higher way of living. A poem by Rainer Maria Rilke, "Archaic Torso of Apollo," portrays an individual who beholds a radiant sculpture of a beautiful young man and in that contemplation realizes the need to change his life. Painting, sculpture, literature, dance, architecture, and drama can uplift our perception,

---

20. Csikszentmihalyi and Csikszentmihalyi, "Introduction to Part III," 183, 185, 187.

21. A rich source of cultural and religious resources for artistic living is Sartwell, *Art of Living*.

imagination, feeling, understanding, posture, gesture, movement, dwelling, and character.

Charmed, people listen, read, or watch, caught up in the aesthetic object that addresses the senses, intellect, and soul. Confucius, Plato, Aristotle, and others have discussed the power of the arts to cultivate character by presenting a well-designed work that elicits a sequence of feelings and thoughts so that audiences come out more cleansed, clarified, balanced, and uplifted. Artistic portrayals are so subtle and complex, however, that we could never completely put into words their nuances of feeling.

It takes experience to discern excellence in the arts, especially when there are so many different genres and approaches, each cultivating a different kind of excellence. People develop their artistic discernment by visiting galleries, attending performances, reading poetry and fiction, and by taking classes to find out what it is to paint, sculpt, sing, play an instrument, dance, act, write, or build. Many classes include the classics and also introduce participants to what others in their field are doing today.

Cultivating our appreciation of the arts enhances our art of experiencing in the rest of life. For example, mature aesthetic appreciation makes us less inclined to hasty enthusiasm or repulsion. Discernment grows with the length, breadth, and depth of experience—the time devoted, the variety of what is explored, and the degree to which emotion, intellect, and soul are engaged.[22]

As we contemplate the skills, virtues, and works of, say, a great composer, artist, dancer, or actor, we do well to recall that the arts, ideally, require virtues in the audience too. A text from ancient India portrays the full range of background knowledge required of the ideal theatergoer and then goes on to adjust the ideal so that aesthetic appreciation can be satisfied in the community of different types of viewers—young and old, male and female, with different interests and expertise.

> The spectators . . . should be men of character and pedigree; endowed with composure, conduct, and learning; intent on good name and virtue; unbiased; of proper age; well versed in drama and its constituent elements; vigilant, pure, and impartial; experts in instruments and make-up; conversant with dialects; . . . adepts in arts and crafts; knowledgeable in the dexterous art of gesticulation and in the intricacies of the major and minor emotional states; proficient in lexicon, prosody, and different branches of learning . . . . It is not expected that all these qualities

22. I am not proposing that all artistic expression should be deep and ennobling; some art is simply for fun, and healthy humor, for example, is essential to a balanced life. Artistic living embraces a wide spectrum of modes of recreation.

will be present in a single spectator. . . . Those in youth will be
pleased with the love portrayed, the connoisseurs with the technical elements, those devoted to mundane things with the material activities presented, and the dispassionate ones with the
efforts toward spiritual liberation depicted; of varied character
are those figuring in a play and the play rests on such variety
of character. The valorous ones will delight in themes of loath-
someness, violence, fights, and battles, and the elders will always
revel in tales of virtue and mythological themes. The young, the
common folk, and the women would always like burlesque and
striking makeup.[23]

In traditional Indian aesthetics, the ultimate goal of bringing background
knowledge and diverse modes of attention to a drama is to identify totally
with the *rasa*, the feeling, being portrayed. The more thorough our background knowledge—and our cultivation of feeling—the more fully we can
appreciate a great work of art.

Aesthetic appreciation includes contemplative and cultural phases. A
work of high art attracts contemplation that is fully focused and simultaneously receptive to all aspects of the perceivable form. A connoisseur dis-
cerns its meaning by coming to perceive it as a unified whole comprising its
subordinate unities.[24] Meaning also emerges by the way the work connects
with the wider culture.

Peak aesthetic experiences address us, according to philosopher John
Dewey, in a blended intellectual, emotional, and practical way. They carry
us beyond the work of art or other object or scene to a greater realization of
being at home in the universe.

> The sense of an extensive and underlying whole is the context
> of every experience, and it is the essence of sanity. . . . A work
> of art elicits and accentuates this quality of being a whole and
> of belonging to the larger, all-inclusive, whole which is the uni-
> verse in which we live. This fact, I think, is the explanation of
> that feeling of exquisite intelligibility and clarity we have in the
> presence of an object that is experienced with esthetic intensity.
> It explains also the religious feeling that accompanies intense
> esthetic perception. We are, as it were, introduced into a world
> beyond this world which is nevertheless the deeper reality of
> the world in which we live in our ordinary experiences. We are
> carried out beyond our selves to find ourselves. . . . [A] sense of
> an enveloping undefined whole . . . accompanies every normal

23. Embree, *Sources of Indian Tradition*, 267–68.
24. Dufrenne, *Phenomenology of Aesthetic Experience*, 12–17.

experience. This whole is then felt as an expansion of ourselves.
. . . Where egotism is not the measure of reality and value, we
are citizens of this vast world beyond ourselves, and any intense
realization of its presence with and in us brings a peculiarly satisfying sense of unity in itself and with ourselves.[25]

What may begin as aesthetic appreciation can culminate in cosmic realization. And Dewey, noting the blend of cognitive, emotional, and practical
dimensions in peak experiences, observed, "No thinker can ply his occupa-
tion save as he is lured and rewarded by total integral experiences that are
intrinsically worth while. Without them he would never know what it is really to think and would be completely at a loss in distinguishing real thought
from the spurious article."[26]

The challenge of the difficult and the ugly

If we aim to move beyond only enjoyable experiences in the arts, the challenge must be faced of how to process artistically the unbeautiful, the difficult, even the painful, aspects of life. I have spoken of the arts at their best,
but talk of the arts as delightful, uplifting, and beautiful is misleading as a
description of much of what is classified as art. Great art may not gratify the
senses because its beauty is on a higher level. Some Zen gardens in Japan
violate norms of perceptual harmony with such subtlety and effectiveness
that they incite visual nausea intended to prompt flight to nirvana. The architecture of the Jewish Museum Berlin is designed to disorient visitors in
order to enhance empathy with unspeakable affliction.

But some art is ugly on the whole, merely an exercise of self-assertion
in which technical skill and intellectual gifts are put in the service of commercial success or the desire to shock or to display a message devoid of
hope. The arts can present a confusing mix of kitsch and chaos, innovative
expression and lostness.[27] At the extreme, we observe the drive to break
every rule, celebrating sheer impulse, asserting a right to do whatever one

---

25. Dewey, *Art as Experience,* 198–99. The idea of artistic experiencing is one that
he develops. In my aesthetics classes, I primarily used Dewey to explain the artistic
living project.

26. Ibid., 44.

27. Everything has beauty in it, even if we need to change the scale by looking
from the disease to the molecules of the infected tissue or from the battle to the good
that eventually prevailed; but neither the disease nor the battle is beautiful as an isolated
phenomenon in human experience.

feels like, and rejecting all critical evaluation: values are reduced to mere preferences.

When a work strikes us intuitively as being ugly, it is natural to respond with disgust, anger, fear, or contempt. This tendency puts special demands on our art of experiencing, and we need to move into soul and commune with spirit. We have been told not to grieve the spirit.[28] God, I think, experiences agony over the ugly, too; and we may well allow ourselves to feel and identify with that agony. To share in such feeling frees us from reactive emotion and makes us ready sooner to find a constructive response.[29]

Skills of experiencing that can be learned in connection with the arts are transferable to the rest of life as well. If we can reach that soulful and divinely social way of going through the awful times when beauty is humanly eclipsed, then our suffering is fully human and we arise out of the ashes to a sense of new life.

On the road to emotional harmony, it is even possible to learn to see our own unbeautiful emotions as part of the friendly universe, alerting us to the consequences of our inferior reaction patterns, which are rooted in a body that needs healing and a mind that needs the sanity that comes from truth, beauty, and goodness. Taking a higher perspective on our own unbeautifulness, we avoid needless guilt feelings and fanatical harshness.

To clarify my use of terms: I use *mind* to include emotion and intellect; when I use the term *heart*, I refer not to the core or spiritual center of the self, nor to an idealized notion of allegedly pure feelings, but to the motivational center of the personality, which responds to the values that we cherish and choose to actualize. I have contrasted (in chapter 3) material emotion with feelings of soul; but let it be understood that not every emotion that might be classified as "negative" is bad or wrong: genuinely righteous indignation, for example, is not unbeautiful. It does not demean the other, but reaches forth to the other to shake the person into realizing the seriousness of his or her mistake.

Zen monk Thich Nhat Hanh gives instructions to promote mental harmony. Using anger as his example, he teaches mindfulness of the emotion: we recognize anger in us and make it our top priority to care for that anger. We neither judge nor repress it; we focus on self, not the other, as an older sister cares for a younger sister. Then we take a walk outside. We

28. This teaching from the Apostle Paul is found in Eph 4:30.

29. I do not wish to imply that all agony is over quickly. In the case of mourning the death of someone close or a loss of similar magnitude, the grieving process typically goes through phases, particularly during the first five years. Thereafter, even with all the spiritual comfort that comes, the bereaved person should never be expected to "move on" in the sense of ceasing to relate to the one who was lost.

remind ourselves that the anger is in us, and though it is unpleasant, it will not endure—and we have the strength to deal with it. When we are calm enough to look directly at the anger, we can begin to see its root causes; he mentions interpersonal misunderstanding, clumsiness, injustice, resentment, or conditioning. The primary roots are in ourselves: our lack of understanding of the causes of anger, and our unbeautiful emotions. The secondary roots are in the other person. When we understand the factors that led to the other's behavior, we can respond with help or discipline from a place of compassion. Next, we learn to let upsetting past experiences come to mindfulness and to become aware of problematic reactions. Practicing breathing and smiling, we learn to look at our difficult emotions without having to turn away from them. Reflecting, we can see the associations with our past experience and can eventually learn how to transform anger into peace, understanding, love, and compassion.[30]

But we don't have to be in a formal meditation session to become more mindful and appreciative. Getting into the shower, we might take the water for granted, indulge ourselves for a long time, or worry about consuming the planet's resources. An alternative is to receive the water as a gift of the cosmos, to be wisely used and enjoyed.

Great art often arises from suffering. A majority of aesthetics students who were reporting on biographies of highly accomplished persons in the arts found that these individuals often had great struggles in their lives arising from both personal problems and the strains and pressures in the civilizations they were part of. Yet they managed to bring forth beauty. In many cases, they drew consciously on spiritual resources and developed great resilience in how they processed their tensions, giving us glimpses of the mission of adversity.

Intelligent design and liberated performance

The last two artistic living basics are intertwined. Design involves intelligent planning, and liberated performance implies freedom. There may seem to be a tension between the two, but integrating them adds structural integrity and power.[31]

30. This paragraph presents guidelines for establishing peace of mind that are scattered throughout Hanh's *Peace Is Every Step*.

31. The creative tension between these two poles is found throughout cultural history. For example, by the Middle Ages, after Confucianism and Taoism had competed for a thousand years, these traditions had developed caricatures of each other. Some Taoists portrayed Confucianism as artificial and uptight in its allegiance to traditional social hierarchy; and some Confucianists portrayed Taoism as immature, impulsive,

Simple or complex, design is required for intelligent action. But design does not artificially thrust itself forward as a necessary first step in every course of action. Wise design avoids the extremes of compulsively planning too much and irresponsibly failing to prepare. The spectrum between these extremes may be sketched by presenting three approaches to planning and one type of professional design.

The minimum framework for liberated spontaneity is a set of decisions, commitments. A great decision becomes part of one's character; after that achievement, we enter situations with fresh questions in the back of our minds, giving us a new way of interpreting experience. Decisions structure the field of action. For example, in any career, the structuring decisions related to character form something like a basic code of professional ethics.

In a second approach, oriented to particular projects, the design component is simply the core idea for a creative process:

> *Expression* is the act of bringing an *idea* into view, of giving it a tangible form. For instance, the idea of giving farmers a place to display their products speedily without having to go through the hands of a middleman, found expression in the building of a farmers' market. The idea of wanting a newcomer to meet your friends leads to the giving of a party. Frequently an appreciation of the idea of beauty and order seen in nature causes one to garden, redecorate his home, or compose a symphony. All expression, be it business, art, social intercourse or science, comes into existence because of an idea—an idea entertained until it becomes so clear that the one seeing it impelled to bring it out in some definite form.[32]

Jessica Somers Driver, who is writing about public speaking, makes it clear that what she means by "idea" is not a subjective opinion but a truth of reality; moreover, she assures her readers that the idea contains within itself everything necessary for its expression. In this approach to creativity, the individual ponders patiently, *listening*, until the idea comes to mind for the true response. Next, the person *values* the idea:

> When you value an idea, you stay with it until you understand it. Valuing also leads you to seek the technique for your particular need. Some persons think that a passing thrill is enough to carry them on to good performance; they often say they work

and socially irresponsible. The predictable solution to this conflict is to realize that orderly structure is inhumane unless it protects, cultivates, and nourishes freedom, and freedom destroys itself without respect for law.

32. This method of creativity is developed in part 1 of Driver, *Speak for Yourself*, 1.

inspirationally and do not need to study technique. Usually they have only glimpsed the idea and are too superficial, or think it too much trouble, to follow through with it. *But an ideal, valued, will not let you be idle.* You are pushed into doing something about it. . . . Nothing is too much work for the one inspired with an idea. An inspired person reaches results much more surely and quickly than the one who works mechanically on technique alone, for the idea is constantly stimulating him.[33]

Then, when the time is ripe, the expression of the idea is vital and spontaneous, guided all the while by one's continually staying in touch with that idea.

A third approach, on the borderline between design and performance, is used by arts professionals who contract to turn in creative work by a particular time. The method has been researched, described, and taught by Robert Fritz, a musician, artist, author, radio host, and seminar presenter. The idea is to create in the mind what he calls "structural tension." The individual brings two things to mind and holds them together. The first item is an honest assessment of the present state of the project to be accomplished. The second item is the vision of the fully completed project, together with its deadline. No energy is invested in planning or wasted in guilt about how little progress may have been accomplished so far. No hype is attached to the vision of the completed project to enhance one's motivation. The mind is deeply and periodically impressed with these conjoined items; and the result is that the work progresses with appropriate acceleration at the end in such a way that the project is completed on time.[34]

In professional design, one first gets clear on the client's goal, the needs to be satisfied, and constraints on the solution. Then the planning and research phase begins, with brainstorming, quick sketches, and mock-ups. Discussion with the client culminates in choosing an approach, and then the detailed work of generating an actual prototype begins. From start to finish, the magic of the creative process involves aesthetic and pragmatic considerations.[35]

Since the professional approach can descend to a technical grind, consider the passion of this architecture student.

33. Ibid., 13–14.

34. For the creative method of setting up structural tension, see Fritz, *Path of Least Resistance.*

35. For professional design specifics I am grateful to Erin Pike. In addition, for the visual arts, the *elements* of design are often said to include line, shape, color, value (light/dark), texture, size, and direction (horizontal, vertical, diagonal); while the *principles* of design include rhythm, repetition, balance, contrast, variation, harmony, texture, value, hierarchy, alignment, and proximity.

The world of design is one where people either live in it or they stand outside. With design you must find that emotional-nerve-striking response from the viewer that makes them want to go grab their friends to come back and see for themselves. For an architecture major, studio is a major portion of our lives. Walking around the studio to see the multitude of designs that everyone has thought up is an inspiring experience, and it still gives me chills to this day. When I see my own model erecting itself in front of me, it always takes me to a place where I think about an open space of land, and suddenly this structure I'm modeling is actually being built and made real. That's what motivates me to improve my model beyond perfection. Design isn't something you learn at school; you live your life through it. Others work with the same geometric shapes, but no one before me has added the exact same flair and ornamentation that I would. I am not just a viewer; I embrace design and want to be part of it.[36]

This statement is from a student in a program that places such high demands even on undergraduates that they are seriously sleep deprived for most weeks of each semester.

A highly complex architectural design typically succeeds by expressing an overarching simplicity. Something similar can be observed in some people's lives. At a time when countless people are seeking to simplify in order to deal with intense global interactivity and accelerated change, simplicity may not require throwing things overboard so much as organizing the multiplicity and subordinating secondary and tertiary matters to what is of greatest value.

To design something is already an action of a certain sort, and it can be done with the quality of liberated performance, to which we now turn. Ideally, the élan of spontaneity graces the whole of life, assuming that we do not distort design and action by regarding the first as a function of reason alone, and the second merely as an expression of impulse.

Artistic living has a spontaneity symbolized by a Swedish practice (a *fartlek*) used to train runners not around a track but at naturally varying velocities on different terrains: charging up a hill, going slower on the way down, sprinting in a meadow.[37] Another example comes from a report of a high school runner whose coach told him to go once around the track as fast as he could. Then the coach told him to do another lap, but in a

36. This excerpt comes from Michael Farver, a student of architecture and aesthetics at Kent State University in 2011.

37. The *fartlek* technique became famous after Percy Cerutti trained Roger Bannister, the first person to run a sub–four-minute mile.

somewhat more relaxed way, at about seven-eighths of his previous pace. The runner came in with an even better time. As we intuit, feel, and follow the movement of life, we let go of anxiety, and the resulting freedom carries us beyond slavish engrossment in the desired goal. It feels *wonderful*.

Liberated performance unites technique and inspiration, as illustrated in this story told by actor and director Laurence Olivier. A performance of *Hamlet* was scheduled outdoors in front of the castle in Elsinore, Denmark, where the original drama had unfolded; but pouring rain forced a quick restaging in the ballroom. The busy director, Tyrone Guthrie, left the task of arranging things to Olivier.

> There is nothing better than a group of actors being presented with a problem of this kind and having to improvise. When time is drifting away and the performance is getting closer, somehow the release of adrenaline creates an excitement that runs through everyone, from the leading actor/actress to the maker of the tea. The entire company pulls together with the one object in mind. It is at such times that you can ask for the impossible, and get it. "I'm afraid the only way you can play this scene is by hanging from the chandelier, dear boy." Without a moment's hesitation, the reply would come back, "Of course—no problem."
>
> Great God! there is something amazing about them, the band of players. There is a comradeship that I have experienced only once elsewhere, but not so happily, in the Services.
>
> Somehow every performance seems to be enhanced in times of unexpected difficulties; there is an edge, a fine edge that hoists the players, even the least inspired, onto another level. All the actors' motors have to be running, but in a low gear for greater acceleration. Nobody dares get a moment wrong. Whereas laziness, even boredom, may have crept in before— and this is very understandable when you think in terms of standing night after night on the end of a spear with somebody else delivering the dialogue that you feel you could do better— that boredom, for a moment, is forgotten and the contribution becomes genuine, energetic, and electric. Everyone becomes a Thoroughbred, muscles alive and alert. The vibrations are high, and this will affect the audience as well. What they witness will be a night that they will always remember. . . .
>
> Whether or not what the audience sees is good we will nev- er know, but the energy that is directed toward them will engulf them in its euphoric state. In Elsinore that night, the actors were heroes, every man Jack of them. I know—I was right in the mid- dle of it. A dignity and excitement was achieved, an atmosphere

in which no one falls on his arse unless it is intended. Everyone
thrills with a sense of achievement and importance—and quite
rightly. The "one for all" society syndrome. Above all, the performance was spontaneous.[38]

The disciplined work of learning lines and rehearsing formed the foundation for the thrilling performance. In daily life, we normally rely on the simplicity of intuition (or what seems like intuition), only occasionally having
the time to do our best thinking in thoroughness; but study and reflection
cultivate our capacity for intuition. Our best thinking prepares our best decisions, which establish a foundation for excellent spontaneous responses.
The integrity of genuine simplicity comes only from laboring in fields of
thoroughness.

But it is also helpful to see what other qualities we need to draw on
when spontaneity is demanded and there is no time to design or cultivate
anything; we must rise to the greatness of the occasion, whatever that may
be. In those situations, life is telling us to wake up: don't make a resolution
for next year. Don't ask for a method or a list of steps. The wisdom you
need is already available, and your present intuition is enough to begin with.
Dare to come into the Presence right now. Truth is here—grasp it. Beauty is
at hand—feel it. Goodness beckons—follow in freedom. This voice speaks
with directness in the Zen gesture, the revelatory proclamation, the decisive
action, the enthusiastic hug.

Unitary concepts become meaningful through experience with complexities, while ventures into thoroughness are kept on track by commitments expressed in a few words. Thus we move back and forth between
affirmations of major concepts and more thorough paths of exploration,
between right-brain simplicity and left-brain complexity. This movement is
the life of our concepts of truth, beauty, and goodness.

In our efforts to coordinate disciplined cultivation with spontaneity, we
seem to face the dilemma of having a mind that operates in predominantly
one of two ways: the first is "intuitive" (though fallible), and the second is
under rational control. According to Daniel Kahneman, "Mood evidently
affects the operation of System 1: when we are uncomfortable and unhappy,
we lose touch with our intuition. [There is] growing evidence that good
mood, intuition, creativity, gullibility, and increased reliance on System 1
form a cluster. At the other pole, sadness, vigilance, suspicion, an analytic

38. Olivier, *On Acting,* 86–88. Olivier makes it clear that (at least for his method)
outstanding performance remains conscious of technique in crafting audience response. Nevertheless, though life is a performing art, it is not about being on stage in
front of an audience, and we do not fashion ourselves so that we can manipulate others'
enjoyment.

approach, and increased effort also go together. A happy mood loosens the control of System 2 over performance: when in a good mood, people become more intuitive and more creative but also less vigilant and more prone to logical errors."[39]

I observe two ways to manage the trade-off. I once taught a seven-week class on the philosophy of living. We began at the middle of the semester, when the students had already formed habits for the term. They were honors students, and their lives were fully scheduled; about a third were heavily overcommitted. Some reported cycling between spurts of high performance followed by collapse. For days or weeks, they would exert themselves to the maximum with no exercise, inadequate sleep, and poor nutrition; once the project was done, they would fall into bed in total exhaustion and only gradually recover their energy. So I developed an artistic living project option that I called "survival plus." The idea is that when demands come thick and fast and the pressure is on, we can survive—and even do better than that. We can hold our head high as we go through the hectic period. But we refuse to abuse our bodies or to subordinate our*selves*—our souls—to deadlines and external task demands. *We* are the ones who will pilot ourselves through the experience. We prune our list of activities if we can, letting go of those that are optional. In some of our remaining activities, we accept the need to do less than we normally would, within the limits of responsibility. We also notice the factors that led to getting overcommitted and determine to avoid repeating those mistakes. We can finish strong in spirit.

Several students took the survival-plus project option and disciplined themselves to programs of sleep, nutrition, or exercise. During class, they supported each other in small-group sharing, and their striving was frequently encouraged in class. They all had successes to report.

A deeper way out of the dilemma is illustrated by the Nobel Prize-winning Bengali poet and educator Rabindranath Tagore:

> I withdrew my heart from my own schemes and calculation, from my daily struggles . . . and gradually my heart was filled. I began to see the world around me through the eyes of my soul. . . . Thus, when I turned back from the struggle to achieve results, from the ambition of doing benefit to others, and came to my own innermost need . . . then the unquiet atmosphere of the outward struggle cleared up and the power of spontaneous creation found its way through the centre of all things.[40]

39. Kahneman, *Thinking, Fast and Slow*, 69. This comment builds on the reference to his research in chapter 2.

40. O'Connell, *Rabindranath Tagore*, 258.

Tagore's path to artistic creativity went through the soul's perspective on truth to the divine center.

When we are working on anything complex and come to see it through the eyes of the soul, we are on the threshold of one of artistic living's greatest gifts to a philosophy of living. We can symbolize that thing (for example a set of ideas, list, quotation, or project) in an image or gesture. Once symbolized, it enters our life of feeling; and we can then combine it with other symbols to facilitate sophisticated creativity.[41]

If I were to select one line to summarize my concept of artistic living, it would be Psalm 118:24. "This is the day which the Lord has made; we will rejoice and be glad in it." Considering the day as already prepared for us suggests that we can do our tasks in a way that fits into the Creator's beautiful mosaic.[42]

Art's mission with meaning and value

When beauty dawns in experiences of the arts, it harmonizes all levels of our being: body, mind (conscious and unconscious), and soul. This result exceeds what philosophy can accomplish. In Rembrandt's painting *Aristotle Contemplating a Bust of Homer*, the portrayal of Aristotle suggests a certain sadness, for golden light falls not on the philosopher but upon the poet. Philosophy excels with reasoning and concepts, but art presents meaning and value in ways that can both include and transcend concepts, expressing particular details, fine shades of difference, or symbols that can never be fully explicated since they awaken responses from beyond the conscious mind.

In every age, eternal truth seeks culturally appropriate expression to illuminate the spiritual struggles of the times. Through his drama *The Suppliant Maidens*, Aeschylus responded to the problems he saw in Athens in the fifth century BCE: intolerant attitudes of Greeks toward "barbarians," the need for religious tradition to open itself to creative transformation, and the necessity for leaders to find new ways of identifying the correct path in a dangerous conflict.

The play begins with the arrival of a ship bringing to the shores of Argos fifty Egyptian women with their father, who speaks for them. They are seeking protection from Egyptian men who are pursuing to force them into incestuous marriage. The women appeal to Pelasgus, king of Argos; and

41. This artistic technique of creativity has been used by geniuses in many fields, according to the autobiographical selections collected in Brewster, *Creative Process*.

42. The metaphor of the Creator's mosaic for the day comes from Russell, *God at Eventide*, 64.

their claim to protection is that they are related by kinship to the Argives. The highly complex and seemingly far-fetched genealogy they offer as evidence reveals a lineage that Aeschylus may not have meant the audience to take literally. To portray these dark Egyptian women as kin to the Argives and as equally descended from Zeus is Aeschylus's spiritual insight, one that his immediate audience would have found challenging.

The king accepts that the women and their father are originally Argives; but there is a further decision to make, and the king is in the throes of uncertainty. From the outset, we have been reminded that the will of Zeus is "not easily traced. Everywhere it gleams, even in blackness." The king acknowledges, "I am at a loss, and fearful is my heart." His dilemma is that if he protects the women, he risks destructive war with the pursuing Egyptians; if he does not protect them, the women threaten suicide upon the altar for suppliants, a move that would bring divine retribution. In this situation, says the king, "We need profound, preserving care, that plunges / Like a diver deep in troubled seas, / Keen and unblurred his eye, to make the end / Without disaster for us and for the city . . . ." In the moment of decision, the crucial factor is "the height of mortal fear" of Zeus; this emotion makes the king resolve above all else that he will not offend the king of the gods.[43] After all, Zeus protects visitors and suppliants.[44]

The king decides to ask the people to protect the women, and he tells them the principle he discovered that governs this situation: "Everyone, / To those weaker than themselves, is kind."[45] The king's courageous effort to struggle responsibly with the ethical implications of the truth of human kinship enables him to successfully plunge like a diver into troubled seas to find the will of God. In the end, the people support the king in his decision to protect the maidens.

The pivotal insight expressed by Aeschylus also motivated Ludwig van Beethoven's *Ninth Symphony*, which continues to draw us into the joy of living in the universal family. This symphony was composed to express portions of *The Ode to Joy*, a poem written in 1785 by Friedrich Schiller, a playwright, philosopher, and poet. In Schiller's philosophy, art is destined to integrate the individual with society, restore our attunement with nature and other human beings, and lead humankind to divine heights. Schiller kept his art from descending to propaganda, religious or otherwise; he held

43. Aeschylus, *Suppliant Maidens*, lines 85–88, 379, and 407–10 (pp. 9, 19, and 20–21).

44. Homer, *Odyssey* IX, 260.

45. Ibid., 488 (23).

that art makes its contribution to humanity not by teaching or preaching but by portraying a vision of living that is both free and moral.

In the *Ode*, Schiller presents joy as a divine gift that kindles the realization of the brotherhood of man that springs from the universal fatherhood of God.

> Joy, beautiful spark of the gods,
>
> Daughter of Elysium,
>
> ... Your magic reunites what custom strictly divided;
>
> All men become brothers
>
> Where your gentle wing lingers.
>
> ....
>
> Brothers, above the canopy of stars
>
> Must dwell a loving Father.[46]

The *Ode* celebrates joy as found in God and the gods; in love, human and divine; in nature; and in heroic exertion. Joy is a divine gift with no attachments to any particular religion. Schiller called joy "daughter of Elysium," a mythological notion of heaven; he turned to ancient Greece for a myth of personal and political wholeness to suggest a possible human future.[47] He blended themes from a variety of cultural and religious sources to portray the heroic venture of becoming like God.

In 1793, when Beethoven was losing his hearing and struggling with near-suicidal depression, he roused himself and made a vow of loyalty to his destiny as a composer, and pledged to set the *Ode* to music. In 1824, three years before his death, he fulfilled that vow in the *Ninth Symphony*.

The first movement of the *Ninth* begins with quiet stirrings, sounds that give an indefinite effect, a reservoir of barely distinguished potentials. Then the main theme enters, moving somewhat rapidly in a minor key. A mood of sternness and driving action dominates, relieved by breaths of tenderness and lightness. Stability and flexibility are manifest in the beginning, whose tensions propel what follows.

The second movement moves faster, driving vigorously in a major key toward its destination, heroic and happy. Now the mood is sunny, strenuous and persistent at moments, often playful, and full of vitality, with echoes of the dignity of the previous movement and anticipations of the lyricism to follow.

---

46. My own translation.

47. I owe this observation on the sixth of the 1792 *Letters on the Aesthetic Education* to Sharpe, *Friedrich Schiller*, 150.

The third movement, slow, achingly beautiful, combines sweetness and heaviness. Its unhurried penetration of sadness, the clarion beams of orchestral brightness, and an irresistible, swelling warmth transport the listener to a meadow of satisfaction.

In the fourth movement, for the first time Beethoven brings lyrics and a chorus into a symphony. There had been debate about which art was higher—music with its capacity to express feelings beyond words, or poetry with its capacity to express concepts beyond the range of music. Beethoven used music and poetry to proclaim the joy of the universal family.

At the outset of the fourth movement, serenity gives way to tension. Themes from the first three movements are quoted in fragmentary form; some synthesis is brewing. A voice breaks in upon the orchestra: "Friends, not these tones." The call goes forth for better music. Neither the tragic-majestic nor the galloping heroic nor the enveloping lyrical mood is adequate to what the poet and the composer have in mind. Then comes the chorus with the lyrics from the *Ode to Joy*.

The melody for the chorus is rhythmically and harmonically simple; the orchestra at times imitates a local town band and then expands to maximum fullness. If we consider the development of the fourth movement in terms of the philosophical aesthetics of its time, we can see that the simple and universally accessible tune that announces the theme of joy expresses the *beautiful*. Then, as the music develops, it rises to a maximally energetic expression of *sublime* height and power. This distinction between the beautiful and the sublime follows Kant: the beautiful indicates a finite order comprehensible to the human mind; the sublime symbolizes the infinite, a mystery to which we respond in awe.[48]

The *Ninth* continues to serve throughout the world as a work that affirms our human unity around the world. In 1989, when the wall separating West Berlin from the formerly communist East Zone was torn down, Leonard Bernstein, then conductor of the New York Philharmonic, flew to Berlin to conduct the symphony with an international orchestra in a live broadcast that could be heard in more than twenty countries. At the opening ceremony of the 1998 Winter Olympic Games in Nagano, Japan, the *Ninth* was conducted by Seiji Ozawa, whose orchestra was linked by satellite with orchestras and choruses performing simultaneously in Australia,

48. James Parsons explains how well the music fits the text according to the eighteenth-century musical and poetical antecedents in English and German culture. Parsons, *Ode to the Ninth*, 308–12. Choir director C. M. Shearer commented that the impression of excess and wildness in the choral finale (for example, in its high notes) has disappeared now that so many choirs are good enough to sing the music as it was written.

China, Germany, South Africa, and the United States. The European Union chose the music of the joy theme as its symbol. No philosophical or religious discourse has such universal and powerful appeal. The symphony proclaims what something deep within us craves to hear.

Art has many functions, and not every work of art has to serve them all; but one of them is to ennoble us. In some circles today, the very idea of ennoblement is unfashionable, but novelist Fyodor Dostoevsky was able to fulfill that mission by probing the darkness of the modern age in a way that undercuts cynicism. For example, his novella *Notes from Underground*, which focuses mainly on the decline and trapped condition of a soul who is lost, portrays failed idealism and failed love. The main character is unable to find any stable basis for thinking or for making decisions and carrying out plans of action—but Dostoevsky gives a clear glimpse of a better alternative. The first part of the novel presents a first-person account of the intellectual plight of the underground man at the age of forty, and the second part goes back to the pivotal time in his life at age twenty-four, when he seems to have permanently spoiled his chance to break through to a better way.

As a young man, the underground man would dream of lofty ideals. He would imagine devoting himself in a glorious love relationship, performing heroic deeds, and embracing humankind. But he could never get himself to *do* anything to actualize these high ideals. Every effort failed, and this humiliated man was drowning in his self-image as a coward. On one fateful escapade with three superficial friends, our protagonist goes to a house of prostitution. Having taken his pleasure and fallen asleep, he awakes at two in the morning and engages the young woman, Liza, in a rousing passionate, moral, and ethical discourse, exhorting her to save herself from this degradation and to take up a life of nobility and true love. As he leaves, he invites her to visit him, which she later does. She comes to offer him her love and—at his crucial moment—he rejects her love in a most ugly way. It is arguably implied that he rapes her.[49] She refuses the money that he puts in her hand, runs out the door, and is lost to his sight in a snowstorm.

The protagonist claims to see beyond the naïve and dogmatic simplicism of the "man of action" who acts directly and spontaneously only because he allegedly fails to see the problems at the root of his own thinking and deciding and acting. The underground man is cynical about hypocritical and sentimental idealism regarding the good and the beautiful. Though he has had moments of emotional involvement with "the sublime and the

49. In "Dostoevsky's Underground Man," Linda L. Williams has analyzed the key passage describing the ugly rejection and argued that it indicates that the underground man responded to his generous visitor by raping her.

beautiful," he cannot sustain loyalty to those ideals in action and rejects them.

The underground man presents himself in the narrative as having the courage to follow up certain insights that we all sense but most of us cover up. He can see only two alternatives: naïveté and the underground. But Liza illustrates a third way. She knows evil, and therefore is not naïve; but she is capable of decision and action. She can love and she also can withdraw her love when it is trampled upon.

The choral finale in the *Ninth* proclaims the message of the universal family as strongly as possible; but artistic expression is usually more indirect. Irish poet Seamus Heaney tells the story of a drive to the ocean, where he found two contrasting and breathtaking scenes. Then, leaving aside religious language, he speaks metaphorically of an awakening of the inner life.

Postscript

And some time make the time to drive out west
Into County Clare, along the Flaggy Shore,
In September or October, when the wind
And the light are working off each other
So that the ocean on one side is wild
With foam and glitter, and inland among stones
The surface of a slate-grey lake is lit
By the earthed lightening of a flock of swans,
Their feathers roughed and ruffling, white on white,
Their fully-grown headstrong-looking heads
Tucked or cresting or busy underwater.
Useless to think you'll park or capture it
More thoroughly. You are neither here nor there,
A hurry through which known and strange things pass
As big soft buffetings come at the car sideways
And catch the heart off guard and blow it open.[50]

The postscript comes, it seems, after a letter to a friend. The poet gently opens a question about the friend's hectic, unsettled pace. From the first line, he plays with the reader's experience, concept, and language of time: "Sometime, make time . . . ." We are slightly displaced, enough to wonder

50. Originally published in *The Spirit Level* (1996), "Postscript" is included in Haney, *Opened Ground*, 411.

whether time is the sort of thing we can make. Then the poem becomes an invitation: come and see. We are told where and when to go and are offered a vivid description of two glorious scenes occurring simultaneously on opposite sides of the road.

If we identify with the description, we can agree that if we came upon such a pair of dazzling scenes, we too might think of stopping to try somehow to capture them, to take in the wide space that exceeds what we can take in at any one time. But the poet tells his friend that to park would be chasing the impossible. Now the poet begins using the word "you" to imply a generality that includes himself; he is not claiming to be above the distortions to which everyday life is vulnerable. Hectic living modifies what it means to be a human being. We are not merely in a hurry: we *are* a hurry. Familiar and strange things pass through us in a jumble without our savoring them.

The poet's friendly command to seek out the beauties of nature is, more generally, an invitation to go where we may be surprised by a gentle power that opens us to what we are typically too rushed to recognize and feel. The poem gives the reader the chance to experience something analogous to the wonders of nature: the poem itself can catch the heart off guard and blow it open.

A culminating concept of beauty

Socrates and Plato realized that our experience of beauty can go beyond temporary enjoyments to become a way of living. In the *Symposium*, Socrates explains an educational process using the image of a ladder whose rungs begin with physical, erotic passion and ascend through appreciation of beautiful minds, admirable customs and laws, and noble philosophical discourse to reach the height—not merely another kind of reality that *has* or *partakes of* beauty, but rather the eternal, unchanging reality that *is* beauty. Then Socrates speaks of a life in divine beauty that would bring forth genuine virtue, friendship with God, and the hope of immortality.[51]

Medieval thought combined Platonic with Aristotelian themes in the light of prophetic religion, and Thomas Aquinas's concept of beauty as experienced in art and nature emphasized the ideas of splendor or radiance in a well-proportioned form, having wholeness or integrity of being. Using examples from science and philosophy, I would propose that the beauty of truth is evident in its radiance.[52]

51. Plato, *Symposium*, 211–12.
52. For this summary of characteristics of beauty in medieval aesthetics I draw on

The high point of the physics career of Albert Einstein (1879–1955) was his discovery of general relativity, which was brought to completion in conversation with Hendrik Lorentz, an eminent Dutch physicist whom Einstein practically revered as a father figure.

> After dinner Lorentz invited his guests to his study, passed cigars around, and with great didactic mastery recapitulated the difficulties that Einstein had to overcome to arrive at the finished form of his [general theory of relativity]. . . . During Lorentz's summary, Einstein drew on his cigar less and less often and, when Lorentz concluded with a subtly formulated question, the cigar had gone out altogether. Einstein was bending over sheets of paper covered with Lorentz's formulas, absently twisting between his fingers a lock of his full mane. Lorentz was smiling at Einstein, as he sat there deep in thought, much as a father would regard his beloved son—confident that he would crack the nut offered him, but tense to discover just how. It took a while, but then Einstein joyously raised his head—he "had it." A little more to and fro, a slight misunderstanding, followed by clarification and complete mutual understanding, and then the two men's eyes shone at the riches of the new theory.[53]

The radiance that they saw I regard as the spiritual quality of truth.

The beauty of spiritual living and the beauty of goodness have already been portrayed in the profile of Jesus of Nazareth in chapter 3. The magnificent simplicity of his poise; his unification of contrasts; his ability to keep his feet on the ground and yet soar to heavenly heights in his thought; his patient compassion and wise teaching; the intelligent design of his mission and the spontaneity of his creative and fearless responses; his touching love, his courage in trial and torture; and the triumph of his final words in the flesh—all these reveal the beauty of spiritual values.

To clarify the expanded concept of beauty needed for a philosophy of art, it is worth considering some thoughts by British philosopher R. G. Collingwood (1889–1943), who observed that beauty is sometimes spoken of very broadly as a synonym for aesthetic excellence, while at other times the beautiful is treated as one specific quality distinguished from the sublime, the comic, the tragic, the lyrical, the romantic, the graceful, and any number of other forms of beauty, which he regards as ways of "cutting

---

Maurer, *About Beauty*, 7–14. Maurer notes the range of meanings for the Hebrew word *hadar*: "splendor," "glory," "beauty."

53. Fölsing, *Albert Einstein*, 396–97.

up and sorting the infinite plurality of beautiful objects." Surely beauty as a general term should not exclude that variety.

> The highest beauty somehow contains within itself, as subordinate and contributory elements, both the sublime and the comic, and indeed all other forms of beauty; so that these forms appear as parts of a whole, the whole being beauty. But where these elements fall apart, where we get one form in apparent isolation, we do not wholly fail of beauty: the one element constitutes a beauty in itself, but a beauty of a truncated and incomplete kind, beauty at a lower level of development.[54]

Beauty can refer to a balance of aesthetic tendencies, which may be taken to extremes:

> The sublime and the comic have been taken . . . as the first and second forms of the beautiful. Each is beautiful, but in an incomplete and one-sided way. In each case there is a discord between the subject and the object which mars the perfection of the aesthetic enjoyment. . . . The disillusionment of laughter is the end of an illusion, but is itself another illusion, equal and opposite. To overcome both illusions would be to attain the stability in which alone the mind can present to itself a truly beautiful object.[55]

Sometimes when we come to understand that which has initially struck us as impressive, we are no longer in awe. In greatest works, the contrasting modes, the sublime and the comic, are integrated so well that we do not experience an oscillation from one mode to another.

> The highest art . . . has come to rest in the centre. The mark of this repose is a feeling which can best, perhaps, be described as one of intimacy with the object. . . . Real beauty is neither "objective" or "subjective" in any sense that excludes the other. It is an experience in which the mind finds itself in the object, the mind rising to the level of the object and the object being, as it were, preadapted to evoke the fullest expression of the mind's powers. The experience of beauty is an experience of utter union with the object; every barrier is broken down, and the beholder feels that his own soul is living in the object, and that the object is unfolding its life in his own heart. Hence arises that absence of constraint, that profound sense of contentment and well-being, that characterizes the experience of real beauty. We feel that it is

54. Collingwood, *Philosophy of Art*, 30 and 32.
55. Ibid., 39–40.

"good for us to be here"; we are at home, we belong to our world and our world belongs to us.[56]

Our expansion of the concept of beauty comes full circle as we return to *hózhó*, which served as our introduction to walking in beauty. Although the Navaho concept is embedded in a culture not all of which outsiders will understand or accept, much of it invites us into its garden.

> *Hózhó* is the intellectual, moral, biological, emotional, and aesthetic experience of beauty. A Navajo experiences beauty most poignantly in creating it and expressing it, not in observing it or preserving it. The experience of beauty is dynamic; it flows to one and from one; it is found not in things, but in relationships among things. Beauty is . . . to be continually renewed in oneself and expressed in one's daily life and activities. To contribute to and be a part of this universal *hózhó* is both man's special blessing and his ultimate destiny.
>
> Navajos generate *hózhó* in their minds and souls or incorporate *hózhó* within themselves by ritual identification with the Holy People who possess it. This ritual identification allows the *hózhó* that radiates from the Holy Person to extend to and be incorporated in the being and mind of the patient through prayer and song, symbol and sandpainting.

The Navajo regard the universe to have been jointly created by a male deity associated with the power of thought and a female deity, sometimes called Earth Woman, associated with speech, whose expression takes on forms including prayer, song, ritual, and various crafts. In the spirit world and in daily life, beauty balances (1) order, control, and balance with (2) forcefulness, energy, and creative dynamism. The three parts of this book portray truth, beauty, and goodness in their particular emphases and interrelations; *hózhó* illustrates how a traditional concept of beauty can function as the hub that integrates an entire philosophy of living.[57]

---

56. Ibid., 42–43. The quotation, "It is good for us to be here" refers to what Peter said to Jesus on the Mount of Transfiguration (Mark 9:5).

57. Witherspoon, *Language and Art*, 178, 191, 17f, 173, and 195. In this fascinating book, which I would classify as philosophical anthropology, he reports that the prayer that we quoted in chapter 4, "With beauty before me, I walk," is for daily use (153). See pp. 17–46 for the implications of the *hózhó* concept in the Navajo language.

Conclusions

Artistic living builds on knowledge, wisdom, spiritual realization, and sensitivity to the wonders of nature. In the practical arena it is skilled, and its social relationships are mature. As beginners, our stirrings in the direction of artistic living contain the ideal of a flow that encompasses all of life. Artistic living expresses true freedom: personal expression cultured by appreciation of others' achievements and loyalty to human community; commitment to values alongside openness to multiple traditions of excellence; and spontaneity based on discipline and design.

Finding creative ways to process experience and embellish others' experience can rise to the heights of joyous cooperation in actualizing divine beauty. And beauty's bonds with truth and goodness enable it to pervade our thinking and doing as well as our feeling.

When we consider the lives of artists and their struggles to bring forth something worthy, we may pause to contemplate the Creator. If God is not finished with us yet, if creation is ongoing, if the eternal God comes forth to participate in evolution, then his artistry is not only about promptly producing perfection in heaven; it also about getting into the trenches to work with us free, finite creatures. If we want to catch more of the spirit of artistic living from Bach and others, we will look for inspiration not only to their most perfect creations; we will also look to their great striving with earthly challenges.

Works of art that lead us toward the realization of high meanings and values express something important in the lives of their creators. A good film, for example, addresses the senses, eliciting perceptions, emotions, and ideas. It captures our attention and whets our appetites to stay with it to the end as the filmmaker leads us to discoveries both predictable and surprising. And artists' strivings, at their best, handle the material aspects of daily life with an uplifting perspective and attitude. Biographical, theological, and artistic resources can help us all acquire an enhanced aesthetic touch in what we do and how we relate. Artistic living is a phase of becoming like the Creator.

Part III. Participating in Divine Goodness

6

As You Want Others to Do to You

Albert Schweitzer, Jane Addams, and Morally Active Living

IN EACH OF OUR three great values, we are not merely spectators; we are players on the field. The concept of living the truth rouses us to share the conviction that we can know the truth and to make it more widely known by putting its implications into practice. The concept of walking in beauty invites us to appreciate beauty and live creatively to add to others' enjoyment and ennoblement. The concept of participating in divine goodness engages our faith, if we choose, in recognizing the Giver behind every genuine value, the Creator whose greatness ranges from the management of the cosmos to his detailed and invisible care for each of his children. Our receptivity to God's care grounds our gratitude, which motivates us to desire to cooperate with his agenda. And he gives us the opportunity to share in his parental ministry of goodness to others. We participate by means of what we do and how we do it, and by who we are in our heart of hearts. In line with these two ways to participate, doing and being, the chapters devoted to goodness focus first on morally active living and next on character crowned by love.

The most loving and effective parent I know is my brother-in-law Charlie Hoeveler. I once asked him his secret of parenting, and he replied, "When you're doing it well, you know." He exudes an attitude of good-hearted and total engagement in whatever he is doing, a quality cultivated by his avocation as a tennis player. Committed to excellence in everything, he has won many national and international championships in singles and doubles tennis, and he leads the business he founded, which runs sports camps across the United States. For more than a decade he gave an annual seminar to help his would-be competitors get started. "I wake up every day asking how I can make the people happier that I'm going to meet today, what I can do to make their lives better, whether it's my wife, tennis partners, business associates. I've been so blessed, and I love to share that."

Morally active living embraces the full spectrum of our projects, duties, and opportunities as we pass through this world. If our quest for truth or beauty in any area becomes excessive and unbalances us, goodness lures us to reorder our priorities. But the true and beautiful way of goodness seems far off in the distance when moral and ethical guidance for the way ahead is unclear, or when our desire to do what is right and good gets swamped by competing attractions.

Ethics does not aim to answer every question about what is right and good, but it can lift our quality of thinking about these questions. This chapter portrays great moral decision-making and world-class social service in the lives of Albert Schweitzer and Jane Addams, whose virtues indicate directions for our own growth. Then we take a closer look at a foundation for excellence in action: three levels of meaning in the golden rule of treating others as we want to be treated. Although the rule is generally regarded as a moral principle that operates in one-to-one relationships, we also touch on a few social, economic, and political applications. When we experience healthy growth toward the virtues we observe in the greats, when our action is meaningful on the levels described, and when we engage to some degree in the various arenas of human responsibility, we enjoy a soul-satisfying participation in goodness.

From my journey

A life that begins well can become unbalanced. I was a "good boy" at home and school. I had some exhilarating experiences of going out with my family to rake leaves for neighbors and doing a little volunteer work in the community. In my teens and twenties, larger opportunities came my way that were satisfying. And then there was the joy of getting back on my spiritual path, dedicating my life to the service of spiritual truth, and organizing my career around the great concepts that fill this book. In my twenties, I dedicated myself to idealistic service, and goodness came to mean striving to make the brotherhood of man a practical reality. When I began using service-learning as a component in my ethics classes, sometimes I was asked about the value of service for learning, and I would reply that without service there's no learning. This summary could give the impression that my life has been increasingly dominated by selfless service; in fact, the story is more complicated.

Over the years, absorbed in my world of books, I could be insensitive to the needs of others. At times I deceived myself by not allowing my background sense of wrong to come into full focus. Despite the amazing things that students in my courses were doing—and I always did projects of my own along with them—I needed to do more with family and community. Making slow progress or none with major growth challenges, I would prop up my self-esteem by identifying with my idealistic projects. Pushing too hard to fulfill great goals, I would dull myself, lose my savor, and attract no one. The furrows in my brow tell of years of strain, struggle, and subterranean anger at self or others. Sometimes my service would be poorly motived, stained by ambition or by a consciousness of duty that was not adequately grounded in understanding and spiritual awareness.

Retirement is bringing new realizations in service. One example came during a season when I volunteered as a reading mentor at Intergenerational School in Cleveland (part of the Breakthrough Schools network). I worked with students in their first years in primary school. It was humbling; I was a beginner. My job was to interact one-on-one for fifteen to twenty minutes per person, doing only a little teaching and more encouragement and interaction, so that the students could learn that reading opens up opportunities for interesting and enjoyable conversation and bonding. I learned to identify with a broad spectrum of students—one who did not manage to learn the alphabet all year, some who were brilliant, a few who were extraordinarily kind, some who were gifted in dramatically expressive reading, and one whose personality, social skills, and attitude were stunningly well integrated. At the beginning of each mentoring day, I was tremendously inspired by interacting briefly with the class to which I had been assigned and observing their outstanding teacher, Mrs. Miller, who managed her class excellently with clarity and a smile.

One day, I discovered a level of mentoring beyond my normal attentive, enthusiastic, and supportive social interaction. When thinking, feeling, and doing go deep, move to the level of *being*, it becomes a soul thing. Sometimes the difference is very clear. I broke through to mentoring from the soul; I was revealing mature love to my students. The content of the interaction was the same; immersed in their reading, the students gave no evidence of sensing anything different qualitatively. But a corner had been turned: service had become ministry. And I came home with a new component of my standard of what it means to be living at my best.

Albert Schweitzer's greatest
decision and discovery

Albert Schweitzer (1875–1965) and Jane Addams (1860–1935) had a lot in common. As children, both of them felt sensitive concern for the poor and had fathers who would not let them enjoy what their classmates could not afford. Both received a classical education, were independent thinkers, established centers to serve the poor, wrote prolifically showing extraordinary learning and original observation, and won the Nobel Peace Prize. I will deal more briefly with Schweitzer than with Addams, since from his life I present only two stories: how he made the decision to begin his main career and how he found the leading theme of his philosophy and his life.

The full range of virtues highlighted in the philosophy of living put forward in this book is exemplified more obviously in Schweitzer than by any other person profiled here. Schweitzer integrated world-class achievements in truth and beauty in a life dominated by goodness. A prominent Bach organist in Europe who was also doing important work as a philosopher and theologian, he subordinated every other interest to go to medical school at age thirty to prepare for service to the poor.

Morally active living is based on decisions, and the great decisions are the ones that guide one's entire life. Schweitzer entered the preliminary phase of his pivotal decision at age twenty-one, when, still immersed in study, he resolved to pursue careers in preaching, scholarship, and music until the age of thirty, and then to devote himself to the service of humanity. This commitment nourished what would be the dominant motive in his life. He began thinking of becoming a physician, and the second phase of his decision occurred in a discovery/insight at age twenty-nine, when he read an article about the need of volunteers for a mission in West Africa. He writes, "Having finished the article, I quietly began my work. My search was over."[1]

The third phase came a few months later on his thirtieth birthday, which he "spent like the man in the parable who, 'desiring to build a tower, first counts the cost whether he have wherewith to complete it.'"[2] In order to arrive at a decision that would be realistic as well as idealistic, Schweitzer lucidly examined whether his own strengths were adequate. "I had considered [the venture] for a long time and from every point of view, and credited myself with the possession of health, sound nerves, energy, practical common sense, toughness, prudence, very few wants, and everything else that might be found necessary by anyone wandering along the path of the idea.

1. Schweitzer, *My Life and Thought*, 88
2. Ibid.

I believed myself, further, to wear the protective armor of a temperament quite capable of enduring an eventual failure of my plan."[3]

A decision sets aside alternative potentials and risks opposition. A great decision, freshly minted, has a self-sustaining momentum. After announcing his plan to serve in Equatorial Africa, and as a physician, not as a missionary, Schweitzer met opposition from friends. In previous years, he had found preaching to be a necessity of his being, but the time had come when he craved service without words. "For years I had been giving myself out in words and it was with joy that I had followed the calling of theological teacher and of preacher. But this new form of activity [medicine] I could not represent to myself as talking about the religion of love, but only as actually putting it into practice. Medical knowledge made it possible for me to carry out my intention in the best and most complete way, wherever the path of service might lead me."[4] Setting aside a career of explicitly religious discourse, he would gain still greater realizations of the religion of love.

An authentic decision launches a course of action, but the follow-through required to actualize the potential may take a further level of commitment. After arriving in Africa and beginning the arduous labors of constructing an adequate medical facility and organizing a medical staff, Schweitzer's inspiration began to be exhausted, and he struggled to find some line of thinking that could remotivate his commitment. A prolonged crisis of meaning prepared him to receive the gift that would become the major premise of his life, the hub around which he ordered other ideas, and the symbol of divine value that he found in all humans, animals, and plants.

Schweitzer observed intellectual and spiritual fatigue in Western civilization, which increasingly tolerated cynical ideas and actions, where material progress in scientific knowledge and mechanical inventions was welcomed despite the lack of balancing ethical vigor. In the horror of World War I, he saw the loss of energetic commitment to "the idealistic attitude toward life."[5] Why had the older ethical commitment collapsed? "The thought out of which [that civilization] arose was noble and enthusiastic but not deep. The intimate connection of the ethical with the affirmative attitude toward life was for it a matter of feeling and experience rather than of proof. It took the side of life affirmation and of ethics without having penetrated their inner nature and their inward connection. [It was] rooted in belief rather than in thinking which penetrated to the real nature of things."[6]

3. Ibid., 90.
4. Ibid., 94.
5. Ibid., 146 and 149.
6. Ibid., 153–54.

He struggled to come up with a satisfying insight into the meaning of life, but nothing would satisfy his mind and soul.

> For months on end I lived in a continual state of mental excitement. Without the least success I let my thinking be concentrated, even all through my daily work at the hospital, on the real nature of the affirmative attitude and of ethics, and on the question of what they have in common. I was wandering about in a thicket in which no path was to be found. I was leaning with all my might against an iron door which would not yield.
>
> All that I had learned from philosophy about ethics left me in the lurch. The conceptions of the Good which it had offered were all so lifeless, so unelemental, so narrow, and so destitute of content that it was quite impossible to bring them into union with the affirmative attitude.[7]

After months with no result, feeling alone in his quest, he became exhausted and depressed. Taking a long, slow journey upriver, he nevertheless kept up his inquiry. Then came the final, pivotal insight that shows the role that spiritual experience can play in the development of a personal philosophy.

> Late in the third day, at the very moment when, at sunset, we were making our way through a herd of hippopotamuses, there flashed upon my mind, unforeseen and unsought, the phrase, "Reverence for Life." The iron door had yielded: the path in the thicket had become visible. Now I had found my way to the idea in which affirmation of the world and ethics are contained side by side! Now I knew that the ethical acceptance of the world and of life together with the ideals of civilization contained in this concept, has a foundation in thought. . . .
>
> At the same time the man who has become a thinking being feels a compulsion to give to every will-to-live the same reverence for life that he gives to his own. . . . A man is ethical only when life, as such, is sacred to him, that of plants and animals as that of his fellow men, and when he devotes himself helpfully to all life that is in need of help. The ethic of Reverence for Life, therefore, comprehends within itself everything that can be described as love, devotion, and sympathy, whether in suffering, joy, or effort.[8]

7. Ibid., 157.

8. Ibid., 156–59. Reverence for life regardless of an organism's level of development has the virtue of recognizing the wonderfulness of life as such. But Schweitzer could also use spray to kill insects in the room where he was about to perform surgery. Maturity recognizes both the universal value of life and the differences of mind and spirit

Schweitzer had insisted on the primacy of rigorous thinking as the way to truth. In this crisis, thinking preceded the gift, and thinking followed it, but thinking did not produce it, nor was the gift a proposition, let alone an inference or a vision of a system. But reverence for life became the main concept around which he would focus his life and thought.

A mark of greatness is the humility that comes from realizing one's continuing need to grow. Schweitzer observed that the idealism of youth must be transformed by constant aspiration for higher attainment: thus "the soft iron . . . hardens into the steel of a full-grown idealism that can never be lost." Then he applies the lesson to himself.

> Does my behaviour in respect of love effect nothing? That is because there is not enough love in me. Am I powerless against the untruthfulness and the lies which have their being all around me? The reason is that I myself am not truthful enough. Have I to watch dislike and ill will carrying on their sad game? That means that I myself have not yet completely laid aside small-mindedness and envy. Is my love of peace misunderstood and scorned? That means that I am not yet sufficiently peace-loving.

Although this thought does not take into account factors beyond one's control, it does well in responding to failure by seeking further growth. Schweitzer encourages those who experience within themselves "the power of the ideas of the good and the true" to accept the gradual emergence of results; they are "producing as much as [their] character allows. . . . No ray of sunlight is ever lost, but the green which it wakes into existence needs time to sprout, and it is not always granted to the sower to live to see the harvest. All work that is worth anything is done in faith."[9] Morally active living, then, as we see it in Albert Schweitzer, harvests a generous crop from all inquiry into truth and devotion to beauty and consecrates one's talents and energies in the service of a better world.

Jane Addams's pioneering initiative, intelligent thinking, and social service

In the life of Jane Addams we see morally active living emerge from a vital spirituality whose concept of universal brotherhood included a special identification with the poor, combined with a growing dissatisfaction with education and culture cut off from the life of democracy and industrial

---

that make species unequal.

9. Schweitzer, *Childhood and Youth*, 101–2.

society. During her college years at Rockford Female Seminary (soon to become Rockford College), she was "clinging to the desire to live in a really living world and refusing to be content with a shadowy intellectual or aesthetic reflection of it."[10] After the death of her adored father, there followed an eight-year struggle to balance competing moral and ethical pulls of family, society, and personal ambition. During that period, she entered medical school, then left it because of poor health and depression, and then went twice to Europe for travel.

On the second trip, she made a life-changing visit to the United Kingdom, where she discovered Toynbee Hall in London and was introduced to the settlement movement as a model of social service. Returning home, she used a modest family inheritance in 1889 to buy a large house in Chicago in a neighborhood largely populated with immigrant families—Italians, Russian and Polish Jews, Irish, Germans, Greeks, and Bohemians. Totally dedicated, with a clear concept in mind, and established in the new home that would house her work, she was now ready to launch her distinguished career of service.

She moved into Hull-House with Ellen Gates Starr, her friend from Rockford College. Promptly they began getting to know the neighbors, learn their needs, and start up programs to help them. They must have been excellent organizers, for they soon had many groups coming and going all through the week: kindergarten, activities for young girls and for young boys, educational and social organizations for adults, and discussion groups. To Hull-House, the central location, were gradually added other buildings in the neighborhood so they could provide a gymnasium, an art gallery, a residence for working women, a coffee house, and other facilities for groups. All these developments emerged naturally, not as the unfolding of a master plan but as needs became evident, opportunities arose, and resources were made available. They assisted civic organizations, did research to support legislation, and occasionally became politically active on issues that could unite and protect a neighborhood.

Their work attracted other capable women, who also came to live in Hull-House, and men too, who took up residence nearby. "From the first it seemed understood that we were ready to perform the humblest neighborhood services. We were asked to wash the new-born babies, and to prepare the dead for burial, to nurse the sick, and to 'mind the children.'"[11] Her ideals of universal brotherhood, democracy, and social equity blended, and she relished the labor that alone makes them a reality.

10. Addams, *Hull-House*, 64.

11. Ibid., 109.

Hull-House had been founded along the lines of the settlement movement, which she described as follows.

> The Settlement . . . is an experimental effort to aid in the solution
> of the social and industrial problems which are engendered by
> the modern conditions of life in a great city. It insists that these
> problems are not confined to any one portion of a city. It is an at-
> tempt to relieve, at the same time, the overaccumulation at one
> end of society and the destitution at the other; but it assumes
> that this overaccumulation and destitution is most sorely felt
> in the things that pertain to social and educational advantages.
> For its very nature it can stand for no political or social propa-
> ganda. . . . The one thing to be dreaded in the Settlement is that
> it lose its flexibility, its power of quick adaptation, its readiness
> to change its methods as its environment may demand. It must
> be open to conviction and must have a deep and abiding sense
> of tolerance. It must be hospitable and ready for experiment. It
> should demand from its residents a scientific patience in the ac-
> cumulation of facts and the steady holding of their sympathies
> as one of the best instruments for that accumulation. It must be
> grounded in a philosophy whose foundation is on the solidar-
> ity of the human race. . . . Its residents must be emptied of all
> conceit of opinion and all self-assertion, and be ready to arouse
> and interpret the public opinion of their neighborhood. They
> must be content to live quietly side by side with their neighbors,
> until they grow into a sense of relationship and mutual inter-
> ests. Their neighbors are held apart by differences of race and
> language which the residents can more easily overcome. They
> are bound to see the needs of their neighborhood as a whole, to
> furnish data for legislation, and to use their influence to secure
> it. In short, residents are pledged to devote themselves to the
> duties of good citizenship and to the arousing of the social ener-
> gies which too largely lie dormant in every neighborhood given
> over to industrialism. They are bound to regard the entire life of
> their city as organic, to make an effort to unify it, and to protest
> against its over-differentiation.[12]

As this account makes clear, Addams adjusted her ideals of service to a scientific understanding of the facts of the persons with whom she worked.

According to Ellen Starr, Addams's spirituality was the source of their
project at Hull-House: "It is as if she simply diffused something which came

12. Ibid., 125–27.

from outside herself of which she is the luminous medium."[13] Her spirituality was free of dogmatism. In college she probed behind the systems of religion, trying to find "a great Primal cause—not nature, exactly but a fostering
Mother, a necessity, brooding and watching over all things, above every human passion . . . . [And I would] go ahead building my religion wherever
I can find it, from the Bible and observation, from books and people, and
in no small degree from Carlyle."[14] She saw the Settlement movement as
expressing a renaissance in Christianity and was convinced that for Christianity to thrive in the modern world, the spirit of social service must have
a new awakening.

Her convictions always had fresh expression. She would speak of universal brotherhood, fellowship, humanity, or kinship. In order to be successful living and working with the poor, one needs the conviction "that the
things which make men alike are finer and better than the things that keep
them apart, and that these basic likenesses, if they are properly accentuated,
easily transcend the less essential differences of race, language, creed, and
tradition."[15] Though Hull-House gave no formal religious instruction, Addams for several years led the residents in Bible readings and prayer.

In her humility, Addams had no trouble seeing altruism alive and well
among the poor she served.

> I became permanently impressed with the kindness of the poor
> to each other; the woman who lives upstairs will willingly share
> her breakfast with the family below because she knows they "are
> hard up"; the man who boarded with them last winter will give
> a month's rent because he knows the father of the family is out
> of work; the baker across the street, who is fast being pushed to
> the wall by his downtown competitors, will send across three
> loaves of stale bread because he has seen the children looking
> longingly into his window and suspects they are hungry.[16]

Needy people sometimes respond more than comfortable folks to others'
needs.

13. Quoted in Farrell, *Beloved Lady*, 61–62.
14. Ibid., 35.
15. Addams, *Hull-House*, 111–12.
16. Ibid., 162–63.

Jane Addams's pragmatism

The flexibility of the Hull-House activities was guided by discovering what "the neighborhood was ready to accept."[17] Addams characterized the 1890s as "a period of propaganda as over against constructive social effort; the moment for marching and carrying banners, for stating general principles and making a demonstration, rather than the time for uncovering the situation and for providing the legal measures and the civic organization through which new social hopes might make themselves felt."[18] Her dynamism came not from naïve passion for an abstract, intellectualized ideal but from concrete care for people.

Although she was lucid about how the social, economic, and political systems obstructed progress and saw that private charity was inadequate for the most difficult cases, Addams never identified with Marxism since its methods of violence contradicted the goal it claimed to pursue. Nor did she identify with socialism; she disliked its doctrinaire one-sidedness, its willingness to regard as brothers only those with a uniform viewpoint, and its abstract and antagonistic rhetoric. She understood the complexities of issues and beliefs, and could see beyond black-and-white characterizations of various movements and groups. She found good in some wealthy capitalists, and was always ready to take a helpful idea from any source whatsoever. Committed to organic social unification rather than polarization, she was noted for her fairness and was frequently invited to mediate conflicts.

Ever practical, she advised leaders to temper their idealism so that they could mobilize social support in order to actually make progress.

> [The leader] has to discover what people really want, and then "provide the channels in which the growing moral force of their lives shall flow." What he does attain, however, is not the result of his individual striving, as a solitary mountain climber beyond the sight of the valley multitude, but it is underpinned and upheld by the sentiments and aspirations of many others. Progress has been slower perpendicularly, but incomparably greater because lateral.
>
> He has not taught his contemporaries to climb mountains, but he has persuaded the villagers to move up a few feet higher. . . . Our thoughts, at least for this generation, cannot be too much directed from mutual relationships and responsibilities. They will be warped, unless we look all men in the face, as if a

17. Ibid., 132.
18. Ibid., 177.

community of interests lay between, unless we hold the mind open, to take strength and cheer from a hundred connections.

To touch to vibrating response the noble fibre in each man, to pull these many fibres, fragile, impalpable and constantly breaking, as they are, into one impulse, to develop that mere impulse through its feeble and tentative stages into action, is no easy task, but lateral progress is impossible without it.[19]

Addams embraced the discipline of evolutionary progress: moving forward at a realistic pace.

Her feminism was a branch of her devotion to humankind. As a college student in 1880, she noted a half-century of women's growing ambitions and aspirations, which were being met with a new approach to education that no longer focused on teaching a woman how to be pleasing, but rather on preparing for new opportunities in the workplace. "We gladly claim these privileges and proudly assert our independence," while expanding the concept of the traditional role of woman as bread giver: "the only true and honorable life is one filled with good works and honest toil."[20] She believed that when women develop understanding of truth by adding scientific education to their intuition, their intuitions will no longer be wasted but will become effective.[21] In her career, she paid a great deal of attention to girls and women, but never by slighting the needs of others.

Her practical, sociological wisdom arose from observations of the individuals she came to know. Social science must often deal in generalities; they have exceptions, but it would be irresponsible to do without them. Addams's approach had "a dual commitment to empathetic understanding as the surest route to social knowledge and to a form of compassion linked to a determination not to judge human beings by 'their hours of defeat.' The requirement that the social commentator make a sympathetic attempt to interpret, to understand, and to criticize in a way that also turns back on the observer herself, demanding a form of self-interpretation and self-criticism as well, lies at the core of Addams's social theory."[22]

Her involvement in working for labor legislation was motivated by a philosophical observation. "Thus confronted by that old conundrum of the interdependence of matter and spirit, the conviction was forced upon us that long and exhausting hours of work are almost sure to be followed by

19. Elshtain, ed., *Addams Reader*, 175–76.

20. Ibid., 8–9.

21. Ibid., 10–12. Note that in *Twenty Years at Hull-House*, Addams criticizes the youthful exaggeration with which she stated her point.

22. Ibid., xxxiii.

lurid and exciting pleasures; that the power to overcome temptation reaches its limit almost automatically with that of physical resistance."[23] And thorough familiarity with the single mothers and their children convinced her that a woman cannot both financially support and nurture children well.

Addams's commitment to pragmatism showed itself in an experimental approach ready to adapt to changing conditions; moreover, her pragmatism was nurtured by friendship with two of the foremost American pragmatist philosophers, William James and John Dewey. Their influence is shown in a remark that she made on truth: she hoped that "young women who had been given over too exclusively to study, might restore a balance of activity along traditional lines and learn of life from life itself; where they might try out some of the things they had been taught and put truth to the ultimate test of the conduct it dictates or inspires."[24] She may have known even better than her philosopher friends that truth does not acquire its fullness apart from practice.

The qualities evident in the lives of Schweitzer and Addams include the following:

- Being well rounded rather than narrowly specialized

- Excellence in decision-making and planning

- Excellence in organization

- Willingness to act on intuition

- A character dominated by universal love

- An appetite to work with real individuals, not just intellectually or aesthetically but practically as well

- A readiness to make necessary compromises in order to stay connected with those they served

These two examples of morally active living feature social service as their way to participate in goodness; and social service—helping strangers with practical problems—is essential in morally active living. Nevertheless, every career requires morally active living and gives opportunities for service, including the careers of scientists, philosophers, prophets, explorers of beauty, and artists—not to mention devoted parents. All who serve in any way participate in goodness.

Next to these famous people, I want to mention two of the many students who made an unforgettable impression on me as they developed

23. Addams, *Hull-House*, 204.
24. Ibid., 85.

outstanding service in class projects. One volunteered once a week for five weeks in a nursing home. On her first visit, she found herself repulsed in her initial meeting with a man who could not walk, sat in a wheelchair, never left his room, was on a feeding tube, and whose mouth foamed with saliva; his tongue was half cut off, so neither she nor anyone else could understand him. She left after only a few minutes and cried. The second time she went to the home, when she was about to leave at the end of her day's work, she went back to this man's room. Before entering, she prayed for courage and strength to be there for him. They managed to communicate for an hour and began a friendship. She came to understand him better than any employee. On later visits she spent a lot of time with him, listening to music, discussing what she was learning in class, and enjoying his brilliance. Coming to regard him as part of the universal family, she looked on him as no different from her grandfather—indeed, no different than herself. Imagining herself in his shoes, she developed a love for him, which expanded into a far-reaching love of service.

The other student was a veteran who had developed bonds of brotherhood with his fellow soldiers and was ready to do anything for them without hesitation; in our ethics class, he challenged himself with a project to develop the same level of brotherly love for strangers. He started looking for people to help; and after the first time—buying dinner for a homeless person who didn't want to talk—the actions of service came naturally. He went to extraordinary lengths, cleaning the house of a disagreeable neighbor who was a hoarder, had just been diagnosed with cancer, had lost her husband, and whose son was a multiple amputee. He changed his attitude toward his family, and began to help them out in various ways—all of which led to a spiritual love for all humankind. His new attitude: there are no strangers, just brothers and sisters you haven't met yet.

Moral living basics: six teachings on the golden rule

What a happy thing to be able to symbolize an entire philosophy of living in one principle, the golden rule—treat others as you want others to treat you! Many people regard this teaching as trivial, while most others who value it have little idea of its depth; but if we choose to take this word of truth as a central concept around which to cluster our understandings of relevant meanings and values, we enter upon a remarkable journey.[25]

25. The past two decades of scholarship on the golden rule have brought to light a freshly emerging principle. The study of this principle in various cultures and academic

This section offers a basis for morally active living by explaining six teachings for understanding and applying this rule. It's helpful when thinking about how to apply it to remember that the golden rule is a searchlight, not a map: no principle can be expected by itself to resolve everything; in that sense, any universal moral principle may seem vague. But the very act of bringing it to mind can transform the shape of a problem.

- Thoughtful application of the rule can begin with a reflection on how we have been well treated

- The golden rule is best seen in the context of a wider philosophy of living

- The golden rule can be interpreted as a rule of sympathy: Treat others with consideration for their feelings, as you want others to do to you

- The rule can be interpreted as a rule of reason: Treat others in accord with reason, as you want others to treat you

- The rule can be interpreted as the principle of the practice of the family of God: Treat others as brothers and sisters, sons and daughter of God

- Imagine yourself in the other person's situation

One caveat before proceeding. Although the golden rule functions primarily in interhuman relations, it has some application to our connection with God and animals. As a person, God has feelings too; and compassion extends to all living things. If we extend consideration in this way, the rule can serve as the foundation for an ethics broad enough to encompass our duties regarding the planet's ecosystems. Ecological care is based on respect for the value inherent in all creation, for our own interests as a species, and for the omnipresent Creator. Living faith in God, expressed in service to humankind, is the core of spiritual religion, but it is not a complete ethics. Faith and service are an ideal basis for cooperation in tackling these wider obligations.[26]

---

disciplines uncovers vast resources of wisdom used to interpret the rule in the context of particular problems that various cultures have worked on. This theme is developed in my book, *The Golden Rule*. For a recent treatment emphasizing the rule as a principle of reason and including discussions of more of the world's religions, see Gensler, *Ethics and Golden Rule*. By far the most thorough treatment of the cultural history of the rule is two-volume history of the golden rule by Olivier du Roy, *Règle d'or: Histoire*; some of his findings are presented in *La règle d'or: retour*. A book that does a fine job of presenting the golden rule in world religions, philosophy, and service organizations is Bauschke, *Goldene Regel*.

26. See my chapter 2 on Confucianism in *The Golden Rule* for a fuller discussion of how the rule works in asymmetrical relations.

Recalling how others have treated us well

We begin a path of discovery with the golden rule by bringing to mind persons who have treated us well. Such persons may include family, friends, teachers, leaders, team members, and strangers. Some supported us when we were down. Some challenged us and helped us grow. Some died before we were born. Some laid down their lives for us. Thinking of these people, we know how we want to be treated; thus, in many types of situations, we may be ready to go forward with the golden rule.

But a thorough review of how we have been well treated may include persons who sacrificed for us in ways that we are not prepared to do for others. If these cases of sacrifice tempt us to interpret the golden rule as implying an unreasonably high standard, we should remember that those who treated us extraordinarily well were probably not anxious and driven about living up to an unreasonably high standard; and they might not have been intending to follow any rule at all. Our readiness to do more for others grows gradually, and we must not allow ourselves to feel bad about our present limitations. In some of the people who treated us well, one thing that came through was love—we could feel it. That love grew naturally, and ours will do the same, nourishing our relationships in the soil of truth, beauty, and goodness.

The golden rule's bonds with truth and beauty

Someone who is going to treat you well needs an adequate understanding of the truth of who you are and the truth of your situation. And that person needs to treat you with the good humor, grace, and delight of one responsive to beauty. When my friend Paul McKenna at Scarboro Mission asked me how my philosophy of living relates to the golden rule, I replied that we like to be treated by those who live the truth beautifully in love.

A rule of sympathy

The golden rule has different levels of meaning. The first level is the golden rule of sympathy. *Act with consideration for others' feelings as you would have others be considerate of your feelings.* The worldwide practice of the golden rule at this level would be enough to transform the world; selfishness and cruelty would be left in the dust.

However, despite its helpful sensitivity, the golden rule of sympathy is shown in some situations to be too low a standard. Sometimes we need to disappoint others' feelings. Suppose a mother has a child who needs a shot at the doctor's office, even though the child always cries pitifully at the approach of the needle. In this case, short-term sympathy would be long-term foolishness. Instead, mothers engage reason and think of the child's long-term well-being.[27] Sympathy is also limited since its response to immediate needs and sensational media images may lead to unwise actions; and sympathy may fail to embrace those we do not see.

Sometimes one hears a sophistical objection to the golden rule: what if a sadomasochist or would-be adulterer treats others as he wants to be treated? This objection ignores the fact that the golden rule is addressed to *you*; it is not an invitation to fantasize about how others might deceive themselves with cynical interpretation and immature self-indulgence. But taking the objection seriously leads us to recognize important truths about the rule: an honest thinker intuitively recognizes it as a *moral* command. The golden rule does not operate in a value vacuum; one of its functions is to summarize a culture's moral wisdom. For example, the Ten Commandments are widely honored, and prohibitions on adultery, theft, and murder are found in every culture. In addition, the rule presupposes a minimum of self-respect and maturity, qualities that are strengthened through the sincere practice of it.[28]

Another objection to the golden rule is expressed by George Bernard Shaw's quip "Don't do to others what you want others to do to you—their tastes may be different." But Shaw's interpretation of the rule is misleading. The rule does not instruct us to attribute all of our particular desires to others, which would be absurd. We learn early that peoples' desires differ, and our common sense often guides us well in making allowances for such differences and asking how others want to be treated in certain situations. Taking a friend out for ice cream, we do not assume that the friend prefers our own favorite flavor. To imply that the golden rule betrays us at the ice cream parlor is sophistry. In general, we all want to be treated well, and this implies due regard for our particular desires. Someone who enjoys all sorts of meats and beverages, for example, would not serve pork to a Muslim friend, beefsteak to a Hindu, or wine to an alcoholic.

Sometimes we do forget to take into account differences that we would recall upon a moment's reflection, and sometimes we do not suspect

---

27. A more complex treatment of golden rule empathy can include spiritual feelings, as du Roy shows magnificently in *Règle d'or*.

28. A fuller discussion is found in Wattles, *Golden Rule*, 176–80.

differences, even deep and important ones, between ourselves and others. The wants and needs of others can differ surprisingly from our own, and sometimes well-intentioned acts of benevolence go awry for this reason. This is Shaw's point, taken charitably; but such problems are inherent in the moral life, and they challenge those who apply any moral principle. I believe that it is worth standing up for the golden rule as a teaching of Jesus and the world's most widely cherished moral principle. And people who have taken this as their rule of living seem to be more trustworthy and powerful in goodness than many others who do not.[29]

A rule of reason

The second level is the golden rule of reason. *Treat others in accord with reason, as you want others to do to you.* To invoke reason is to open the interpretation of the golden rule to the entire field of ethics; we will take two samples.[30]

One challenge of this level of the golden rule is that sometimes we do not want to be treated with reason. We want the sympathy; we want to *feel* good. But some of the people who have treated us well challenged us constructively. They loved us, respected us enough, had enough faith in us to tell us what we did not want to but needed to hear.

The golden rule has stimulated some philosophers to formulate its intellectual implications in a more sharply defined way, as can be seen in two major modern ethical theories, one by Immanuel Kant and the other by John Stuart Mill, each of whom presents a highly developed account of an essential side of ethics.

Certain features in Kant's early life make it plausible that he developed his unconditional moral principle, the categorical imperative, partly to give intellectual precision to the golden rule.[31] Kant's principle requires, first, that we act only according to specific maxims that we could will to be universal law (put very roughly, this requirement is the test, "What if everyone did that?").[32] Kant's principle requires, second, that we treat each person,

29. This paragraph is adapted from Wattles, *Golden Rule*, 174–76.

30. More details on basic ethics are available at https://sites.google.com/a/kent.edu/jwattles/home/ethics.

31. For Kant's criticisms of the golden rule, see his footnote in the second section of the *Grounding for the Metaphysics of Morals* (AK 430), where he discusses the second major formulation of the categorical imperative. Kant grew up in a Pietist home, which emphasized not formal religion but Bible reading and a deeply moral life; he would surely have imbibed the golden rule during his boyhood and youth.

32. A maxim specifies the type of situation, the type of action, and the motive for

including ourselves, not merely as a means but as an end. The *humanity* in us implies that we each have equal and awesome—he calls it infinite—dignity. It takes profound self-respect for the golden rule to flourish. Third, we should act autonomously on principles that could function in an advanced civilization (or help such a civilization evolve).

Another influential modern ethical theory associated with the golden rule is utilitarianism. One of its founders was John Stuart Mill, who advocated acting for the good of the whole. This theory, despite its problems, contains insights that enrich the interpretation of the rule. In fact, Mill saw the golden rule as expressing the heart of his theory. "As between his own happiness and that of others, utilitarianism requires him to be as strictly impartial as a disinterested [nonpartisan] and benevolent spectator. In the golden rule of Jesus of Nazareth, we read the complete spirit of the ethics of utility. To do as one would be done by, and to love one's neighbor as oneself, constitute the ideal perfection of utilitarian morality."[33]

A strength of utilitarianism is its attempt to consider all beings directly or indirectly affected by an action; utilitarianism thereby provides a bridge from a moral principle of one-to-one relationships to an ethics applied to social systems of three or more. For example, utilitarianism realizes that sometimes what seems right between two persons must be adjusted to take into account the interests of the group.

Kant and Mill recognized a key component of moral reason: we should look not only at the particulars of a situation and decision but also what those particulars indicate about the wider meaning of the action. The morally responsible person uses general terms to think about the *type* of situation, and describes the action and motive in terms that could apply to countless other cases. For example, whenever I am tempted to make a deceptive promise in order to borrow money (situation type), I will refuse to do so (action stated in general terms) on grounds of principle (universal motive).

But what if a would-be assassin demands that I reveal the location of his intended victim? Mill described the process of making a responsible exception to the moral rule of telling the truth. Not only do I need to realize

---

the action.

33. Mill, *Utilitarianism*, chapter 2, 288. Mill was a hedonist in the sense that he defined good in terms of happiness, and happiness in terms of pleasure; but his hedonism was neither individualistic nor vulgar: he emphasized the greatest good for the greatest number over the greatest length of time, thereby directing moral agents to estimate the *consequences* of their actions (an aspect of scientific living). This is the context for his statement about the good of the whole, which comes immediately after the quotation just cited.

the tremendous importance of truth-telling; I also need to define the precise kind of situation in which an exception is justified (when telling the truth would bring great harm to those affected directly and indirectly by the action). If I do not make the exception precise, I leave things fuzzy and may start making unjustified exceptions, corrupting my character and contributing to social decline.

Note that virtues are expressed in general terms that relate to situation types. Courage, for example, pertains to situations that are threatening (and there are kinds of courage pertaining to specific kinds of threats). We take our moral life to the next level by reflecting on these meanings.

When I began my study of ethics, the debate between Kantian ethics and utilitarianism occupied center stage. The utilitarians attacked the Kantians for their let-there-be-justice-even-if-the-world-perishes fanaticism. ("Would you would insist on following ideal justice procedures after capturing a terrorist who knows where the nuclear bomb has been set to explode in New York City?") They found the idea of absolutizing particular duties at the cost of human welfare repugnant. Kantians attacked utilitarians for jeopardizing minority rights and implying that it was acceptable to sacrifice individuals to the common good ("Should a doctor harvest the organs of a healthy patient in order to save five critically ill ones?").

The heart of the solution to this clash of theories comes, in my opinion, from Jesus' use of the parable of the lost sheep in a context of introducing a social teaching about stages in a process of forgiveness. The lesson highlights the transcendent value of the individual person, at the same time acknowledging the need of the group to take action to protect itself from seriously and persistently troublesome individuals.

In the parable, the good shepherd leaves the ninety-nine sheep while he goes out to seek for the one that has wandered off and gotten lost. Finding that sheep, he brings it back with great rejoicing. "There will be more joy in heaven over one sinner who repents than over ninety-nine righteous persons who need no repentance."[34] If the sheep were on their way to green pastures and cool water, they had to wait, endure suffering, because of the wayward individual. A utilitarian wanting to maximize happiness would

34. Luke 15:7. In Matt 18, the story of the good shepherd's success and rejoicing is followed by a three-stage grievance procedure marked by mercy, patience, and power, and then a concluding parable. Many current discussions of mercy emphasize the need for forgiveness for the sake of the psychological health of the person who has been harmed; but the grievance procedure in Matthew aims also at the rehabilitation of the offender and the protection of the community. Although mercy should be a constant component of our attitude, forgiveness requires a *process* when an offender deliberately and persistently does serious harm. Conditions that should ideally be fulfilled by offender and victim are portrayed in Griswold, *Forgiveness*, 48–51 and 54–58.

have to honor the shepherd's action. This shepherd's act symbolizes an attitude of complete loving mercy for the individual who needs it.

But the attitude of thoroughgoing love and mercy is not all. It functions as the pervasive motivation for Jesus' range of possible responses. The next part of his teaching was the three-stage grievance procedure: If your brother (a member of your spiritual community) sins against you, approach him personally and try to achieve mutual understanding; if he listens, you have won him back into the circuits of loving community. If not, go with a few others to speak together once more. If he persists in deliberate, seriously disruptive behavior, bring him before the large group, which may decide to exclude him from their fellowship. And if any who heard this teaching were imagining themselves sitting in judgment on the accused, the perfect antidote comes in the parable of the unforgiving servant, which subverts arrogance by reminding them how much they have been forgiven to be welcomed into the spiritual family of God: "And should not you have had mercy on your fellow servant, as I had mercy on you?"[35] Thus the infinite and equal value of the individual is proclaimed as the first and last word, and the merciful and tough social procedure to protect the group is sandwiched in between. Spiritual insight can grasp the coherence of the social-ethical procedure in context, sandwiched between two parables.

The parable contains the lessons for making peace between those who insist on the infinite dignity of the individual person and those who insist on group rights. It takes faith to believe that in the long run, the interests of the individual and the group are the same. On this assumption, if we could ever humanly know with certainty what is best for the individual, then we could trust that that action would work out best for the group. And if we could ever humanly know what is best for the group, then we could trust that this course of action would work out best for the individual too.

The God of moral meanings loves each person infinitely, which provides a reason in support of the best version of Kantian ethics. And, in support of the best version of utilitarianism, God loves every person equally, which brings together all the children of God into relationship as a family, providing a reason to treat everyone with profound respect and to work for the good of the whole.

A spiritual rule

Emotional sympathy and moral reason, despite their essential contributions, do not solve every moral problem. We can be well attuned emotionally and

35. Matt 18:33 (substituting "servant" for "slave").

well informed, but sometimes our best thinking does not find the answer, and spontaneously we reach out for higher wisdom. Or we know *what* we should do, but *how* to do it is beyond us. These situations call for a spiritual level of interpretation of the golden rule.

On a spiritual level, the golden rule may be regarded as the principle of the practice of the family of God: *Treat others as brothers and sisters, as sons and daughters of God, as you want others to treat you.* Or we can imagine treating others as God would treat them; we can participate in the goodness of God, the highest possible interpretation of the rule.[36] Imagine how others need to see you: brimming with God, balanced, and shining in the mystery of your unique personality.

The spiritual interpretation of the golden rule opens new vistas. As we come to know God better, we begin to sense a new purpose in living. Our wonderful friend, awesome Creator, and loving Father has a will for us. If we are wholehearted and persistent, we can even find it and do it. The golden rule becomes equivalent to the law of neighbor love: we are to love and our neighbor as ourselves.

Imagining ourselves in the other person's situation

To imagine oneself in another person's situation is a common practice, widely associated with the golden rule, even though the rule does not explicitly require it. Note that the golden rule is neither necessary nor sufficient for moral insight: we can find the right way intuitively, without the detour of an act of imagination; and the mere fact of imagining oneself in the other person's situation does not guarantee that we will come up with the right answer to a moral question.

The imaginative role reversal has other limits. It does not add new knowledge. It is not a substitute for personal acquaintance, scientific knowledge, or sensitivity cultivated through the arts. It cannot compensate for failing to consult with others when our decisions will affect them; or for the knowledge gained by interacting to find out whether our empathic sense is correct about what the other person has said and what feelings the other person is expressing. Research shows that even helping professionals significantly overestimate their empathetic capacity to discern the needs of their clients. Once again, caution is in order about what we naturally take to

36. I regard Scarboro Missions in Ontario as the leading center for the golden rule movement in world religions: https://www.scarboromissions.ca/. See also Neusner and Chilton, eds., *Golden Rule: Reciprocity*, and *Golden Rule: Analytical Perspectives*.

be our intuitive understanding. It takes training and practice to learn, to test our perceptions of what others say and the feelings they convey.[37]

Moreover, when the other is very different from us, our imagination is less instructive. When the other is familiar, we may err by confusing familiarity with understanding. And a habit of seeing ourselves through the eyes of the dominant social group may be discouraging, especially to minorities. Imagining how others will see our action can help moral reflection, but its greatest usefulness is in helping us clarify our *own* intuition.

Nevertheless, despite its limitations, we have reason to imagine ourselves in the situation of another person. Most of us live with the more-or-less continuous background of self-centeredness that we grew up with. That self-centeredness performs legitimate functions in the evolving creature, but it is destined to be outgrown. Imagining our proposed action from the perspective of another person's situation can awaken sympathy, understanding, moral reason, spiritual insight, and love.

> Whoever practices the golden rule opens himself or herself to a process of change. Letting go of self to identify with a single other individual, or with a third-person perspective on a complex situation, or with a divine perspective, one allows a subtle and gradual transformation to proceed, a transformation with bright hope for the individual and the planet. The rule begins by setting forth the way the self wants to be treated as a standard of conduct; but by placing the other on a par with the self, the rule engages one in approximating a higher perspective from which the kinship of humanity is evident. To pursue this higher perspective is to risk encountering the divine and the realization that every step along the forward path is illumined by the Creator.[38]

Imagining oneself in the other's situation gently displaces our customary self-centeredness. We turn to focus on the other person and their needs. Thus the self-concerned self is decentered, and recentered in self-forgetting identification with the other. If we identify with the other, our own desires are transformed; if we initially desired benefits only for self, we come to desire also the other's good.[39]

37. Hughes et al., "Learning to Use Empathy."

38. Wattles, *Golden Rule*, 183. See also my "Philosophical Reflections on the Golden Rule," in Neusner and Chilton, eds., *Golden Rule: Analytical Perspectives*.

39. Olivier du Roy develops a broad and deep concept of empathy; the transformation of desires is mentioned in the discussion of Louis Lavelle in du Roy, *Règle d'or*, vol. 2, 129.

There is evidence that imagining oneself in the other's *situation*—imagining how one would perceive the world from the other's perspective—is more productive than the emotions of sympathy or pity aroused by the spectacle of the other's *suffering*. In other words, productive involvement sidesteps pity. A high degree of empathy can be associated with a counterproductive level of physiological and psychological arousal.[40] In an extreme case, the individual may experience paralyzing fascination while witnessing a crime or panic at the scene of a horrible accident. In less extreme cases, the sense of "*I ought* to do something—what am I going to do?" can shift our focus from the urgent situation to our own need to measure up. Subjects who report feeling very upset by witnessing another's suffering often do little to help; and when they do help, they often appear to be motivated more by desire for personal relief than by concern for the one suffering. These more egoistical "altruists" tend to be compliant and nonassertive.[41]

Finally, we all have love inside of us that may get imprisoned by self-consciousness or by some other obstacle. The decision to move toward another person in empathy and imagination can activate love's self-forgetting flood, an identification with the other that is not emotional but spiritual.[42]

40. These problems regarding the psychology of helping others are discussed in my *Golden Rule*, 118–20. "Arousal" is a term that covers many phenomena. Arousal can be produced by extraneous environmental factors that impede altruism. It is not difficult to guess the effect of heightened pedestrian and traffic flow, abundance of visual stimuli, and a constantly high noise level on altruistic behavior. Nor will we be surprised at the following report:

[Princeton Theological Seminary students were] asked to prepare and deliver a short talk on the parable of the Good Samaritan and then to deliver their talks in another building, requiring a short walk between campus buildings. Darley and Batson used the walk as an analogue of the road between Jerusalem and Jericho, and to complete the scenario, positioned a student confederate along the way who was slumped over, shabbily dressed, coughing and groaning. Darley and Batson wanted to see how much the students would help the "victim." The factor that made a large difference in helping behavior was the time pressure put on the subjects. Quoted from James Rest in Wattles, *Golden Rule*, 224–25.

But arousal may also connote the positive mobilization of one's powers stimulated by a good mood. People who feel good as the result of succeeding at a task, thinking happy thoughts, reading "elation" statements, receiving unexpected gifts, or finding money, subsequently show increased altruism. See Rosenhan, "Attention and Altruism."

41. See, e.g., Batson et al., "Reactions to others' distress."

42. The best book I know on the golden rule practice of empathetically putting yourself in the position of others brings together neuroscience, ethology, psychology, humble and gripping autobiographical narratives, moving stories of friends and neighbors, and a generous supply of quotes and biographical bits from various religious traditions with a gentle emphasis on Buddhism: Barasch, *Compassionate Life*.

Most of the time, the power in the golden rule is quiet and undramatic. The rule has no monopoly on this power; but this is the power we need in order to face and solve serious ethical problems. This power is greater than our own; personal decision must be complemented by something from beyond or within. This power is a participation in the goodness of God.[43]

A dilemma for an ethics centered on the will of God

How do we know whether or not a particular action is right? One answer is that an action is right if and only if it is the will of God. But this answer is challenged today by a classic dilemma. The original version is found in Plato's *Euthyphro* where Socrates criticizes a form of religious thinking that falls far short of a mature religious ethics. A dilemma presents us with a forced choice between two horns, neither of which is acceptable. The alleged defeater for a will-of-God–centered ethics comes in the form of a question: *Is an action right because God wills it, or does God will it because it is right?*

If we take the first option, then an objection arises: "What if God wills an atrocity?" In the modern discussion of this dilemma, the first option— that an action is right simply because God wills it—has been interpreted to imply the danger that to regard the will of God as the criterion of what is right and good could lead us to disregard moral reason in our search for moral guidance. The danger is real. Various books that have been used as reliable sources of information about God or the gods have sometimes portrayed questionable actions as being commanded by higher beings; and people do sometimes neglect moral reason in their quest for the will of God. When Euthyphro defined the good as whatever the gods command, Socrates pointed out that in Homer they don't always agree. Kierkegaard's famous "teleological suspension of the ethical" is a strategy that can be used to block moral reason from playing a role in the assessment of religious experience.[44]

---

43. The golden rule assumes a deep equality between agent and recipient, but in human affairs there is often a marked asymmetry of power. The spiritual golden rule obliges the strong to exercise power with love and mercy, and it obliges weaker persons to connect with the power of God so that, as the situation calls for it, they can stand up for justice.

44. Kierkegaard, *Fear and Trembling*, 54–67. What Kierkegaard does show, in my opinion, is that moral reason cannot be regarded by someone who believes in God as sufficient ground for making a serious moral decision. I believe that an answer to prayer does not overturn moral reason at its best; but it does often raise our own moral thinking to a greater fullness, reorient it, enhance it, and add higher meaning and value

If we reply that God is good and would never will an atrocity, we are appealing to ideas of divine goodness that go beyond the seemingly arbitrary will-of-God criterion implied in the first option. So we might prefer to take the second option to the dilemma question and say that God wills an action because it is right. But then another objection arises: if God always wills what is right, then God must have a standard or pattern or criterion that he is following—which seems to subordinate God to whatever he is following. Moreover, if the criterion has been revealed—for example, in the golden rule or the law of love for the neighbor—then we could simply apply that criterion by ourselves, and we would have no need of God. The two horns of the dilemma allegedly show that, in ethics, religion is either dangerous or superfluous. But the second horn of the dilemma misleadingly assumes that we can fully understand and apply the love command or the golden rule without divine aid. A mature religious perspective can affirm that God's goodness as an expression of who he is and that our good requires that we increasingly come into closer relationship with him.

Sometimes an ethics centered on the will of God is challenged by an objection about how difficult it is to find the will of God. This book can be read as an answer to that question. We can affirm that divine principles of fairness and love are stepping stones to progressive participation in the universal family. If we are infinitely loved sons and daughters of a true, beautiful, and good God, whose will can be progressively known if we persist in every available method of sharpening our moral and spiritual intuition, then religion and ethics require each other in order to flourish.

Any proposed definition of "right" or "good" can be criticized, and objections can be raised to any criterion for sound moral judgment. The real question, then, is whether a particular ethical theory orients inquiry in a helpful way. I believe that an action is right if and only if it is the will of God, and that understanding divine truth, beauty, and goodness, and using moral reason in preparation for prayer, is an excellent path of inquiry to discover that will. Our moral reason is fallible, and so is our spiritual discernment. And it is precisely our privilege and challenge to evolve by divine aid as we do our best with these imperfections. *That* is the will of God.

Moral wisdom and the planet's problems: The tip of the iceberg

As moral reason develops moral wisdom, we apply the moral lessons of person-to-person relationships to the ethics of social systems comprising

---

to the decision so as to transform the experience of moral living.

three or more persons.[45] Sooner or later, after continuing to learn lessons the hard way, humankind will turn to the work of reorganizing its institutions. As a start, we will do better at protecting the environment; society will strengthen family life as well as individual self-realization; economic life will increasingly balance the profit motive by the service motive; and political life will pursue the good of the planet as well as the interests of the nation. An extensive and encouraging answer to the despairing question "What can one person do?" is given in a book by Jared Diamond describing how various societies in history rose (or failed to rise) to the challenge of making the great decisions that would allow them to avoid ecological collapse.[46]

One of our greatest social problems is to combine recognition of the eternal truth of our spiritual equality as human beings in the family of God with realism about the empirical facts of our inequalities as groups. The spiritual and humane approach needed to address this topic can be found in the 1903 African American classic by W. E. B. Du Bois, *The Souls of Black Folk*. Du Bois earned a Harvard PhD and did additional study in Germany before he returned to the United States to do research, writing, teaching, and organizational leadership. As an interdisciplinary work of history and sociology, this book combines empirical studies of individuals, cities, counties, institutions, races, and a nation by means of biography, quantitative studies, and "ideal types"—descriptions that highlight typical features in groups.[47]

45. The significance of this distinction is brought home in Sartre, *No Exit*, which portrays the devastating way that each person in a group of three can interrupt the relationship that arises between the other two. Levinas in "Peace and Proximity" traces a path from the relation to the Other to a group that includes a third person, and shows steps toward a cosmopolitan world order. Levinas's condensed thinking portrays biblical proximity—neighborliness— as requiring Greek objectivity, truth, and knowledge. With the presence of the third, justice enters the scene and becomes the foundation of consciousness; in the resulting social order, philosophy akin to the wisdom of love is needed.

46. Diamond's dozens of ideas about what one person can do include finding a group to join and writing letters of appreciation to those who are doing a good job. See Diamond, *Collapse*, 556–60.

47. "Ideal types" is a term linked to sociologist Max Weber, whose lectures Du Bois heard during his time in Germany. The term names a way of describing a group, and by no means does it imply idealizing the group; rather such a description is like a statistical generalization without the mathematics; it is a simplified sketch of a group in terms of some of its prominent features. It is common to use such descriptions when contrasting generations, e.g., millennials and baby boomers; but they are avoided in some other areas due to the danger of supporting abusive stereotypes. Plato used them in one way toward the end of the *Republic*; Jesus used them in another way during his open warfare with the religious leaders; Marx used them; Maurice Merleau-Ponty defended them in

The book portrays the condition of blacks in their relations with whites in the United States at the beginning of the twentieth century. It sets the stage with the story of the era of Reconstruction after the US Civil War, when former slaves, newly freed, struggled to make their way. With great learning and poetic and religious sensitivity, Du Bois administers prophetic moral clarity and warning along with universal compassion, qualified generalizations, and nuanced understanding of individuals in his call to awaken brotherhood. His uncommon fairness in recognizing the many-sidedness of issues does not keep him from taking clear positions. He looks forward, lucid about the slowness of most historical process, offering a vivid portrait of ideals and a core agenda for progress. He criticized success-oriented education and exalted what he regarded as the real goals of education: truth, beauty, and goodness.[48]

Du Bois criticized the separation of blacks from whites in the American South as "so thorough and deep that it absolutely precludes for the present between the races anything like that sympathetic and effective group-training and leadership of the one by the other, such as the American Negro and all backward peoples must have for effectual progress." To tell his story, he avoids simplistic apology or fault finding in favor of empirical honesty.[49]

Du Bois's writing is dialectical. He presents a series of arguments on behalf of blacks in rebuttal to criticisms of their race by "Southern Gentlemen." Then he comments:

> I will not say such arguments are wholly justified,—I will not insist that there is no other side to the shield; but I do say that of the nine millions of Negroes in this nation, there is scarcely one out of the cradle to whom these arguments do not daily present themselves in the guise of terrible truth. I insist that the question of the future is how best to keep these millions from brooding over the wrongs of the past and the difficulties of the present, so that all their energies may be bent toward a cheerful striving and co-operation with their white neighbors toward a larger, juster, and fuller future.[50]

"The Crisis of the Understanding." In my opinion, Du Bois showed the understanding, courage, and humanity needed to rehabilitate this important form of social description today. He knew that "superior" and "inferior" do not mean good and bad, that civilizational differences do not impair spiritual equality, and that right responses to racial and other differences can lead to a much better world.

48. Du Bois, *Souls of Black Folk*, 417; cf. 476.

49. Ibid., 429.

50. Ibid., 436–37.

Conditions have changed since 1903, and today's excellent descriptions of these groups would differ; but the virtues visible in Du Bois's classic are needed as much as ever. If he were alive today, I believe he would recognize that Jesus' core teachings, shared by many religions, not only address the spiritual difficulties of various groups of people; he would also recognize that these difficulties are among the root causes of our ecological, social, economic, and political problems.

An example of the kind of network for social uplift that gives me the most hope is the eleven Breakthrough Schools in Cleveland, whose educational models are based on the KIPP schools and the Uncommon Schools that have proven to be very successful around the country. Each of the Breakthrough Schools uses one of four approaches: one features high discipline, like a military or religious school; another makes extensive use of intergenerational contacts between students and mentors or older people whom the students visit regularly; a third emphasizes citizenship education; and another uses expeditionary education centered on experiential projects in a variety of classes. Breakthrough School students are 97 percent minorities and 87 percent low-income; for 90 percent of their students, the achievement gap between African Americans and nonminority students vanishes. Not only are state-of-the-art educational methods used, but in each school, faculty and administrators cooperate in their chosen educational approach, so that no enlightened instructor with high ideals has to struggle alone against the momentum of a failed educational system. And parents are enlisted in the effort.[51]

Inspiring ourselves with the best that individuals, groups, and organizations are doing motivates hope that is not overwhelmed by the worst that people deal with. One of the great service organizations on the planet, the Tzu Chi Foundation, was collecting funds after the Nepal earthquake of May 12, 2015; and members were handing donors a card with a lovely photo of plants in the sunlight and a quote from Dharma Master Chen Yen: "If we work with a joyful heart, no matter how tiring and demanding the task is,

51. Breakthrough Schools are K–8, tuition-free, nonprofit public charter schools that persist through many legal financial inequities to serve students; they do not have selection criteria for the students they admit. By the standards of the 2013–14 Ohio Achievement Assessments, Breakthrough Schools surpassed the average of Cleveland and Ohio schools in student growth. Receiving only two-thirds of the money that public schools receive, they rely on foundations, corporations, and individuals to make up the difference. https://www.breakthroughschools.org/. In Ohio, on the tests established for grades three through eight by the federal program, No Child Left Behind, 75 percent of all students pass, but only 45 percent of African Americans pass. For 90 percent of Breakthrough students, that difference vanishes.

we will be rewarded with a sense of bliss and joy." The spirit of loving and compassionate service knows no boundaries.

Despite the best efforts of individuals and groups, it is understandable that many people see the world as going downhill short-term and long-term. To address discouragement, we need to face a question long discussed in philosophy, one that arises especially when disaster strikes.

The facts of suffering and evil and the truths of God's goodness

When something terrible happens, it is common to ask, "Why me?" or "What did he do to deserve something like that?" or to say, "All her life she was so good to people, and look what happened to her." Whoever rejoices in the beauty and goodness of truth also needs to deal with the shock of facts that are ugly and cruel. The question "Why?" mingles a cry of unknowing with complaint and doubt. We have an instinct for justice and fairness. We understand when destructive persons harvest the bitter consequences of their actions, but some persons suffer far beyond what they deserve. Some people react to terrible events by denying God's existence or goodness; others turn to religion's profound resources.

To justify injustice insults the victims. Nothing of what is said here denies the fact of evil in finite, mortal experience. For many people, life is, in the words of Thomas Hobbes, "solitary, poor, nasty, brutish, and short"; many know cruel blows, monotony, cataclysms, galling corruption, complacent greed, culture wars and clashes of civilizations, physical and verbal abuse, agonizing disease, bad religion, sophistic philosophy, misleading science, environmental pollution, anti-art, ethnic antagonisms, overwhelming complexity of modern life, gross economic inequities, and war.

For all that, life in our world is not, on the whole, a pool of misery, despite the fact that commercial media would go out of business if they published too much good news. On balance, there is much to be thankful for; and everyone who finds a constructive way to deal with the most distressing obstacles in his or her path gains leverage in bringing a better day closer.

To respond to suffering with simplistic answers can discount the reality of the other's pain and falsify the mystery of the Creator's plan. Silent companionship and compassionate listening are often the best we can offer. I would normally assume that philosophical ideas about the problem of evil are not what one communicates to a person who is in the midst of suffering. But a young friend told me of his saintly mother's longtime anguish over the assaults of a brutal adult son who would break into their home from time to time to steal from his parents. I sent her a version of the following list, and was moved to hear that it helped her profoundly.

Even with the contradictions of pain, suffering, and evil, the following thoughts can bolster faith in an eternally perfect, all-knowing, and all-powerful Creator. None of these ideas by themselves—nor all of them taken together—can bear the entire weight of the problem, but they set forth a perspective that can support prayer for help from the God of unlimited love.

1. The most powerful defense against being overwhelmed by suffering is personal experience of the goodness of God. "Taste and see that the Lord is good."[52] The more deeply we know God, the less likely we are to have our faith shaken by appalling things that are part of this mortal life.

2. We cannot discern how terrible things fit into the eternal wisdom of God's plan for us and our future. "As the heavens are higher than the earth, so [God's] ways are higher than your ways."[53] To acknowledge mystery is an essential part of the total response to suffering, the I-don't-know part of the response. God is the First Cause, but primal causation is beyond our comprehension; science knows only secondary causes. Faith regards God as sovereign, but we cannot trace the outworking of universal law.

3. Not everything is good, but faith can embrace the thought that evil gets recycled. God and those who cooperate with God so labor that all things eventually do work together for good; and we have a responsible part to play in the process.[54] The time frame of the cosmos spans billions of years; humans have walked this planet for, more or less, a million years. Having hurt one another so much, it may take millennia to achieve the practical realization of brotherhood in our world, which will show that we have learned the lessons. If all earthly phenomena are ultimately part of the outworking of a divinely governed evolutionary process, we can make ever-new discoveries that confirm faith in a friendly universe.

4. We should not assume that this world is the best the Creator could do. There is a heaven of eternal perfection where the will of God is done, as well as this evolving realm where human beings are invited into the adventure of becoming perfect. Jesus prayed, "Your will be done on

52. Ps 34:8.
53. Isa 55:9.
54. Rom 8:28.

earth as it is in heaven."[55] Some of the needed healing and justice happens after this life.

5. Natural processes follow their course; accidents and mistakes have their consequences. But an earthquake should not be called an act of God. We live in a realm of everlastingly dependable causal law. It is tempting to take a limited human snapshot of a universal process and to blame God for the suffering highlighted in that snapshot. But this picture does not reflect that truth, beauty, and goodness of the cosmic and divine scale.

6. We bring suffering on ourselves and others by misusing our free will when we violate—deliberately or not—laws of health, sanity, morality, or happiness.

7. Suffering can result from our failure to exercise vigorous, positive attitudes. An athlete who holds back from self-forgetting, totally committed playing because of fear of injury is more likely to be injured.[56]

8. Anxious craving causes suffering.[57]

9. Some suffering is needed to develop a noble character.

10. The powerful will of the far-seeing God upholds the gift of free will to the creature. The possibility of evil is inherent in his choice to make beings that are both free and imperfect. The Creator's purpose is not to "balance good and evil" but to allow us to climb the ladder of goodness by making real choices between potential alternatives. The Creator is not to be blamed for our wrong choices that result in actual evil.

11. It is misleading to think that God gives permission to wrongdoers to do as they please without limits. A human lifetime is over surprisingly quickly, and judgment must be faced.

    Much evil is corrected in this life. God-given moral reason and righteous indignation (as distinguished from anger, which unconsciously contains the seed of murder) rouse responsible people to bring justice to outrageous wrongdoers.[58]

    God goes through everything with us and does not leave us alone. "In all their afflictions he was afflicted."[59]

55. Matt 6:9.

56. Kyle and Hodermarsky, *Object of the Game*.

57. I use "anxious craving" to translate the Buddhist concept of *tanha*—attachment or desire that binds us.

58. Matt 5:21–22a.

59. Isa 63:9 (RSV).

12. Once a minor but painful episode is over—really over—we look back and the suffering no longer feels substantial. If healing can take place on a small scale, it can occur on a large scale, no matter how long it takes. Evil can exist only for a time by being parasitical on realities that are good. Eventually the good will outshine and recycle the evil. "Those who sow in tears shall reap in joy."[60]

In sum, these lines of reasoning offer ways to interpret our experience in the light of a concept of divine purpose being worked out in evolution.

Conclusions

We have watched two inspiring leaders put the truth of the universal family into action with mature decisiveness and pragmatic effectiveness. We have surveyed meanings in the golden rule, glimpsed the ethics of social systems, and considered reasons supporting faith in the goodness of God despite facts that some regard as obstacles to faith. The resulting perspective integrates moral reason with other dimensions of the self. Ethics thus becomes a preparation for doing the will of God.

Once we overcome the resistances to giving ourselves to the service of others, a veil lifts, and the family of God becomes a new reality in our experience. Doing the will of God requires, first, the supreme *desire* to do it. In the light of that desire, it is easier to discern *what* to do. And *how* we carry that out matters greatly and is grounded in *who* we have become, which is the subject of the last chapter.

60. Ps 126:5 (NKJV).

7

"You Shall Be Like a Watered Garden"

Pitirim Sorokin and Character Pervaded by Love

AFTER THE DAYTON ACCORDS of 1995 brought to an end the devastation of Bosnia in the conflict between ethnic and religious groups, Franciscan Friar Ivo Markovic returned to his home from which he had fled as his father and six brothers were being killed. The house had been taken over by others, but he did not contest their appropriation of what was not theirs. His mission focused solely on service. In his now peaceful and partly ruined territory, he began traveling around to assist the clergy of every faith, helping them in material ways so that they could continue their ministries.

Markovic founded the Pontanima Interreligious Choir, composed of Jews, Christians, and Muslims, half of whom were also members of the same distinguished national symphony choir he was already part of in Sarajevo. Pontanima sings religious music expressing each of these traditions and performs not only in concert halls on ordinary days but also on the holidays of the various religions and in their places of worship. They quickly gained a reputation as the best choir in southeastern Europe. After concerts at New York's Lincoln Center and Washington DC's Kennedy Center, they came to Kent State University, where I was teaching at the time, to honor the hometown of Amy Gopp, one of their new members. Their concert included several choral pieces as inspiring as any I have heard.

Halfway through the concert, we made time for questions and answers. It was an extraordinary exchange, but it left me with the conviction that doing things together—as the choir was doing—was far stronger than dialogue. I had gotten to know them a bit, feeling their power as they got off the bus and walked into the church, even though they were tired from the long ride from Washington after being delayed by a winter storm; and when we gathered again for lunch the next day I spoke at length with Markovic. In stalwart character I found them to be the most impressive group of persons I had ever met. One more occasion to ponder the meaning of greatness.

Thus far in this book, we have operated on the premise that we develop virtues by doing the appropriate kinds of activities. As the proverb goes, "Sow an action, reap a habit. Sow a habit, reap a character. Sow a character, reap a destiny." Now we consider a complementary thought: to truly *do* good we must first *be* good. Each of these ideas contains truth. The first one suggests that persons acquire strong character by doing actions that are true, beautiful, and good. The second one hints at the insight that strong character is needed for action to have cosmic leverage.

Focusing on character, this chapter begins with a sketch of the life of Russian revolutionary leader and Harvard sociologist Pitirim Sorokin, whose life of action and study led him to a concept of love that was intimately bound up with truth, beauty, and goodness. The remaining sections set forth a twofold relationship between unified character and the virtues portrayed in the previous chapters. On the one hand, cultivation of intellectual, spiritual, aesthetic, and moral virtues contributes to character. On the other hand, character has a spiritual core—righteousness, the gift of God. For our righteousness to be true, beautiful, and good, God infuses our soul with love. In its simplicity and in its more complex outworkings, love motivates divine living. The way of righteous, loving service is the basis for continuing growth.

Our glimpse of Sorokin emphasizes again what we have seen in previous biographical sketches: excellence is less a product of self-conscious self-cultivation than of self-forgetting engagement with the real. And growth comes gradually and naturally in a process that can take the average person to remarkable heights.

From my journey

I have had plenty of practice in cultivating the soil for growth. I strove for self-mastery over a lustful heart, then for courage; then I became acutely aware of anger, contempt, ugly competitiveness, and intolerance in quick succession until I burst out laughing with the recognition that these were all variations on the theme of pride—failing to give due recognition to my relation with our heavenly Father and to that living spiritual reality that I call the brotherhood of man.

I look forward to being held accountable in the next life for my misdeeds, and to participating in the magnificent outworking of the perfect blend of God's justice and mercy.

In the spiritual core of character, I have not yet reached continuous communion with God; my listening falls short of what I know is possible; and I do not know how far I am from that goal. But I cherish the present, dappled experience as a precious phase of evolution, fully trusting that I will arrive.[1]

Recently I had a vision of truth rolling into our planet like a powerful, gentle, and beautifully curved wave. I plunged in and discovered my center: love. Here is my interpretation of what I saw and felt: The magnitude of the wave is so great that the role I can play in its mission is infinitesimal, and yet it is my duty and privilege to swim with it, adding my physical, intellectual, and spiritual energies. The wave does not come like a tsunami with revolutionary force; its goodness is to bring the truth we can use now, in light of the world's present cultural development. Cosmic wave and human swimmers join in the process of actualizing value in time; and the God of eternity is at the heart of it all.

Sorokin's early formation

The writings of Pitirim Sorokin (1889–1968) reveal him as a great thinker and human being who developed outstanding concepts of love and values. Sorokin's life displays all the components emphasized in this philosophy of living, beginning with a realization of beauty in nature and the arts, truth in religion and the intellectual life, goodness in political activity, and service to a world struggling in transition.

He was born of an Ugro-Finnish mother and a Russian father and grew up in a village near two great rivers and surrounded by a vast forest in northern Russia. The rivers with their "effervescent flow" and "crystal-clear waters" were "bounded by fine sandy beaches, steep hills, fragrant meadows, and trees and bushes growing down to the very edge of their banks." He was enraptured by the tall pine and spruce trees, which "rose like the most wondrous spires ascending to the sky in columns, now silent and mysterious, as though lost in prayer, now roaring and agitated as though fighting their raging enemies.[2] The beauty, sublimity, refreshment, and invigoration

1. The word "dappled" alludes to "Pied Beauty," by Gerard Manley Hopkins: "Glory be to God for dappled things— / For skies of couple-colour as a brinded cow; / For rose-moles all in stipple upon trout that swim; / Fresh-firecoal chestnut-falls; finches' wings; / Landscape plotted and pieced—fold, fallow, and plough; / And áll trádes, their gear and tackle and trim. / All things counter, original, spare, strange; / Whatever is fickle, freckled (who knows how?) / With swift, slow; sweet, sour; adazzle, dim; / He fathers-forth whose beauty is past change: / Praise him."

2. Sorokin, *Long Journey*, 11–12. An excellent, thirty-page autobiography is also

of nature would be essential to Sorokin's balance throughout his life. The time he took to relax, his many outdoor hobbies, and his vacations sustained a rhythm that nourished his creativity. And his physically demanding ventures in the wilderness formed a stepping stone to the fearlessness that he carried into later conflicts. He exemplified both sides of his sociological insight that rural folk tend to be strong in direct experience, and urban people develop excellence in indirect experience.[3]

Sorokin's engagement in the arts showed in his wide appreciation of literature, his cultivated sensitivity to music, and in the trade he learned as a youth from his father: he became highly skilled in "writing" icons, at gilding and silvering parts of Russian Orthodox churches, and in using icons as a basis for making sculptures.

Sorokin's religious formation began among the Komi people, whose customs included practicing religious tolerance, honoring the Ten Commandments and the golden rule, and helping one another. He never joined a religious institution, but he developed solitary methods of communion with God by plunging into the forest for fasting and prayer. He appreciated ascetic disciplines, which he regarded as useful for the few who can thrive on them; and he came to regard the *Yoga Sutras* of Patanjali as the model for similar systems of training practiced in diverse traditions around the world. Later on, he saw the heights of prayer in political prisoners about to be executed or praying for one who had just been shot.

Sorokin's philosophies at each stage of life

As a youth, Sorokin was largely self-educated through extraordinarily wide reading, and during his entire life he was intellectually voracious. His first philosophy was the synthesis that crowned the years of his youth.

> The moral precepts of Christianity, especially of the Sermon on the Mount and the Beatitudes, decisively conditioned my moral values not only in youth but for the rest of my life. . . . Combined with my itinerant way of life and the social life of the Komi people the religious climate of my early age played an important part in the formation of my personality, the integration of my system of values, and the crystallization of my early philosophy. All in all mine was an idealistic world-view in which God and nature, truth, goodness and beauty, religion, science, art, and ethics were all united into one harmonious system. No sharp

available as the lead essay in Allen, ed., *Sorokin in Review*.

3. This finding is reported in Smith, "Sorokin's Rural-Urban Principles," 188–205.

conflict and no inner contradiction between these values as yet marred my peace of mind. Despite material hardship and the sorrows and trials of human life, the world appeared to me a marvelous place in which to live and to strive for life's great values.[4]

The simple and youthful idealism of his first philosophy collapsed from the impact of Sorokin's expanding education at the University of St. Petersburg, which brought him into contact with a broad range of persons with diverse scientific, philosophical, and political views.

As his second philosophy, Sorokin adopted positivism, which offered a science-centered humanism that was optimistic about progressive human evolution. Sorokin's university training centered on sociology; and sociology at that place and time placed empirical studies in the context of a vast, integrative vision. Sorokin's early publications showed such distinction that he was invited to create the first Department of Sociology at the University of St. Petersburg.

By then, Sorokin had already begun his career as a revolutionary leader and organizer in opposition to the Czarist government, which three times imprisoned him.[5] During one period in prison, he was told each day for several weeks that he would be executed the next day. Under this extreme and prolonged stress, he forged a loyalty to values that could not be shaken by threats of death. During the first months after the Russian Revolution overthrew the Czar, Sorokin was chosen as secretary to Prime Minister Kerensky; but then the Bolsheviks plunged Russia into anarchy as they took over the revolution.

After the Bolsheviks overturned Kerensky and took power, they expelled Sorokin from his post at the University of St. Petersburg. In the winter of 1921, his task for the government was to study the mass starvation that resulted from the Bolsheviks' disruption of the country's agriculture. Sorokin writes, "My nervous system, accustomed to many horrors in the years of the Revolution, broke down completely before the spectacle of the actual starvation of millions in my ravaged country. If I came out less an investigator, I do not think I came out less a man, less an enemy of any group of men capable of inflicting such suffering on the human race. . . . The

4. Sorokin, *Long Journey,* 41.

5. Political events in 1904 and 1905 discredited the Czar's regime. These events included the surprising and humiliating defeat of Russia by Japan and a revolution in which Czar Nicholas II agreed to major structural reforms to preserve his regime, despite continuing unrest, which led to the February Revolution of 1917.

memory of what I saw and heard made me absolutely fearless in denounc-
ing the Revolution and the monsters who were devouring Russia."[6]

Sorokin's positivistic, humanistic optimism was shaken by world war
and Bolshevik barbarism.[7] This second philosophical crisis led him to
striving further for a coherent understanding of life's contradictions. His
struggle culminated in his third philosophy. It was the synthesis that served
him to the end of his life—an integration of values into "the Supreme Trinity of Truth, Goodness, and Beauty." "Integralism," he wrote, "has given me
a firm foundation for maintenance of my integrity and has wisely guided
my conduct amidst the bloody debris of the crumbling [materialistic]
civilization."[8] Character and conduct, guided by supreme values, enabled
this leader to preserve his effectiveness in a crisis. Integralism would pervade his scientific work as well.

An integrated philosophy is no substitute for courage, but it does guide
and reinforce it. We learn courage in part by seeing others' courage and
being fortified by it. As a sociology professor during the revolution, Sorokin
taught without fear or favor the truths he had found. Another example was
the refusal by the famous scientist Pavlov of benefits offered to him by the
Communist regime in 1921. Others were equally heroic, refusing to accom-
modate to Communism. Sorokin testified, "Let anyone who seeks moral
heroism turn his eyes to the thousands of people in Russia who, for years,
from day to day, from night to night, despite persecution and temptation,
have steadfastly replied to the Bosheviki: 'Man does not live by bread alone,'
and 'You shall worship the Lord your God, and Him only shall you serve.'"[9]
The moral and spiritual courage of "ordinary" people inspired and upheld
this bold leader.

The conclusion of Sorokin's 1924 *Leaves from a Russian Diary* expresses the attitude that would characterize the rest of his life:

> *Whatever may happen in the future, I know that I have learned*
> *three things which will forever remain convictions of my heart as*
> *well as of my mind. Life, even the hardest life, is the most beauti-*
> *ful, wonderful, and miraculous treasure in the world. Fulfillment*
> *of duty is another beautiful thing, making life happy and giving*

6. Sorokin, *Long Journey*, 189, 191.

7. "Humanism" in this context implies atheism; positivism sets aside religion and
metaphysical philosophy while advocating science as the way to engineer an advanced
civilization.

8. Sorokin, *Long Journey*, 325.

9. Ibid., 183, modifying the translation of the Bible to substitute newer forms, such
as "you shall" for older forms, such as "thou shalt." The quotations may be found in the
New Testament, Matthew 4, verses 4 and 10.

to the soul the unconquerable force to sustain ideals—this is my
second conviction. And my third is that cruelty, hatred, and injus-
tice never can and never will be able to create a mental, moral, or
material millennium. [italics in the original][10]

By age thirty-five, Sorokin had learned to find high value in the most difficult situations and stay resolutely committed to morally engaged living
while never relinquishing hope for a new age and a much better world. After
Sorokin's third incarceration in a Communist prison, Lenin allowed him to
immigrate to Czechoslovakia. He visited the United States to give lectures,
which led to an appointment at the University of Minnesota for six years.
He came to Harvard in 1924 to create a sociology program, remaining there
until his retirement.

Sorokin's vision of history

Sorokin saw the drama of our time as instability and transition: a civilization of egoism and materialism is subverting itself, while a new civilization is beginning to emerge to integrate material values with rational and
spiritual values. He predicted World War II and gave this expression to his
"prophetic sociology" in 1941: "Sensate values will become still more relative and atomistic until they are ground into dust devoid of any universal
recognition and binding power. The boundary line between the true and
false, the right and wrong, and beautiful and ugly, positive and negative
values, will be obliterated increasingly until mental, moral, aesthetic, and
social anarchy reigns supreme."[11]

By contrast, in the emerging civilization, spiritual values will prevail
and integrate all other values. Love will sponsor the coming age of truth,
beauty, and goodness. To usher in the better age, we need a general increase
of altruism and leadership that draws on the creativity of the inner life.[12]

The program that Sorokin worked out for civilizational transformation begins with the transformation of the individual, to be followed by
institutional changes, and finally by reaching out to engage an increasing
proportion of the world's population in the transformation.[13] The transfor-

10. Ibid., 197.

11. Quoted in Hillery Jr. et al., "Empirical Assessment," 172. The term "prophetic
sociology" was coined by Johnston, in *Intellectual Biography*.

12. We have already seen Sorokin's hope for a better future. My own view is that the
integration he predicts will emerge only in the wake of the moral and spiritual renaissance that he calls for.

13. Sorokin, *Reconstruction of Humanity*, 233–36. Sorokin's historical reasons

mation of the individual changes the center of gravity from egoistic and material interests to the dominion of love. Sorokin saw creative intuition and altruistic activity as being inspired from beyond the conscious mind.

Sorokin's idealism recognized the need for creative geniuses and heroes of love, but his plan for planetary transformation did not depend on everyone becoming a hero. If ordinary people join the ranks of good neighbors, refuse to do violence to others, and organize themselves more intelligently, they will contribute massively to a tremendous forward step. A summary of his 1950 study of American good neighbors clarifies the standard. "Most good neighbors were motivated by the Golden Rule and a love of humanity. For them altruism came from religion, parents, and family. . . . Good neighbors were also regular participants in voluntary organizations, and 86 percent belonged to between one and five such groups."[14]

Sorokin on love and values

Sorokin developed an enhanced concept of God as love. "On the religious plane love is identified with God, the highest value in the Christian and other great religions. . . . 'God is love and he that dwells in love dwells in God and God in him,' says the New Testament. . . . [As qualitative and quantitative infinity, love] cannot be defined by any words or concepts; at best these can be only symbolic indicators of the infinite cosmos of love."[15] Sorokin's appreciation of love kept his mysticism in touch with a personalist concept of God.

Sorokin's studies taught him an ordered and universal scale of values:

> The scale of values of all genuine religions unanimously puts at the top the supreme value of the Infinite Manifold itself (God, Brahman, Tao, the Holy, the Sacred), and then, in descending order, the highest values of truth, goodness, and beauty, their inferior and less pure varieties, and finally the sensory and sensate values. Likewise, the moral commandments of all genuine religions are fundamentally identical. Their ethics is the ethics of unbounded love of man for God, for his fellow men, for all living creatures, and for the entire universe.[16]

---

supporting hope for a spiritual renaissance were presented in chapter 1.

14. Johnston, *Intellectual Biography*, 183.

15. Sorokin, *Ways and Power of Love*, 5, changing "dwelleth" to "dwells." I make similar changes elsewhere in citing Sorokin's quotations from the Bible.

16. Sorokin, *Reconstruction of Humanity*, 155.

Sorokin did well to recognize truth, beauty, and goodness as divine qualities while also recognizing their mixed expressions on other levels.

Next, Sorokin recognized essential interconnections of truth, beauty, and goodness; and he also saw love functioning in ways akin to how other values function. "Love is viewed as the essence of goodness inseparable from truth and beauty. All three are unified aspects of the Absolute Value or God. Real goodness is always true and beautiful; pure truth is always good and beautiful; and genuine beauty is invariably true and good."[17] "Love is, side by side with truth and beauty, one of the highest forms of a *unifying, integrating, harmonizing, creative energy or power.*"[18]

The ethical aspect of love Sorokin identified with goodness itself. "As a creative energy of goodness, love . . . raises man as a biological organism to the level of divinity, infinitely enriches the human self, and empowers humanity with a mastery over the inorganic, organic, and sociocultural forces, up to the potential rescue of an individual and mankind from even biological death."[19] Among the trio of main values, Sorokin places the greatest emphasis on goodness, which he most closely identifies with love.

Once he had penetrated into the interior of love and these great values, there was no end to fresh discoveries of the relations between them:

> *Love is the experience that annuls our individual loneliness*; fills the emptiness of our isolation with the richest values; breaks and transcends the narrow walls of our little egos; makes us co-participants in the highest life of humanity and in the whole cosmos; expands our true individuality to the immeasurable boundaries of the universe. . . . Making us full-fledged co-participants in the lives of others, love infinitely enriches our lives by the greatest and noblest values of all humanity. In this sense it fills us with *knowledge*, because the co-participation and co-experience in the richest experience of all the generations of humanity—rather than only in one's pitifully poor individual experience—is the most efficient method of learning and the most fruitful way to truth and knowledge. In this sense the love experience leads to a true cognition and *love becomes truth*. . . .
>
> *Love beautifies our life* because the love experience is beautiful by its very nature and beautifies the whole universe. To love anything or anybody means literally to immortalize the mortal, to ennoble the ignoble, to uplift the low, to beautify the ugly.

17. Sorokin, *Ways and Power of Love*, 6.

18. Ibid.

19. Ibid.

Anything that one looks at through loving eyes becomes "love-ly," that is, beautiful.

By its very nature *love is goodness itself*; therefore *it makes our life noble and good. Love experience means freedom at its loftiest.* To love anything is to act freely, without compulsion or coercion. And vice versa: to be free means to do what one loves to do. In this sense, *love and true freedom are synonyms; love is the loftiest form of freedom.* Compulsion and coercion are the negation of love. Where there is love there is no coercion; where there is coercion there is no love. And the greater the love the greater the freedom. . . . The love experience is marked further by a "feeling" of *fearlessness and power.* . . . A loving mother does not hesitate to throw herself against any danger menacing her child; a loving person does not hesitate to lay down his life—is not afraid even of death—saving the loved ones. Fear comes from a selfish idea of cutting one's self off from the universe. The smaller and the more selfish I make myself, the more is my fear. . . . *The most effective and most accessible way to acquire the maximum of constructive power is to love truly and wisely.*[20]

Love's knowing of other persons gives truth; love's elevating our perspective on anything whatsoever brings beauty; love's fearlessness and freedom empower goodness.

Sorokin's scientific perspective complements the idea of love as a gift of God. Sociologically speaking, love does not simply descend from above; it needs to be maintained by groups with "the necessary minimum of solidarity, co-operation, good will, and peaceful relations among their members: in the family, community, state, nation, labor union, political party, or religious group. Love solidarity and peaceful relationships in any group do not fall by themselves from heaven."[21] According to Sorokin, as a result of our participation in different social groups, the self contains a variety of clusters of meanings and values, beliefs, norms, and habits.[22] This observation gives us all the more reason to welcome love as a unifier of human character.

Sorokin's broad and integrated concept of love made it accessible to scientific research. He proposed the study of love energy in its production, accumulation, and distribution. He wrote of five dimensions of love.

- Intensity, or the degree to which one's full energies are mobilized

- Breadth of inclusiveness toward all of humankind

20. Ibid., 11–13.
21. Ibid., 36 (cf. 24f).
22. Ibid., 90.

- Durability, from a moment to a lifetime

- Purity or the degree of admixture of base motives

- Adequacy in the subject (the love must not be unwise, misled, igno-
  rant, or blind) and effectiveness in bringing good to the recipient

And he did not claim that his survey was complete: "The religious,
ethical, ontological, physical, biological, psychological, and social phases of
love do not exhaust it; on the contrary, they show the infinite richness of
this participant in the Absolute."[23] His sense of the infinity of divine love
prevented him from attempting to construct a complete or formal system
that would preempt new discoveries.

One more biographical essential qualifies Sorokin to represent character achievement. Until late in life, his response to what he found intoler-
able was fearless denunciation; but eventually love dominated his character,
enabling him to let certain things go and respond to other things constructively. For example, his autobiography, published five years before his death,
sets aside his notorious polemics against his Harvard colleagues and others.
He shows himself to be more than a scholar in learning his own lessons of
transformation.

Sorokin's writings form an integral part of his unified life, which
stands as a refutation of the criticism of love as weak, eroticized, narrowly
Christian, or one-sided. The prominent virtues we see in the character of
Sorokin are these.

- Integration of the seven main phases of truth, beauty, and goodness, in
  a balance of science and spirituality, realism and idealism

- Wholeheartedness, intensity, and stamina—sustainable heroism

- Unceasing commitment to excellence

- Faith in God

- A character dominated by love

Although Sorokin's sweeping generalizations about religions and civilizations do not fit the precision of today's scholarship, his insights remain
powerful; and we may be moved by him without agreeing with his every

23. I generally use *wholeheartedness* rather than Sorokin's word *intensity* to avoid
connoting pathological extremes. I reserve the word *love* for potentially mutual relations between persons, whereas Sorokin also uses it for what I call identification with
cosmic reality. And Sorokin's concept of adequacy is twofold: the subject is more or less
adequate in loving, and the recipient is more or less benefited as a result of the subject's
action. See ibid., 13, 15–36.

step. For love to become real, we do not need perfect concepts or perfect selves.

Natural and gradual character growth: The individual supported by society

The long-range perspective of spiritual wisdom relaxes the anxious and driven pursuit of idealistic goals. Most of the time, growth is gradual. Discoveries and decisions are frequent, but sudden leaps forward in personal growth are rare. In leading persons through six-week projects, I repeatedly insist that the goal is not growth, which has its own rhythm and occurs in its own time. The goal is to *cultivate the soil* for growth. Mencius called for a mean between extremes, and he satirized misguided self-cultivation in this story of a farmer.

> You must work at [rightness] and never let it out of your mind. At the same time, while you must never let it out of your mind, you must not forcibly help it grow either. You must not be like the man from Sung. There was a man from Sung who pulled at his rice plants because he was worried about their failure to grow. Having done so, he went on his way home, not realizing what he had done. "I am worn out today," said he to his family. "I have been helping the rice plants to grow." His son rushed out to take a look and there the plants were, all shrivelled up. There are few in the world who can resist the urge to help their rice plants grow. There are some who leave the plants unattended, thinking that nothing they can do will be of any use. They are the people who do not even bother to weed. There are others who help the plants grow. They are the people who pull at them. Not only do they fail to help them but they do the plants positive harm.[24]

We all need to keep growing. It is impossible to cease efforts to grow and simply coast, holding on to a certain level of attainment. We either go forward or backward; and the next segment of our path may require a steep climb and a good working relationship with our spirit guide in order to gain the true success that awaits us. But trying too hard to grow is counterproductive. In this story, to weed means to gently and patiently uproot our bad habits, continuing to make course corrections as we go. To pull on the plants means compulsively examining our failures and weaknesses; it implies trying to build character through a regime of behavioral self-control in which

24. Mencius, *Mencius*, 2A2, 78.

we are so focused on self that we miss the faith, trust, patience, and love that nourish genuine growth.[25]

Emphasis on character achievement has been one of the great strengths of Confucianism. A traditional Confucian teaching says that "if there is righteousness in the heart, there will be harmony in the home; if there is harmony in the home, the nation will be well-governed; if the nation is well-governed, there will be peace in the world."[26] This sequence represents the primary emphasis for a philosophy of living; but the complementary truth is that goodness in society helps individuals to manifest good character. Indeed, another traditional strength of Confucianism has been its emphasis on proper relationships in family and society.

Cleveland's Breakthrough Schools do a good job of supporting character growth. On my first visit to a school in this network, I was amazed by the outstanding behavioral habits demonstrated by three classes of eighth graders. I thought to myself, "In my projects at Kent State, breakthroughs are common in three to six weeks, but habit formation requires far more than that. This school is doing an awesome job." These students in their early teens focused on me and the other visiting speakers *continuously*; I had never seen such attention in any other audience. When asked for responses to a question, their spirit of participation was superior on average to that of my college students.

The school, E-Prep Academy's Woodland Hills Campus, does not overemphasize virtues. Their approach is not heavy handed, but they establish an unmistakable atmosphere of excellence, and they do insist on certain behaviors. Students rate themselves twice a year on a scale of 1 (very unlike me) to 5 (very like me) on a cluster of virtues: zest, self-control in schoolwork, self-control in interpersonal behavior, gratitude, curiosity, optimism, grit, and social intelligence. The virtues are defined in ways that express principles or rules, behavior patterns. For example, zest is defined by three behavior patterns: "actively participates," "shows enthusiasm," and "approaches new situations with excitement and energy." Gratitude includes "notices when others need help" and "does something nice for someone else

25. Character is not the product of piecing together disjointed activities—physical training, intellectual development, and spiritual exercises—at various times during the day. Rather these activities go best when all dimensions of the personality are fully engaged in each one.

For a historical account of the development from self-conscious, awkward, unbeautiful conformity to social-ethical norms to the beautiful moral spontaneity of genuine goodness, see "A Confucian Path from Conscientiousness to Spontaneity" in my *Golden Rule*, 15–26.

26. The sequence of rectification proceeding from the individual to the family, nation, and world comes from the very brief Confucian classic titled *The Great Learning*.

as a means of saying thank you." Optimism includes "believes that effort will improve the future," "when bad things happen, thinks about what could make it better next time," "stays motivated even when things don't go well," and "believes you can improve on things you're not good at."[27]

The best example I know of world-class character manifest in a society was discovered by Navy SEAL Marcus Luttrell on a mission that ended in a harrowing ambush by Taliban fighters in which his three comrades were killed; he survived thanks to the extraordinarily brave and resourceful generosity of Muslim villagers in a remote area of Afghanistan. When I heard Luttrell tell his story, it made sense to me in the light of a book about Albanian Muslims who rescued Jews during World War II. These Albanians had a tradition of honor that they held as individuals, families, and communities; it was part of their sense of national and religious identity. Their code includes the concept of *besa*, which requires a fully generous response to anyone who comes to them in serious need. They sought no recognition and would take no money from those they sheltered.

I believe it is worthwhile to read some excerpts from the statements made by the rescuers. The first is by Beqir Qoghja.

> My father owned a general store with food provisions. It was the only store of its kind for many miles around. One day a German transport rolled by with 19 Albanian prisoners on their way to hard labor, and one Jew who was to be shot. My father spoke excellent German and invited the Nazis into his store and offered them food and wine. He plied them with wine until they became drunk. Meanwhile he hid a note in a piece of melon and gave it to the young Jew. It instructed him to jump out and flee into the woods to a designated place. The Nazis were furious over the escape, but my father claimed innocence. They brought my father into the village and lined him up against a wall to extract information about where the Jew was hiding. Four times they put a gun to his head. They came back and threatened to burn the village down if my father didn't confess. My father held out, and they finally left.

---

27. The E-Prep, Village Academy Alumni Character Strengths and Character Growth Card is adapted from the KIPP Character Report Card; see www.breakthroughschools.org and www.kipp.org. Each of the four different educational models in the Breakthrough network has its own approach to educating the whole child—intellectually, emotionally, and socially. One school focuses on virtues, another on values, a third on beliefs; but they all promote grit, responsibility, and a sense of purpose.

Medi Frasheri, the prime minister of Albania at that time, gave a secret order: "All Jewish children will sleep with your children, all will eat the same food, all will live as one family."

Nadire Proseku: "We saw the Jews as brothers. As religious but liberal Muslims, we were only doing our duty. Now my grandson is an evangelical Christian. This is fine with my son and me. There is only one God."

Orhan Frasheri: "For eighteen months we all lived as brothers and participated in all the celebrations, both Muslim and Jewish."

Isak Kormaku: "It is in the Koran that in the name of God we help all humans."

Petrit Kika: "We are secular Muslims. We were never afraid. It was both a great pleasure and an honor to shelter the Jews. We were old friends. It is our tradition."

Sazan Hoxha: "My father's words to those he took in: 'Now we are one family. You won't suffer any evil. My sons and I will defend you against peril at the cost of our lives.'"

Aferdita Gjergjani: "Sara and I were like sisters. . . . I didn't have enough milk for my son—Sara nursed both. It is an Albanian tradition that when the same woman feeds two babies, they become brother and sister. . . . I was once asked if I mind that a Jewish mother had fed my baby. I answered, 'Jews are God's people like us.'"

Agim Sinani, when asked why his family sheltered the Jews: "We had the biggest house in the village. Any villager would have done the same. . . . We did nothing special. We did what any Albanian would do. We are all human."

Agim Islam Trimi: We Shengjergj villagers have big hearts. Our village is a righteous Muslim village. We believe that to do good is to get good."

Kasein Jakup Kocerri: "The Jews and Muslims of Albania are cousins. . . . I salute all the Jews. . . . To save a life is to go to Paradise."

Drita Veseli: When my husband was asked about the possibility of Albanians reporting the presence of Jews to the Germans, my husband said that if an Albanian did this he would disgrace his village and his family. At a minimum, his home would be destroyed and his family banished. . . . Our home is first God's house, second our guest's house, and third our family's house."[28]

---

28. Gershman, *Besa*, 94, 4, 16, 20, 32, 36, 62, 72, 80, 84, 70, and 74. The book consists of photos of individuals, couples, and families whom he interviewed, accompanied by brief statements they made in explanation of their service. Marcus Luttrell's story is portrayed in the book and film *Lone Survivor*.

Philosophical ideals of virtue and the spiritual gift of righteousness

Striving for growth reaches toward an ideal, an often vague sense of completeness or wholeness. Aristotle conceived of the fulfillment of one's purpose as being analogous to the way an acorn fulfills its purpose by becoming a mature oak tree. The word *teleion*, "perfect," was used to denote this achievement. Aristotle defined a virtue as a trustworthy habit of acting on a firm and constant disposition to do the right thing in the right way in a specific type of situation. For example, courage is the virtue of reliably responding excellently to situations of fear, pain, and danger. Self-mastery regarding pleasure ("temperance") requires moderation or restraint when the opportunity for self-indulgence arises—a person who has the virtue no longer struggles with desires that are strong and base. Among the social virtues, justice involves taking no more than one's proper share—and, we might add, *contributing* one's proper share.

According to Aristotle, deficiencies and excesses arise when we lack the appropriate disposition or fail to act on it, or when we deploy one particular strength when the situation calls for a different one; and it takes good judgment to consistently hit the mean between these extremes. We acquire a virtue by doing the right thing in the right way in the relevant type of situation until we *have it*—a habit that has become second nature. Thus the exercise of moral virtues requires practical wisdom (involving keen deliberation), the virtue that unites and contains them all. Aristotle also recognized intellectual and technical virtues of thinking and of making any type of product, from bricks to paintings. His ideal of perfection comprised the complete fulfillment of one's growth potentials.

Despite the nobility of Aristotle's ideals, it is understandable that the word *virtues* is generally well received among philosophers, theologians, religious believers, and older people, while many others dislike the term and find it stuffy, laden with obsolete constraints; and they prefer the term *strengths*. As it often happens, the implied critique is partly insightful, partly not. In my view, Aristotle's approach emphasizing a cluster of self-cultivated virtues can be modified in two ways. First, ongoing striving toward remote ideals of perfection can be regarded as completed in heaven. Second, efforts for continued growth can be remotivated by the spiritual transformation of one's character as a whole.

On the surface, Jesus' teaching is akin to Aristotle's when he says, "Be you perfect, even as your Father in heaven is perfect."[29] Jesus' teaching is very

29. Lev 19:2 and Matt 5:48. We can narrow the gap between Jesus and Aristotle in

different, but it takes some work to understand it. The quest for perfection gets a bad reputation because people associate it with perfectionism, which is narrow, compulsive, and counterproductive. And the word *righteousness* also has some unbeautiful connotations; it can imply a harsh, judgmental, aggressive, hostile, prideful, and moralistic attitude. But righteousness in its wholeness is none of these.

Jesus' concept of perfection was not static, and he never gave it an outward, behavioral definition. But I believe that his concept included a sense of a perfection that is possible in this life—perfection-as-righteousness. That humanly attainable achievement begins by responding to God's call with a wholehearted commitment to the will and way of God. That level of living in grace includes spiritual self-mastery, which liberates one from struggling with unruly desire, fear, or pride. When coupled with persistent prayer, dedication to the will of God sooner or later leads to soul-satisfying integration and harmony.

In *The Golden Rule*, addressing the question of whether the teachings of Jesus in his Sermon on the Mount presented an unrealistically high standard, I set forth an interpretation that makes sense of the idea that Jesus expected his apostles to live according to a higher standard than what was expected of the average believer or disciple.

> The call to be perfect [*teleios*] is addressed to all, not in the sense that apostles or disciples are expected to have completed their personal growth, but in the sense that every believer is expected to be wholehearted. As Joachim Jeremias clarifies, we need not "take *teleios* in a perfectionist sense; rather, Matthew will have understood *teleios* in the sense of the Old Testament *tamim* ('intact,' 'undivided') as the designation of who belongs to God with the totality of his life." "You cannot serve God and wealth." Abandoning anxiety, the disciple is to "strive first for the kingdom and his righteousness," and is to trust God for other essentials.
>
> The specific constraints on the apostles must of course not be substituted for the gospel message itself and taken as legalistic requirements for anyone seeking to enter the kingdom . . . . Jesus' eschatological presence sets up a gravitational attraction that strictly holds the apostles in a close orbit; partly similar

---

three steps: (1) recall that in *Nichomachean Ethics* X.6–7, Aristotle sets forth the highest happiness as contemplative and as bringing friendship with the gods; (2) abandon Aristotle's separation of theoretical and practical virtue; and (3) reinterpret Aristotle's insistence that virtuous conduct is intrinsically enjoyable: Aristotle did not consciously realize that his enjoyment of eternal and divine truth and his friendship with God were nourishing his own enjoyment of virtuous action.

requirements hold for the seventy who were also commissioned to preach the gospel; and other disciples and the crowds are accelerated into its vortex of righteousness. The presence of Jesus generates a movement of desire and commitment to live like him: the core of his new community is to share his specific requirements, while teachings such as the golden rule function spiritually to help a morally diverse humanity to live in an increasingly God-like way.[30]

The desire for wholeness, for perfection in that sense, is widespread; and religious faith routes our quest to fulfill that desire through the relationship with God. The divine gift of perfection-as-righteousness does not replace the long quest for perfection.

The gift of perfection-as-righteousness is a *connection* with God that brings spiritual truth, beauty, and goodness into our thinking, feeling, and doing. It does not impart knowledge or wisdom; nor does it exempt a person from the need for moral and ethical reflection. And the humbling wonder of it all is that this participation in divinity can be enjoyed by mortals who remain cognitively, emotionally, and behaviorally imperfect.

Righteousness flourishes on the basis of meaningful integration of scientific and spiritual living; emotional maturity and sensitivity to beauty; and dedication to some important work, no matter how humble it may seem. But it would be unreasonable to require advanced attainment in any of these areas; an average person can attain the required balance, and any realistic concept of perfection-as-righteousness must make room for our status as learners.

Love as the crowning unification of excellent character

Facing the problem of how we are to acquire the great many virtues needed for an ideal character, it is not surprising that teachers of philosophy and religion have tended to simplify the list, presenting a single virtue or a small number of virtues for emphasis.[31] Plato portrayed four cardinal virtues

30. The New Testament quotations in this paragraph are from Matt 6:24 and 6:24–33; and see Jeremias, *New Testament Theology*, 230.

31. In contrast to the tendency to simplify long virtue lists, it is worth mentioning a carefully organized and thorough discussion of forty-two character strengths presented by a team of psychologists. The recent movement of positive psychology uses experimental techniques to probe human flourishing, and the systematic treatment by Peterson and Seligman, *Character Strengths and Virtues*, shows significant kinship to the philosophy of living being presented in the present book. For example, among

(self-mastery regarding pleasure, courage, justice, and wisdom) as sufficient
to establish a solid core of excellence. Aristotle proposed practical wisdom
not as a shortcut but as a methodological unity comprising the moral virtues. To crown Aristotle's list of virtues, Aquinas added faith, hope, and love.
Kant and Mill each set forth a supreme moral principle as the key to character. While I find enrichment in these and many other sources, I agree with
Aquinas about love being the highest virtue.

In contrast with the Aristotelian program, in this emerging philosophy
we do not compose a beautiful character by acquiring a set of virtues: think
how impossible it would be for most of us to acquire anything close to the
excellences of Darwin, Socrates, Jesus, Muir, Bach, Addams, or Sorokin to
apply in daily life. Rather, noble character is best understood as a quality of
an integrated whole—engaged in fact, meaning, and value, responsive to the
actuals and potentials of beauty, and consecrated to goodness. Perfection-
as-righteousness as total engagement in the divine way is the *core* of greatness of character; and other qualities continue to develop naturally around
that ever-growing core.

Love surrounds us and indwells us. This truth intuitively feels right
to some persons who do not believe in God. Persons who choose to open
themselves to receive God's love find experiences that vary from so faint as
to be uncertain to so full as to be beyond words. As we grow in knowing

---

the chapters are included discussions of curiosity, love of learning, open-mindedness,
wisdom, spirituality, the appreciation of beauty and excellence, humor, creativity, and
several moral strengths of character; and the strengths listed are methodically selected.
The editors harmonize input from forty-two contributors, each providing a chapter fea-
turing a thumbnail biography of a paradigm case of the virtue; a consensual definition;
theoretical traditions; measures; correlates and consequences; enabling and inhibiting
factors; development (in the life course); gender, cross-national, and cross-cultural aspects; deliberate interventions; what is not known; and must-read articles and books.
Though the editors appear to regard to psychology as having supplanted philosophy in
investigating the virtues, it is heartening to see calls for a new philosophy to complement the new psychology. Nancy Eisenberg and Vivian Ota Wang write, "In many ways,
nurturing peace, human strengths, and prosocial behaviors between and within similar
and different cultures will eventually have to involve a new philosophy of thinking,
learning, and being that must be capable of accommodating to the new and unforeseen
demands and challenges of the 21st century" ("Toward Positive Psychology," 125).

And Mihalhy Csikszentmihalyi, a founder of positive psychology, frankly notes a
need: "[Positive psychology] lacks theoretical coherence. It is not unified by a central
conceptual apparatus. In fact, the many contributions are not even linked in what one
might call a nomological network—they remain discrete ideas or findings that share
only a common attitude toward what matters about human experience and behavior.
This lack of a unifying theory might be remedied with time" ("Introduction" to *Optimal
Experience*, 6). Proposals for a unifying theory should emerge as more philosophers
and scholars of religion interact with psychology and more psychologists interact with
them.

God and receiving his love for us, it becomes natural for us to love him in return. Thus we complete the circuit of love in the most direct way. We can also complete the circuit of love by expanding it: we receive our Father's gift of love and then pass it on to others. This may be regarded as an expanded circuit because God dwells in us all and we in him.[32]

Divine love as the source of beauty of character is celebrated by the Sufis, partly based on traditions that "Muhammad used to pray, 'O God, Thou hast made my creation beautiful, so make my character beautiful too!' He also said, 'The most beloved of you to God is the most beautiful of you in character.'" Building on the Qur'an and on such traditions, Abu'l-Hasan al-Daylalmī, author of the first Arabic treatise on love from a largely Sufi perspective, says that when someone loves God,

> God beautifies his character traits, for He bestows upon him a robe of honor from His love and character traits from His character traits. He dresses him in a light from His light, a beauty from His beauty, a splendor from His splendor, a generosity from His generosity, a forbearance from His forbearance, a kindness from His kindness, a munificence from His munificence, and so on with the other attributes.
>
> Love is the very Reality of God Himself. Love gives rise to the universe and permeates all of creation. God singled out human beings for special love by creating them in His own form and bestowing on them the unique capacity to recognize Him in Himself and to love Him for Himself, not for any specific blessing. The mark of this capacity is that they alone receive the command instructing them on what they are to do. Human beings alone are offered the choice of loving Him or rejecting Him. The creative command instills them with love, but He cannot force them to recognize who it is that they truly love without depriving them of their humanity. As the Qur'an puts it, "There is no coercion in religion" [2:256], for coerced love is no love at all.[33]

This passage comes close to another idea that I regard as insightful: in its fullness, every virtue is a fruit of the spirit.

According to Thomas Aquinas, God infuses love in the soul as the crowning virtue in excellent human character. The giver of this gift is infinite and eternally perfect; and his will is expressed in his love of us all, a love that ever seeks to enable us to participate in his goodness. Love infuses joy

32. "In him we live and move and have our being." Acts 17:28.

33. The writer is Abu'l-Hasan al-Daylalmī (d. ca. 1000), author of the first Arabic treatise on love from a Sufi perspective. The two quotations come from Chittick, "Love in Islam," 168.

in the will. "The soul's joy, flowing over into the body, fills it with happiness in the form of health and incorruptible vigor."[34] As God's love descends to us, we rise toward God, the root of our happiness. Loving God wholeheartedly brings us toward union with God, a union that we can already sense, though the feeling is not a sign that we *are* divine.

As our love grows, it becomes more intense, more deeply rooted in us, and it embraces more and more in its compass. The scope of our love expands to identify with the good of all creation, and it is fulfilled in friendship with God, a participation in the social life of God, whose love communicates itself to every being who may possibly share in that intelligent and intelligence-transcending love. Love in its fullness enables us to love our neighbors, near and far. And sometimes, Thomas observes, love overcomes evil with good and warms an enemy.

Although Thomas speaks of love as a virtue, love is hard to classify. Love illumines understanding, but it is more than a way of seeing. Love is felt, but it is a more than a feeling. Love is the supreme motivation, but it is more than motivation. A person can be loving, but love is more than a virtue.

Divine love: theme and variations

In my opinion, the simplicity of divine love encompasses many kinds of love. Our human experience of love begins, typically, at mother's breast. Growing up, we learn to love family and friends, then romantic partners, and maybe God, so it is natural to distinguish types of love in terms of these circles of relating. But I regard these types of love as varieties of love in the fullest sense—as Godly love. Divine love (*agape*) can be expressed in various kinds of relationship, including friendship (*philia*) and romantic love (*eros*). In friendship or romance, motivations may arise that compete with divine love; but friendship and erotic attraction are part of the Creator's plan, and when divine love is the effective core of the friendship or romance, then those relationships are truly loving, because each partner seeks the other's good. The same applies to love within the family and other spheres of love.

Shakespeare in Sonnet 105 expresses the height of romantic love:

> Let not my love be call'd idolatry,
> Nor my beloved as an idol show,
> Since all alike my songs and praises be

---

34. Aquinas, *Summa Theologiae*, Ia IIae 59.5 (cf. 2a2ae 23.2). The following two paragraphs draw especially on 2a2ae 23.3 and 25.5.

To one, of one, still such, and ever so.

Kind is my love to-day, to-morrow kind,

Still constant in a wondrous excellence,

Therefore my verse, to constancy confin'd,

One thing expressing, leaves out difference.

"Fair," "kind," and "true" is all my argument,

"Fair," "kind," and "true" varying to other words,

And in this change is my invention spent,

Three themes in one, which wondrous scope affords.

Shakespeare defends himself against the charge of idolatry, devotion to an unworthy substitute for God. By contrast, his relationship is romantic affection pervaded by divine love. The poet testifies to the unity and constancy of his love and to the fact that his love is not focused on outward charms but on the character qualities of the beloved, who is kind with a wondrous excellence. Although the poet uses different words, he uses his creativity to express this one triune theme. Then the poet sets forth the unity of love in terms of its three ingredients: beauty, goodness, and truth. First, the beloved is fair; in this context, "fair" refers not to a kind of justice but rather to beauty: the beloved is beautiful; in this context, physical beauty cannot be the whole story, since there is beauty in wondrous kindness. Second, the beloved is kind, a quality of goodness. Third, the beloved is true, and "true" here means "genuine and trustworthy." These three values are one in the beloved, giving rise to a wide range of creative expressions.[35]

Godly love functions as the unifying source and inspiration for the different varieties of applied love distinguished by Stephen G. Post, medical ethicist and founder and president of the Institute for Research on Unlimited Love.

When I rise in the morning, which is usually quite early before people have had a chance to intrude on the quietness, I pray a bit for the gift of Godly love, and then I take a while with eyes

35. Because of the Christian and romantic associations with the word *love*, some thinkers prefer *compassion* or *caring*. Without trying to do justice to Buddhist or feminist discussions, I would suggest that each of these terms may be used to stand for all three, whose meanings may be distinguished and interrelated as follows: love is the motivation inherent in both the attitude of compassion that looks mercifully on another's plight and also the acts of caring that make love real. Spiritual love does not see the other person first and foremost as someone suffering and in need of care, but as a unique, spiritually indwelt, infinitely precious child of God. In order to interact with that person, we also need to express love in word and deed in light of our understanding of the person's factual situation.

closed but imagination open, to visualize the interactions to come during the course of the day. I usually know my schedule, so I visualize each interaction, from those with my wife and children to those with the many people I will be meeting that day, from the groups to whom I may be speaking, to the individuals scheduled for a conference call. I ask myself, one by one, how can that person or those people best be loved? What does my heart and what does Godly love want me to give them? Some people need compassion, some a little carefrontation, others an expression of loyalty or perhaps celebration. By very briefly visualizing these interactions I set the stage for the day before it really begins. I gain a sense of genuine intentionality—"I am living today to express the ways of love, and to draw on Godly love in every interaction without exception." I ask God to help me in this endeavor to spread love in small ways throughout the course of the day. Godly love becomes my partner for the day. And then I try to act accordingly, to make these loving intentions and rehearsed interactions become reality. They usually do. Actions are key; otherwise this is a purely internal exercise of no great value or purpose.[36]

Post's research and practice find love specifically expressed in a series of responses that he portrays on a wheel with no beginning or end: respect, listening, compassion, helpfulness, creativity, forgiveness, carefrontation (confrontation modified by love), celebration, mirth, and loyalty. Decades of Christian living in love, and years of consciously channeling energies into these ten expressions of love, show in Stephen's radiant personality.

Among the various types of love widely spoken of today, one that could use a fresh perspective is self-love, an important topic because so many people struggle to love themselves. The effort is understandable. When we look in the mirror, it is common to see pluses and minuses in our body. When we introspect and observe our minds, it is common to see both pluses and minuses in our mind. The image seen in the mirror and derived from the contents of one's mind shows nothing that could justify *wholehearted* love for the self.

---

36. Post's institute is the leading supporter today of research on love. He has made love his top priority from his teenage years, and is able to fluently handle questions on a wide range of concerns in a way that makes faith and wisdom concrete as he cites research studies that bring hope and suggest lessons on how to make love effective. Post, *Godly Love*, 139–41. Post's many books range from academic to popular. For information on his Institute for Research on Unlimited Love, see http://unlimitedloveinstitute. org/.

But thinking of ourselves simply in terms of mind and body makes us vulnerable to low self-esteem and places unnecessary limits on love. What primarily makes us lovable does not show up in the mirror or register in the mind's field of objects for introspection. If our deepest craving is to love and be loved, then an honest, mixed review of the body-and-mind self raises a problem and stimulates the search for a solution.

The idea of loving oneself is meaningful in the following senses: we *can* come to respect ourselves profoundly, accept the facts of our present condition, harmonize the different parts of ourselves, be responsible in caring for ourselves, and enjoy our personal uniqueness. All these achievements are part of a full solution, and they find their place in a still wider framework.

We feel good about ourselves most of all when we are not thinking about ourselves, but rather when we forget ourselves in devotion to worthy projects, including doing things for others. That's when we allow self to move into the background; and occasionally we sense our invisible self when it is functioning wonderfully. Those who truly love us do not do so primarily because of physical or intellectual features, but because of who we are and are becoming: our personality, our growing soul, and the divine spirit within.[37]

And true love not only delights in the best and most beautiful, but also gets actively involved. It does not pretend that the other person is perfect. Mature love coordinates realism with its idealism. The test of the reality of love comes when another's imperfections interfere with our own contentment. Love in its fullness embraces the entire person wholeheartedly. If we mercifully and realistically interpret what we understand of those imperfections, we can do what is appropriate to support the other's growth—which can sometimes require tough action.

In my view, love in its fullest sense and expression is interpersonal and mutual. To be loved, and to love, is so deeply satisfying because the love we receive touches the very core of our being and the loving we give comes from our spiritual center. In this sense, love is not something we can give ourselves. It is what we receive from and give to others, whether that is a friend, a spouse, a child, a co-worker, a parent, a stranger in need, or God.

---

37. Shakespeare's Sonnet 55 celebrates the beloved without a single descriptive word. "Not marble, nor the gilded monuments / Of princes, shall outlive this powerful rhyme; / But you shall shine more bright in these contents / Than unswept stone, besmear'd with sluttish time. / When wasteful war shall statues overturn, / And broils root out the work of masonry, / Nor Mars his sword, nor war's quick fire shall burn / The living record of your memory. / 'Gainst death, and all oblivious enmity / Shall you pace forth; your praise shall still find room / Even in the eyes of all posterity / That wear this world out to the ending doom. / So, till the judgment that yourself arise, / You live in this, and dwell in lovers' eyes."

In the end, human love relationships, for all their beauty and mutuality, can never substitute for the love relationship with the Father whose "I love you" is spoken from within. Those who know the love of God have a foundation for self-esteem beyond human opinion. When we let go of our resistance to his embrace, and abandon the feeling that we need to conceal from him what we are ashamed of, we can receive the One who pours out unlimited love and fills us to overflowing.

Back down to earth one last time

After seeing challenging stories of heroism and exalted concepts of values, we need a balancing pause before we conclude. For all the cosmic importance of truth, beauty, and goodness, it is possible to overemphasize them. There other high and worthy concepts, other ways of expressing wisdom and insight. Piotr Jaroszyński, for example, gives strategic advice that we pursue truth, beauty, and goodness *indirectly* by engaging ourselves in concrete ways.

> Instead of searching for a quality of truth, it is better to bring
> our cognition in harmony with reality. Instead of searching for
> a quality of the good, it is better to love a right and real good.
> Instead of striving after the quality of being, it is better to look at
> being with complacency, or to create something while seeking
> unity for the many elements of the work that must ultimately
> be joined together, since this guarantees the intelligibility and
> availability of a work. Truth, good, and beauty will be there.[38]

I take a both/and approach that proposes to *add* supreme value concepts to our ideas of our concrete tasks; but Jaroszynski's point is well taken, and it is reinforced by the fact that large numbers of people today are put off by talk of truth, beauty, and goodness, which requires that our communication of these realities be indirect and artistic.[39]

A second way to come back down to earth is by recalling the humble level from which we begin if we choose to face our front-burner issue, our number-one growth priority. The power of this honest and direct approach

38. Jaroszyński, *Beauty and Being*, 220. To "regard being with complacency" means to take pleasure in being. Jaroszyński insightfully argues that beauty is a *relation*; and I would argue the same for truth and goodness.

39. This observation is developed in Wilson, *Preaching as Poetry*. My experience with lower-division undergraduates is that skepticism about truth, beauty, and goodness disappears when people are invited to put such concepts in their own words and use their own interpretations as the launching pad for their growth.

to growth can manifest quickly, as we see in the case of a student who devoted a week to the project of cultivating the virtue of friendship. She reported, "I have been very shy and insecure ever since I was a young child. In
the past I would let feelings of embarrassment or shame wash over me and
affect my mood for the rest of the day. The negativity would spill onto others, and the whole day would be one big mess. Any sort of ambition would
be lost; a whole day would be unproductive, because my energy would be
wasted. I realized I had to take on the issues. . . . After reading Jessica Somers
Driver, I became inspired. By being truthful with myself and keeping some
of her advice in mind, I made some small yet wonderful improvements."
The student quoted these lines from Driver: "A truth is discovered, not created by someone. See an idea clearly, eliminating any sense of inadequacy or
personal responsibility, and you may rest assured that you can show it forth
in some form."

Here she describes the beginnings of her breakthrough:

> I began to realize that I was not the only one with a sort of so-
> cial anxiety, and that I too could get past them. I could walk
> anywhere with my head up and smiling. I could walk through
> the Kent State Student Center with my head up, and as I did
> so I made contact with many smiling faces. I suddenly felt
> motivated.
>
> As the week progressed I made many changes to my daily
> routines. Instead of seeking refuge in my dorm room, where I
> would eventually fall asleep due to slight depression and bore-
> dom, I ventured outdoors. I sat outside under the shade of a
> tree, studied, and listened to the soft breeze. I stopped by the
> library and checked out some new books. Walking alone I
> stopped and talked with some who seemed interested in talking
> with me, making some new friends. The world had become less
> frightening and more welcoming.

With this newfound confidence came a readiness to study and work with
others:

> There is a feeling of capability now. I began to listen, I mean re-
> ally listen, to others speak. Everything sounded interesting and
> new to me. How wonderful it can be to listen to others' thoughts
> and to find that you have much in common! There are so many
> different and wonderful ways of expressing ideas. It is incredibly
> fulfilling to embrace differences and variety. It is also a joy to
> find that those whom you believed to be so foreign to you are
> not really so different. Now that I was making a point to listen,
> my conversations with others were so much more meaningful;

so much so that at certain points I was so overcome with joy or
sorrow that tears would form in my eyes.

Even with her family she had experienced awkwardness, partly due to feelings of inferiority toward her gifted, outgoing, and lovely sisters; but at her
grandfather's seventy-second birthday party, things changed: "I was able to
open up and actually make everyone laugh."

> Driver's advice leads me to the conclusion that we are God's
> children, and each one of us is a special being. By having faith
> and praying, our Creator will help us through all obstacles. Our
> thoughts are a privilege, and one should never be afraid to share
> them with others. During my experience, the time I spend pray-
> ing increased daily, and I will continue with my new manner of
> prayer. Each morning I awake with a prayer for all I know and
> all I will meet, and everyone on this beautiful planet. I pray for
> everyone to be led through a virtuous path and to recognize its
> greatness. When I am faced with a conflict, instead of becoming
> upset, I ask for God's assistance to make the correct decision. I
> then thank God. As I pray I feel love and warmth in my soul,
> and it feels lovely. Even when I feel as if no one else cares for
> me, I know God loves me. By realizing this, I have gained so
> much love for everyone else. As my faith in God has grown, so
> has my faith in my fellow brothers and sisters on earth, who are
> experiencing many of the same fears as I have.
>
> The main points that Jessica Driver makes in her article are
> to listen, value, and spontaneously to express the idea.[40] By in-
> corporating her reasoning and beliefs into my own experiences
> I have come closer to one day helping the world become a better
> place. Right now I am starting small, and learning to appreci-
> ate those around me and what I already have been given. I am
> learning that I am very capable of helping others, and they are
> capable of helping me, even if that help is just a sincere smile and
> hello. There is a need to let go of yourself and to expect to make
> mistakes. When things go unexpectedly or mistakes happen you
> must learn from them. One must be humble and grateful for all
> they have been given. If one is grateful for what they have, there
> will be room in their soul to genuinely help others.
>
> I am aware now that I want to share my ideas with others.
> I know that I want to give them genuine ideas, and stay true
> to myself and God. I also want to listen to others and encour-
> age them to find the freedom that can occur when they express

40. Our discussion of design and spontaneity in chapter 5 presented Driver's concept of the *idea* as the core meaning or truth to be expressed.

themselves. These new feelings I have are things achieved through my experience this past week. Again, I feel they are small achievements, but they are a large step in helping others. If everyone lends a helping hand of encouragement and compassion, we can all help humanity.[41]

Conclusion: Love's bonds with truth, beauty, and goodness

Philosophers can always say more; but within the limits of the human mind, this book project, and my own growth, this is as far as I have come in being able to set forth my thesis: the values that most deeply guide our thinking, feeling, and doing are more than hopeful projections. There is a reality to these core values, and that reality is God.

To enable us to participate in the divine life, God reaches toward us, extending ladders of value, helping us to realize and participate in truth, beauty, and goodness. If we welcome the spirit of the God of love as our center, we can reflect that the center cannot function fully except through vital interaction with what surrounds it. Spiritual living flourishes in connection with the other aspects featured in these chapters.

Looking back on the path set forth in these chapters, we can see love presented as its culmination; but love also underlies it from the beginning. The long path to mature love takes patience and pondering, and it is designed to complement the short path—the immediate availability of love found in communion with the spirit. The long path depends at all times on the short path, and the short path is enriched by each forward step on the long path. Fortified by values, love matures all along the way.

If we braid insights from some of the persons who have been our main guides on our path through this book, we see the intimate bonds between love and our trio of supreme values. As Socrates sensed, the truth seeker comes to recognize truth as a gift.[42] As we saw in Bach, the soul filled with beauty knows God's love as the source of beauty. And, as Schweitzer and Addams show, the great person attains goodness by diligently and responsibly expressing love. Love is the *origin* of truth, beauty, and goodness.

Next, as Sorokin understood, the search for truth leads to the God who is love; our hunger for beauty leads to experiences of divine love; and

41. This experience report on a project for Introduction to Ethics was done in April 2003, and the student's name is withheld by her request. Significantly, Driver's book has very little spiritual teaching in it.

42. Plato, *Republic*, 507b-509b.

our active participation in goodness leads us toward perfection in love. Love is the goal that truth, beauty, and goodness ultimately lead us to.

Finally, as Jesus showed, love comprises truth, beauty, and goodness. All those qualities are found in true love. Love cannot be itself without these values. Love without truth is blind; without beauty, graceless; without goodness, a self-centered illusion. When we are living at our best, these values fill our thinking, feeling, and doing; and they are all implicit in love.

Love is the divine source, the spiritual destiny, and the unity of truth, beauty, and goodness.

Acknowledgments

I CANNOT BEGIN TO do justice to all the help I have received—visible and invisible—in my decades of work on this book. The postmodernist attack on the image of the solitary author has merit in this case. I cannot measure my debt to the thousands of students who did projects with me: they are my real colleagues on this frontier. The tolerant and supportive environment provided by the Kent State University Department of Philosophy enabled a large proportion of the essential research to take place. And much of the quality of this product is due to the many objections, rejections, and obstacles that caused delay, allowing me to ripen.

Philip Rolnick has been my longest and most stalwart supporter on this project, commenting on multiple drafts of the whole. Elianne Obadia, "The Writer's Midwife," has been a priceless editor, incisive in fine details and in matters of structural and conceptual importance. I am also grateful to Rodney Clapp, my editor at Wipf and Stock Publishers, for his stabilizing good judgment on matters big and small. The people at that press with whom I have interacted have given me an enhanced sense of what it means to integrate spirituality with business. Michael Hill and Susan Owen also made helpful comments on the whole manuscript. Byron Belitsos at Origin Press has significantly encouraged this work for decades.

For many years, I prided myself on not having to put the standard apology in the acknowledgements to the wife and family who suffered in various ways due to an author's arguably excessive diligence. Now I know better. I join those ranks and joyously acknowledge my wife Hagiko and our son Ben who have shared the burden of my labor.

I am also grateful for help of various kinds from Grace Boyett, Susan Cook, Gard Jameson, Margie Ray, Victoria Stertzbach, and Tom Wattles.

Bibliography

Addams, Jane. *Twenty Years at Hull-House*. New York: Macmillan, 1926.

Aeschylus. *The Suppliant Maidens*. Translated by Seth G. Bernardete. In *Aeschylus II: Four Tragedies*, 1–42. Chicago: University of Chicago Press, 1956.

Allen, Phillip J. *Pitirim A. Sorokin in Review*. Durham, NC: Duke University Press, 1963.

Alston, William P. *Perceiving God: The Epistemology of Religious Experience*. Ithaca, NY: Cornell University Press, 1991.

———. *A Realist Conception of Truth*. Ithaca, NY: Cornell University Press, 1996.

Aquinas, Thomas. *Summa Theologica*. http://www.newadvent.org/summa/.

Aristotle. *Nicomachean Ethics*. 2nd ed. Translated by Terence Irwin. Indianapolis: Hackett, 1999.

Audi, Robert. "Intuition and Its Place in Ethics." *Journal of the American Philosophical Association* 1 (Spring 2015) 57–77.

Badè, William Frederic. *The Life and Letters of John Muir*. In *John Muir: His Life and Letters and Other Writings*, edited by Terry Gifford, 12–388. Seattle: The Mountaineers, 1996.

Barasch, Marc Ian. *The Compassionate Life: Walking the Path of Kindness*. San Francisco: Berrett-Koehler, 2009.

Batson, C. Daniel, et al. "Adults' emotional reactions to the distress of others." In *Empathy and Its Development*, edited by Nancy Eisenberg and Janet Strayer, 163–84. New York: Cambridge University Press, 1987.

Bauschke, Martin. *Die Goldene Regel: Staunen, Verstehen, Handeln*. Berlin: EB-Verlag, 2010.

Bengtsson, Jan Olaf. *The Worldview of Personalism: Origins and Early Development*. New York: Oxford University Press, 2006.

Berdyaev, Nicolas. *Slavery and Freedom*. Translated by R. M. French. London: G. Bles, Centenary, 1934.

Berger, Peter L., ed. *The Other Side of God: A Polarity in World Religions*. Garden City, NY: Doubleday, 1981.

Bernstein, Jessey H. and Richard M. Ryan. "Vitality." In *Character Strengths and Virtues: A Handbook and Classification*, edited by Christopher Peterson and Martin E. P. Seligman, 273–80. New York: Oxford University Press, 2004.

The Book of Common Prayer. New York: Church Publishing, 1986.

Brewster, Ghiselin. *The Creative Process: A Symposium*. New York: New American Library, 1952.

Brown, Montague. *Restoration of Reason: The Eclipse and Recovery of Truth, Goodness, and Beauty*. Grand Rapids, MI: Baker Academic, 2006.

Buford, Thomas O. *Personal Philosophy: The Art of Living*. New York: Holt, Rinehart, and Winston, 1984.

Caruna, Louis. *Science and Virtue: An Essay on the Impact of the Scientific Mentality on Moral Character*. Aldershot, England: Ashgate, 2006.

Chan, Wing-tsit, ed. *A Source Book in Chinese Philosophy*. Princeton, NJ: Princeton University Press, 1963.

Chang Tsai. "The Western Inscription." In *A Source Book in Chinese Philosophy*, edited by Wing-tsit Chan, 497–98. Princeton, NJ: Princeton University Press, 1963.

Chittick, William C. "Divine and Human Love in Islam." In *Divine Love: Perspectives from the World's Religious Traditions*, edited by Jeff Levin and Stephen G. Post, 163–200. West Conshohocken, PA: Templeton, 2010.

Chuang Tzu. "The Secret of Caring for Life." Translated by Burton Watson. In *Chuang Tzu, Basic Writings*, 46–49. New York: Columbia University Press, 1964.

Cohen, Michael P. *The Pathless Way: John Muir and American Wilderness*. Madison, WI: University of Wisconsin Press, 1984.

Collingwood, R. G. "Outlines of a Philosophy of Art" [1924]. In *Essays in the Philosophy of Art*, edited by Alan Donagan, 43–154. Bloomington, IN: Indiana University Press, 1964.

Cottingham, John. *On the Meaning of Life*. London: Routledge, 2003.

Csikszentmihalyi, Mihaly. "The Future of Flow." In *Optimal Experience: Psychological Studies of Flow in Consciousness*, edited by Mihaly Csikszentmihalyi and Isabella Selega Csikszentmihalyi, 364–83. Cambridge: Cambridge University Press, 1988.

———. "Introduction." In *A Life Worth Living: Contributions to Positive Psychology*, edited by Mihaly Csikszentmihalyi and Isabella Selega Csikszentmihalyi, 3–17. New York: Oxford University Press, 2006.

———. "Introduction." In *Optimal Experience: Psychological Studies of Flow in Consciousness*, edited by Mihaly Csikszentmihalyi and Isabella Selega Csikszentmihalyi, 183–92. Cambridge: Cambridge University Press, 1988.

Csikszentmihalyi, Mihaly, and Isabella Selega Csikszentmihalyi. "Introduction to Part III." In *Optimal Experience: Psychological Studies of Flow in Consciousness*, edited by Mihaly Csikszentmihalyi and Isabella Selega Csikszentmihalyi, 183–92. Cambridge: Cambridge University Press, 1988.

Darwin, Charles. *On the Origin of Species by Means of Natural Selection*. Edited by Joseph Carroll. Peterborough, Ontario: Broadview, 2003.

———. *Journal of Researches into the Natural History & Geology of the Countries Visited During the Voyage of the H. M. S. Beagle Under the Command of Capt. Fitz Roy, R. N.* New York: Heritage, 1957.

Darwin, Sir Francis. *Charles Darwin's Autobiography*. New York: Henry Schuman, 1950.

David, Hans T., and Arthur Mendel, eds. *The Bach Reader: A Life of Johann Sebastian Bach in Letters and Documents*. Rev. ed. New York: Norton, 1966.

Davies, Paul. *The Last Three Minutes: Conjectures about the Ultimate Fate of the Universe*. New York: Basic, 1994.

De Luca, Anthony J. *Freud and Future Religious Experience*. New York: Philosophical Library, 1976.

Descartes, René. *Meditations on First Philosophy*. Translated by Donald Cress. In *René Descartes: Philosophical Essays and Correspondence*, edited by Roger Ariew, 97–141. Indianapolis: Hackett, 2000.

———. *Rules for the Direction of the Mind*. In *René Descartes: Philosophical Essays and Correspondence*, edited by Roger Ariew, 2–28. Indianapolis: Hackett, 2000.

Desmond, Adrian, and James Moore. *Darwin*. New York: Warner, 1991.

Dewey, John. *Art as Experience*, vol. 10: 1934. The Later Works of John Dewey, 1925–1953. Carbondale, IL: Southern Illinois University Press, 1987.

Diamond, Jared. *Collapse: How Societies Choose to Succeed or Fail*. New York: Viking, 2006.

Dickinson, Emily. *The Complete Poems of Emily Dickinson*. Edited by Thomas H. Johnson. Boston: Little, Brown, 1960.

Dihle, Albrecht. *Die Goldene Regel*. Göttingen: Vandenhoeck and Ruprecht, 1962.

The Doctrine of the Mean. Translated by Wing-tsit Chan. In *A Source Book in Chinese Philosophy*, edited by Wing-tsit Chan, 95–114. Princeton, NJ: Princeton University Press, 1963.

Donald, David Herbert. *Lincoln*. New York: Simon and Schuster, 1995.

Dostoevsky, Fyodor. *Notes from Underground*. Translated by Ralph E. Matlaw. New York: E. P. Dutton, 1960.

Driver, Jessica Somers. *Speak for Yourself: Essentials of Reading Aloud and Speaking*. Rev. ed. Los Angeles: n.p., 1956.

Du Bois, W. E. B. *The Souls of Black Folk*. In W. E. B. Du Bois, *Writings*, 357–548. New York: The Library of America, 1986.

du Roy, Olivier. *La Règle d'or: histoire d'une maxime morale universelle*. Two vols. Paris: Cerf, 2012.

———. *La Règle d'or: Le retour d'une maxime oubliée*. Paris: Cerf, 2009.

Dufrenne, Mikel. *The Phenomenology of Aesthetic Experience*. Translated by Edward S. Casey. Evanston, IL: Northwestern University Press, 1973.

Eagleton, Terry. *The Meaning of Life: A Very Short Introduction*. Oxford: Oxford University Press, 2008.

Eisenberg, Nancy, and Vivian Ota Wang. "Toward a Positive Psychology: Social Developmental and Cultural Contributions." In *A Psychology of Human Strengths: Fundamental Questions and Future Directions for a Positive Psychology*, edited by Lisa G. Aspinwall and Ursula M. Staudinger, 117–29. Washington, DC: American Psychological Association, 2003.

Elshtain, Jean Bethke, ed. *A Jane Addams Reader*. New York: Basic, 2002.

Embree, Ainslie, T., ed. *Sources of Indian Tradition*, vol. 1, *From the Beginning to 1800*. 2nd ed. New York: Columbia University Press, 1988.

Farrell, John C. *Beloved Lady: A History of Jane Addams' Ideas on Reform and Peace*. Baltimore: Johns Hopkins University Press, 1967.

Fölsing, Albrecht. *Albert Einstein: A Biography*. Translated by Ewald Osers. New York: Viking, 1997.

Foucault, Michel. *The Order of Things: An Archaeology of the Human Sciences*. New York: Random House, 1970.

Fowler, James. *Stages of Faith*. San Francisco: Harper San Francisco, [1981] 1995.

Frankl, Viktor E. *Man's Search for Meaning: An Introduction to Logotherapy*. Translated by Ilse Lasch. New York: Simon and Schuster, 1962.

Fredrickson, Barbara L. *Positivity: Top-Notch Research Reveals the 3-to-1 Ratio That Will Change Your Life*. New York: Three Rivers, 2009.

Fritz, Robert. *The Path of Least Resistance: Learning to Become the Creative Force in Your Own Life*. Rev. ed. New York: Fawcett/Random House, 1989.

Gandhi, Mahatma. *All Men Are Brothers: Life and Thoughts of Mahatma Gandhi as Told in His Own Words*. Edited by Krishna Kripalani. New York: UNESCO, 1965.

Gardner, Howard. *Truth, Beauty, and Goodness Reframed: Educating for the Virtues in the Twenty-First Century*. New York: Basic, 2011.

Gensler, Harry J. *Ethics and the Golden Rule*. New York: Routledge, 2013.

Gershman, Norman H. *Besa: Muslims Who Saved Jews in World War II*. New York: Syracuse University Press, 2008.

Gladwell, Malcolm. *Outliers: The Story of Success*. New York: Little, Brown, 2008.

The Great Learning. Translated by Wing-tsit Chan. In *A Source Book in Chinese Philosophy*, edited by Wing-tsit Chan, 86–87. Princeton, NJ: Princeton University Press, 1963.

Griswold, Charles L. *Forgiveness: A Philosophical Explanation*. New York: Cambridge University Press, 2007.

Grout, Donald J. *A History of Western Music*. New York: Norton, 1960.

Haney, Seamus. "Postscript." In *Opened Ground: Selected Poems 1966–1996*, 411. New York: Farrar, Straus and Giroux, 1998.

Hanh, Thich Nhat. *Peace Is Every Step: The Path of Mindfulness in Everyday Life*. New York: Bantam, 1991.

Harnack, Adolf von. *What Is Christianity?* Translated by Thomas Bailey Saunders. New York: Harper & Row, 1957.

Hegel, G. W. F. *The Phenomenology of Spirit*. Translated by A. V. Miller. New York: Oxford University Press, 1977.

Heidegger, Martin. "The Origin of the Work of Art." In *Martin Heidegger: Basic Writings*, edited by David Farrell Krell, 139–212. San Francisco: HarperCollins, 1993.

Heiler, Friedrich. *Prayer: A Study in the History and Psychology of Religion*. Translated by Samuel McComb. New York: Oxford University Press, 1958.

Hillery, George A., Jr., et al. "An Empirical Assessment of Sorokin's Theory of Change." In *Sorokin and Civilization: A Centennial Assessment*, edited by Joseph B. Ford et al., 171–86. New Brunswick, NJ: Transaction, 1996.

Homer. *The Odyssey*. Translated by Robert Fagles. New York: Penguin Putnam, 1996.

Hughes, Jean R., et al. "Learning to Use Empathy." In *Empathy in the Helping Relationship*, edited by Ruth C. MacKay et al., 107–19. New York: Springer, 1990.

Institute for the Advancement of Philosophy for Children. http://www.montclair.edu/cehs/academics/centers-and-institutes/iapc/.

Jaroszyński, Piotr. *Beauty and Being: Thomistic Perspectives*. Translated by Hugh McDonald and Piotr Jaroszyński. Toronto: Pontifical Institute of Medieval Studies, 2011.

Jeremias, Joachim. *New Testament Theology*. Translated by John Bowden. New York: Scribner's, 1971.

Johnson, Elizabeth A. *She Who Is*. New York: Crossroad, 1993.

Johnston, Barry V. *Pitirim A. Sorokin: An Intellectual Biography*. Lawrence, KS: University Press of Kansas, 1995.

Jones, Richard D. P. *The Creative Development of Johann Sebastian Bach*, vol. 1: 1695–1717, *Music to Delight the Spirit*. Oxford: Oxford University Press, 2007.

Kahneman, Daniel. *Thinking, Fast and Slow*. New York: Farrar, Straus and Giroux, 2011.

Kant, Immanuel. *Grounding for the Metaphysics of Morals*. Translated by James W. Ellington. In *Immanuel Kant, Ethical Philosophy*, 1–69. 2nd ed. Indianapolis: Hackett, 1994.

Kaplan, Wendy. "Design for the Modern World." In *The Arts and Crafts Movement in Europe and America, 1880–1920: Design for the Modern World*, edited by Wendy Kaplan, 11–19. New York: Thames and Hudson, 2004.

Kekes, John. *The Art of Life*. Ithaca, NY: Cornell University Press, 2002.

Keller, Evelyn Fox. *A Feeling for the Organism: The Life and Work of Barbara McClintock*. San Francisco: W. H. Freeman, 1983.

Kierkegaard, Søren. *Fear and Trembling*. Translated by Howard V. Hong and Edna H. Hong. Princeton, NJ: Princeton University Press, 1983.

Klemke, E. D., and Steven M. Cahn. *The Meaning of Life: A Reader*. 3rd edition. New York: Oxford University Press, 2007.

Koenig, Harold, et al. *Handbook of Religion and Health*. New York: Oxford University Press, 2000.

Kreeft, Peter. "Lewis's Philosophy of Truth, Goodness and Beauty." In *C. S. Lewis as Philosopher: Truth, Goodness, and Beauty*, edited by David Baggett, Gary R. Habermas, and Jerry L. Walls, 23–36. Downer's Grove, IL: InterVarsity, 2008.

Kyle, Charles, and Mark Hodermarsky. *The Object of the Game*. Dubuque, IA: Kendall Hunt, 2008.

Le Mée, Jean, ed. *Hymns from the Rig-Veda*. Translated by Jean Le Mée. New York: Alfred Knopf, 1975.

Levinas, Emmanuel. "Peace and Proximity." In *Basic Philosophical Writings*, translated by Simon Critchley, 161–69. Bloomington, IN: Indiana University Press, 1996.

Lurie, Yuval. *Tracking the Meaning of Life: A Philosophical Journey*. Columbia, MO: University of Missouri Press, 2006.

Martin, Calvin Luther. *The Way of the Human Being*. New Haven, CT: Yale University Press, 1999.

Maurer, Armand A. *About Beauty: A Thomistic Interpretation*. Houston, TX: Center for Thomistic Studies, 1983.

McFague, Sallie. *Models of God: Theology for an Ecological, Nuclear Age*. Philadelphia: Fortress, 1987.

McIntosh, Steve. *Evolution's Purpose: An Integral Interpretation of the Story of our Origins*. New York: Select, 2012.

———. *The Presence of the Infinite: The Spiritual Experience of Beauty, Truth, and Goodness*. Wheaton, IL: Quest, 2015.

McLeod, W. H. "The Teachings of Guru Nanak." In *Sikhs and Sikhism*, 148–226. Oxford: Oxford University Press, 1999.

Medina, John. *Brain Rules: 12 Principles for Surviving and Thriving at Work, Home, and School*. Seattle, WA: Pear, 2009.

Mencius. *Mencius*. Translated by D. C. Lau. Harmondsworth, UK: Penguin, 1970.

Merleau-Ponty, Maurice. "The Crisis of the Understanding." Translated by Nancy Metzel and John Flodstrom. In *The Primacy of Perception and Other Essays*, edited by James M. Edie, 193–210. Evanston, IL: Northwestern University Press, 1968.

Mill, John Stuart. *Utilitarianism*. In *Utilitarianism and Other Essays*, edited by Alan Ryan, 272–338. London: Penguin, 1987.

Miller, Mitchell H., Jr. *Plato's Parmenides*. University Park, PA: Penn State University Press, 2004.

Muir, John. *The Mountains of California*. New York: Century, 1922.

———. *My First Summer in the Sierra*. Boston: Houghton Mifflin, 1911.

———. *Our National Parks*. Boston: Houghton Mifflin, 1901.

———. *The Story of My Boyhood and Youth*. New York: Houghton Mifflin, 1913.

———. *Travels in Alaska*. Boston: Houghton Mifflin, 1915.

———. *The Yosemite*. New York: Century, 1914.

Neusner, Jacob, and Bruce Chilton, eds. *The Golden Rule: Analytical Perspectives*. Lanham, MD: University Press of America, 2009.

———. *The Golden Rule: The Ethics of Reciprocity in World Religions*. New York: Continuum, 2008.

Newberg, Andrew, et al. *Why God Won't Go Away: Brain Science and the Biology of Belief*. New York: Ballantine, 2001.

Nichiren. *Dedication to the Lotus*. In *The Buddhist Tradition in India, China, and Japan*, edited by William Theodore de Bary, 349–50. New York: Random House, 1972.

Nichols, Aidan. *A Key to Balthasar: Hans Urs von Balthasar on Beauty, Goodness, and Truth*. Grand Rapids, MI: Baker Academic, 2011.

Nicolson, Marjorie Hope. *Mountain Gloom and Mountain Glory: The Development of the Aesthetics of the Infinite*. New York: Norton, 1963.

Norman, Philippa. "Feeding the Brain for Academic Success." http://www.healthybrainforlife.com/articles/school-health-and-nutrition/feeding-the-brain-for-academic-success-how.

Nozick, Robert. *The Examined Life: Philosophical Meditations*. New York: Simon and Schuster, 1989.

O'Connell, Kathleen M. *Rabindranath Tagore: The Poet as Educator*. Kolkata, India: Visva-Bharati, 2002.

Olivier, Laurence. *On Acting*. New York: Simon and Schuster, 1986.

Parsons, James. *Ode to the Ninth: The Poetic and Musical Tradition Behind the Finale of Beethoven's Choral Symphony*. PhD diss., University of North Texas, 1992.

Pedersen, Olaf. "Christian Belief and the Fascination of Science." In *Physics, Philosophy, and Theology: A Common Quest for Understanding*, edited by Robert J. Russell, et al., 125–40. 3rd ed. Vatican City State: Vatican Observatory, 1997.

Pelikan, Jaroslav. *Fools for Christ: Essays on the True, the Good, and the Beautiful*. Eugene, OR: Wipf and Stock, 2001.

Peterson, Christopher, and Martin E. P. Seligman. *Character Strengths and Virtues: A Handbook and Classification*. New York: Oxford University Press, 2004.

Pinnock, Clark H. "Annihilationism." In *The Oxford Handbook of Eschatology*, edited by Jerry L. Walls, 446–61. New York: Oxford University Press, 2008.

———. "The Conditional View." In *Four Views on Hell*, edited by William Crockett, 135–66. Grand Rapids: Zondervan 1992.

Plantinga, Alvin. "Creation and Evolution: A Modest Proposal." In *Intelligent Design: Creationism and its Critics*, edited by Robert Pennock, 779–91. Cambridge, MA: MIT Press, 2003.

Plato. *Complete Works*. Edited by John M. Cooper. Indianapolis: Hackett, 1997.

———. *Symposium*. In *Plato: Complete Works*, edited by John M. Cooper. Indianapolis: Hackett, 1997.

Poloma, Margaret M. *Main Street Mystics: The Toronto Blessing and Reviving Pentecostalism*. Walnut Creek, CA: AltaMira, 2003.

Post, Stephen G. *Godly Love: A Rose Planted in the Desert of our Hearts*. Conshohoken, PA: Templeton Foundation Press, 2008.

Post, Stephen, and Jill Neimark. *Why Good Things Happen to Good People*. New York: Broadway, 2007.

Ramos, Alice M. *Dynamic Transcendentals: Truth, Goodness, and Beauty from a Thomistic Perspective*. Washington, DC: The Catholic University of America Press, 2012.

Ratey, John J., and Eric Hagerman. *Spark: The Revolutionary New Science of Exercise and the Brain*. Boston: Little, Brown, 2013.

Rizzuto, Ana-Maria. *The Birth of the Living God: A Psychoanalytic Study*. Chicago: University of Chicago Press, 1979.

Roberts, Robert C., and W. Jay Wood. *Intellectual Virtues*. Oxford: Clarendon, 2007.

Rolnick, Philip A. *Origins: Evolution, Big Bang, and Creation*. Waco, TX: Baylor University Press, 2015.

———. *Person, Grace, and God*. Grand Rapids, MI: Eerdmans, 2007.

Rosenhan, David. "Focus of Attention Mediates the Impact of Negative Affect on Altruism." *Journal of Personality and Social Psychology* 38 (1980) 291–300.

Ross, Stephen David. *The Gift of Beauty: The Good as Art*. Albany, NY: State University of New York Press, 1996.

Runzo, Joseph, and Nancy M. Martin, eds. *The Meaning of Life in the World Religions*. Oxford: Oneworld, 2000.

———. *The Gift of Truth: Gathering the Good*. Albany, NY: State University of New York Press, 1997.

Russell, A. J., ed. *God at Eventide: A Companion Volume to God Calling, by Two Listeners*. New York: Dodd, Mead, 1950.

Sartre, Jean-Paul. *No Exit*. In *No Exit and Three Other Plays*, translated by Stuart Gilbert, 1–46. New York: Vintage, 1989.

Sartwell, Crispin. *The Art of Living: Aesthetics of the Ordinary in World Spiritual Traditions*. Albany, NY: State University of New York Press, 1995.

Schweitzer, Albert. *Memoirs of Childhood and Youth*. Translated by C. T. Campion. New York: Macmillan, 1931.

———. *Out of My Life and Thought: An Autobiography*. Translated by C. T. Campion. New York: Holt, Rinehart and Winston, 1949.

Seachris, Joshua W., ed. *Exploring the Meaning of Life: An Anthology and Guide*. Malden, MA: Wiley-Blackwell, 2012.

Sharpe, Leslie. *Friedrich Schiller: Drama, Thought and Politics*. Cambridge: Cambridge University Press, 1991.

Shotwell, Thomas. "An Essay on Beauty: Some Implications of Beauty in the Natural World." *Zygon* 27 (1992) 479–90.

Shusterman, Richard. *Body Consciousness: A Philosophy of Mindfulness and Som-aesthetics*. New York: Cambridge University Press, 2008.

Small, Gary, and Gigi Vorgan. *iBrain: Surviving the Technological Alteration of the Modern Mind*. New York: HarperCollins, 2009.

Smith, T. Lynn. "Sorokin's Rural-Urban Principles." In *Pitirim A. Sorokin in Review*, edited by Phillip J. Allen, 188–205. Durham, NC: Duke University Press, 1963.

Smith, Wilfred Cantwell. *Faith and Belief*. Princeton, NJ: Princeton University Press, 1979.

Sorokin, Pitirim A. "Autobiography." In Allen, Philip J. ed., *Pitirim A. Sorokin in Review*, 1–30. Durham, NC: Duke University Press, 1963.

———. *A Long Journey: The Autobiography of Pitirim A. Sorokin.* New Haven, CT: College and University Press, 1963.

———. *The Reconstruction of Humanity.* Boston: Beacon, 1948.

———. *Ways and Power of Love: Types, Factors, and Techniques of Moral Transformation.* Philadelphia: Templeton Foundation, 2002.

Strong, Mary, ed. *Letters of the Scattered Brotherhood.* New York: Harper and Row, 1948.

Tatum, W. Barnes. *In Quest of Jesus.* Rev. ed. Nashville: Abingdon Press, 1999.

Thomson, Garrett. *On the Meaning of Life.* Toronto: Wadsworth: 2002.

Tillich, Paul. *The Courage to Be.* New Haven: Yale University Press, 1962.

Todes, Samuel. "Sensuous Abstraction and the Abstract Sense of Reality." In *Body and World*, by Samuel Todes and Hubert Dreyfus, 269–76. Cambridge, MA: MIT Press, 2001.

The Urantia Book. Chicago: The Urantia Foundation, 1955.

Wallwork, Ernest. "Thou Shalt Love Thy Neighbor as Thyself: The Freudian Critique." *Journal of Religious Ethics* 10 (Fall 1982) 264–319.

Wattles, Jeffrey. *The Golden Rule.* New York: Oxford University Press, 1996.

———. "Husserl and the Phenomenology of Religious Experience: A Sketch and an Invitation." In *Being Amongst Others: Phenomenological Reflections on the Life-World*, edited by Eric Chelstrom, 244–61. Cambridge, UK: Cambridge Scholars, 2006.

———. "John Muir as a Guide to Education in Environmental Aesthetics." *The Journal of Aesthetic Education* 47 (Fall 2013) 56–71.

———. "Teleology Past and Present." *Zygon: A Journal of Religion and Science* 41 (June 2006) 445–64.

White, Richard. *The Heart of Wisdom: A Philosophy of Spiritual Life.* Lanham, MD: Rowman & Littlefield, 2013.

Whitehead, Alfred North. *Adventures of Ideas.* New York: Macmillan, 1961.

Williams, Linda L. "Dostoevsky's Underground Man: A Question of Meaning." *Studies in the Novel* 27 (Summer 1995) 129–40.

Wilson, Paul Scott. *Preaching as Poetry: Beauty, Goodness, and Truth in Every Sermon.* Nashville, TN: Abingdon, 2014.

Witherspoon, Gary. *Language and Art in the Navaho Universe.* Ann Arbor, MI: University of Michigan Press, 1977.

Wolff, Christoph. *Johann Sebastian Bach: The Learned Musician.* New York: W. W. Norton, 2000.

Index

Whitehead, Alfred North, 31–32, 53,
    113n45
wholeheartedness, 6, 38, 75, 80, 83, 90,
    115
    in relation to God, 84, 85n66, 88,
        170, 198, 202
    unites dimensions of experience,
        101, 113, 114
    See also feeling and heart

wisdom, xix, xxiv, 16, 160, 170, 174-78,
    179, 193
    foolishness, xxiv, 15, 24, 38, 41, 49,
        50, 72n34, 154, 165, 178
    and love, 24, 175n45, 191, 192
    and philosophy, 30–31, 34, 38–39,
        50–51, 59, 61, 163n25, 165
    spiritual, xxii, 16, 70, 71, 75, 77,
        83–84, 170, 179, 193